Floating on a Malayan Breeze

Floating on a Malayan Breeze

Travels in Malaysia and Singapore

Sudhir Thomas Vadaketh

NUS PRESS
SINGAPORE

香港大學出版社
HONG KONG UNIVERSITY PRESS

© Hong Kong University Press 2012

First published by:
Hong Kong University Press
14/F Hing Wai Centre
7 Tin Wan Praya Road
Aberdeen, Hong Kong
Fax: 852-2875-0734
E-mail: hkupress@hku.hk
Website: http://www.hkupress.org

ISBN 978-988-8139-31-6 *(Paperback)*

Published for distribution in Southeast Asia by:
NUS Press
National University of Singapore
AS3-01-02, 3 Arts Link
Singapore 117569
Fax: (65) 6774-0652
E-mail: nusbooks@nus.edu.sg
Website: http://www.nus.edu.sg/nuspress

ISBN 978-9971-69-647-4 *(Paperback)*

National Library Board, Singapore Cataloguing-in-Publication Data
A catalogue record for the book is available from the National Library, Singapore

10   9   8   7   6   5   4   3   2   1

Printed and bound by Liang Yu Printing Factory Company Ltd., Hong Kong, China

Contents

Key

0 _____ 100 km

⌇⌇⌇⌇➤ Bicycle journey

Map of Malaysia

Preface

This book is about Malaysia and Singapore as seen from the ground. As the Singapore-born son of a Malaysia-born father, I have great affection for both places. Yet I have often lamented the shortage of this bottom-up perspective in national discourse. This book is my humble attempt to help address that.

This story began when my best friend, Sumana Rajarethnam, and I decided in 2004 to spend a month cycling around Malaysia on a daily budget of RM10 (US$3) each, meeting people wherever we went. Though the impetus for the trip was our own desire—naive as it was—to "better relations" between our two countries, it ended up being a wonderful journey of observation, interaction and self-discovery.

Most importantly, I have to thank Sumana, both for accompanying me on that jaunt and for contributing his time and editorial expertise towards the completion of this book. As contributor and main editor, he helped with the writing of several passages, and provided feedback and guidance throughout.

Additionally, I must thank a number of other people who urged us on right from the start. It required a bit of gumption for us to embark on this crackpot trip in the summer of our Masters programmes—rather than doing a more "normal" internship that might have led to a proper job. We would not have made the leap without the encouragement of Linda Lim, Sharon Siddique, Pete Gosling, Koh Buck Song and our parents, families and friends.

I am grateful to Yayasan Strategik Sosial (YSS), a Malaysian NGO, for writing a letter on our behalf before the trip, explaining who we are and what we are doing in Malaysia. That gave us legitimacy in our interactions with some Malaysians.

Finally, I also received financial assistance from the Harvard International Development Internship Fund (HIDIF) at Harvard's Kennedy School. Though the money itself was undoubtedly helpful—subsidising the purchase of my bicycle—it was HIDIF's belief in the trip that was also invaluable in fuelling our own confidence. Helaine Daniels was especially supportive.

In the past seven years, there have been many other people who have assisted with the production of this book. For editorial and intellectual guidance, I would like to thank my colleagues at The Economist Group, particularly Simon Long, Graeme

Maxton, Bala Shetty and Justin Wood. Farah Cheah deserves special mention for agreeing to help as a research assistant but then morphing into a quite extraordinary reviewer and source of new ideas.

For assistance with additional research in Malaysia and Singapore, I am grateful to Aileen Goh, Kiran Grewal, Wan Mardiyanti, Yap Mun Ching, Reuben David, James and Molly Kingham, Chan and Momo, Nuno Santos, James and Leela, Sam and Roshni, Buah and Ravi, John and Bina, and Peter and Natasha. For assistance with digital, marketing and social media, I would like to give special thanks to Allanjit Singh and K. J. Tan.

I am indebted to several people who took the time to read through my manuscript, correcting errors, offering new points of view, and suggesting improvements to structure, grammar and language. These were Farah Cheah, Jen Wei Ting, Sharon Siddique, Neil Khor, Koh Buck Song, Simon Long and Kevin Tan. I am thankful for the help and guidance offered by the editorial team at Hong Kong University Press, particularly Clara Ho and Christopher Munn, as well as NUS Press, especially Paul Kratoska.

Over the course of the past eight years, I have interviewed hundreds of Malaysians and Singaporeans. Some of them appear in the following pages; many others do not, though their words and thoughts have influenced my writing greatly. In their own way, they have all contributed to this book. Though there are too many to list, I am eternally grateful to all for their time, patience and insights.

I am especially thankful to the people who provided us with room and board around Malaysia. It must have been unnerving for some to welcome into their homes two foreign men whom they had only just met. Their hospitality kept us going then, and the memories of those encounters still regularly humble us.

Finally, I have to thank my family for their support. My father's love of Malaysia has always inspired me to learn more about the country. My mother's encouragement of my writing, and her reminders about the need to chart one's own course in life, are among the main reasons I am doing what I want to do today. My siblings Vidhya, Jaymit and Shaleen have frequently offered words of encouragement to prod me on. Throughout the book's entire production process, my wife's patience, undying support and her tolerance of my many foibles have been invaluable.

Introduction

This is a story about Malaysia and Singapore—or Malaya, if you will.

I use "Malaya" because I grew up thinking of the two countries as one. As a little boy, I remember travelling from Singapore to Malaysia, sitting in the backseat of my dad's car, swerving through Malaysia's old single-lane highways, evading smog-emitting trucks piled high with oil palm fruit. We would visit relatives, sometimes five or six homes in a day, popping our heads in to sip tea, nibble cakes and watch the oldies play Cupid—"Is there a nice boy for her in Singapore?"

We would stop at roadside vendors, slurping up tropical fruits for a song, and yet still wonder, all the way home, whether we had just been fleeced. We would, in short, soak in Malaysia, her people, her nature, everything about this vast country.

Our country, we sometimes thought. Well, if not exactly our countrymen, then our cousins, our brothers from another mother. Malaysia is a 20-minute ride away. Malaysians speak the same languages and eat the same food. We had a separate passport that allowed us entry to (peninsular) Malaysia and nowhere else, as if to signify that we were special, less different than the rest. It was as if God had created another Singapore, right next to us, and blessed it with more land and lower prices.

Political divisions and developmental ideologies didn't bother me back then. I was young and eager and just wanted to go on a road trip, to leave Singapore's urban madness for some country adventure and *kampung* durians. As I grew older, my youthful naiveté slowly gave way to curiosity.

Malaya, as I slowly realised, is actually made up of two quite different countries. How can that be? Malaysia and Singapore are, after all, physically divided by only a narrow strait. They were connected politically for centuries.

So how come the countries are so different now? Why is Singapore so much more economically developed today than Malaysia? How is it that the ideologies, cultural narratives and ways of thinking vary so much across the narrow border? Is it all because of the invisible political line that divides us?

Sumana, my best friend, and I were seeking answers to these questions eight years ago when our real journey through Malaya began. *Real*, because before 2004, we had never really made an effort to dig deep below the surface, to venture beyond the comfort of cosy conversations and public presumptions.

It is frighteningly easy, after all, to live in Singapore with tunnel vision, not needing to think too much outside the daily grind. Life here goes on, day in and day out, with that unmistakable beat of clockwork consumerism. Singapore just works.

The comfortable monotony can also numb one's senses. It was a conversation in the US, oddly, that forced me to sit up and think a bit more about Malaya. Sitting in a campus pub, in 2003, I had been teasing my American grad school classmates about their country. "Where next are you guys exporting democracy to?"

Foreign students in the US tended to huddle together, seeking the comfort of fellow outsiders. We shared much in common, strangers in a strange land. This natural alignment allowed for some rollicking US vs. Foreign debates, which were fuelled by egos, perceived enlightenment and pints of beer.

American misadventure in Iraq had provided us with plenty of fodder. We spewed "neocolonialism", "torture", "WMD" and other words of the moment at our hapless American friends, as they cringed, embarrassed, for the most part, at what was going on in the Middle East. It was all very unfair, particularly since most of them did not support the war. But who cared? It was great fun seeing them stumped, torn between their ideals and nation.

In class, our professors asked us to get into groups and theorise about the best way to reconstruct Iraq. Before long, we were recommending policies for the Shias and suggesting ways to accommodate the Kurds. It all seemed a bit misplaced. We were just a bunch of students, sitting 6,000 miles away.

Most worryingly, in our view, was that nobody there really knew much about the people, the Iraqis, having never met one in their lives. Was this how policy in the US was formulated? Based on just research papers, historical boundaries and academic discussion? We grilled our classmates.

"So how well do you know the people in your neighbouring countries?" one of them asked us. Cocksure, I shot back with some drivel about having visited Indonesia, Malaysia and Thailand many times. They weren't buying it. "How many different Thai beaches have you been to, again?" they laughed.

I felt a bit stupid. The truth is that I really didn't know *that* much about our neighbours. I was somewhat oblivious to the many strata of society in Singapore, let alone Malaysia.

Many Singaporeans only really know the mainstream, establishment view—what our governments tell us through their media channels. There is little alternative dialogue in our countries. What did ordinary Malaysians really think? What inspired them, motivated them, disgusted them? We had lived all these years, in our tiny little bubbles, without bothering to find out more.

Sumana and I could have easily gone our whole lives without caring. Yet something inside us tugged away. Perhaps it was our grandparents and their friends, whose stories, filled with romance and tragedy, provided a bridge to the colonial era, when Malaysia and Singapore were one.

Or perhaps it was just the endless contradictions that we had trouble dealing with. Malaysia is beautiful; Malaysia is dangerous. Malaysia is multicultural; Malaysia is racist. Which is it? We yearned to find out more.

But how exactly should we go about this? American education, for better or worse, filled us with dreamy hope, idealism and bravado. We felt younger and more energised than we had in high school, eight years before in Singapore.

And so we hatched a plan. We would walk across Malaysia in our sarongs and talk to people. It was a cheap and simple idea that had us suitably stoked. We soon realised it would be nigh well impossible. For one, our legs would likely buckle under the weight of our beer and durian-fed pot bellies. What's more, in our sarongs, and carrying giant backpacks, we looked less like Gandhian pilgrims than wayward buffoons.

Restless, we quickly came up with an alternative idea. We would cycle around Malaysia for a month, visiting every state in peninsular Malaysia and meeting random people along the way. We also decided to subsist on RM10 (about US$3) a day each, a limit that would force us to live simply and seek out help and assistance whenever we could. An early working title for this book was *On the Benevolence of Malaysians.*

We sought advice from friends, family, and professors. A few urged us on. Most said the idea was crazy. And quite a few confirmed what our mums had always told us—that we are, indeed, wayward buffoons.

But we had made up our minds and there was no turning back. And so our journey through Malaya, our *real* journey through Malaya, began eight years ago. With two bicycles, a tent and RM600, we spent a month cycling around the whole of peninsular Malaysia.

We visited hundreds of towns, met many fascinating people, had countless conversations, and landed in several comedic capers. It was a random, rollicking, rip-roaring exploration through Malaysia and, also, through ourselves—our own emotions, misconceptions and prejudices.

What started out as a dive into Malaysia, therefore, quickly became a look at our home, Singapore, as well. We found ourselves constantly comparing the two countries. Each became a sounding board for the other. During that time, the kernel for a story had grown, but only just. Our one-month bicycle trip had merely whetted our appetites.

We spent the next eight years speaking to many different people in Malaysia and Singapore—analysts, economists, farmers, managers, ministers, politicians, professors, senior business executives, shopkeepers, students, taxi drivers, and others, laypeople, from all walks of life.

Our interactions with these people serve as the backbone of this story, which I have divided into 11 chapters. Chapters 1 and 2 explore the relationship between Malaysia and Singapore—our shared history, imagined identities and separation anxieties. Chapters 3 and 4 look at politics and government in our countries. Chapter 5 examines the roles of the media, judiciary and civil society in our countries. I talk about business and economic development in Chapters 6 and 7. Chapter 8 deals with issues surrounding ethnicity and race. Chapter 9 discussed the influence of religion in our two countries. Finally, I spend Chapters 10 and 11 pondering something that rarely gets enough attention here—happiness.

It would be arrogant and foolish for me to suggest that I really understand Malaya now. Our story is, undoubtedly, more a collection of insights than a comprehensive study. Every time we spoke with somebody different, or visited a new place, we realised that there is something else we don't know.

There is also a geographical omission in this work that I must explain. Modern Malaysia is spread out over two separate land masses. There are eleven states and two federal territories on Peninsular Malaysia (West Malaysia), and two states and one federal territory on the island of Borneo (East Malaysia).

My research covers mostly West Malaysia and not East Malaysia. There are several reasons for this. Throughout this book, I have tried to consider what happens when one country is split apart and each subdivision pushed on its own developmental path. Using this lens, it is West Malaysia that has deep-rooted cultural, historical, political and social bonds with Singapore. East Malaysia is different from both West Malaysia and Singapore in many ways, not least its peoples' provenance.

East Malaysia joined the Federation of Malaysia only in 1963, in the face of much local opposition.[1] It has never been an easy union. All this put together, there seems much less reason to compare East Malaysia's development to Singapore's.

Still, it may seem negligent for any book on Malaysia to ignore those two beautiful states of Sabah and Sarawak, particularly given how they have become key battlegrounds for control of the Federal government. Unfortunately this book's scope does not permit me to give them the treatment they deserve; I hope to one day.

There is so much more to this complex region that has yet to be written about. I can really hope only to contribute a bit to our collective understanding.

What, in essence, did I discover?

The first, perhaps obvious point, is that Malaysians and Singaporeans do indeed have much in common. All across Malaysia we met people who had connections to Singapore. An old man who had lived and worked there under the British administration; a daughter who had been sent to school; a young man who, originally from Kelantan, a northern state, now lives in Johor, the southernmost, in order to commute every day to Singapore for work. Similarly, there are so many people in Singapore with relatives, friends or business contacts in Malaysia—more than 5 per cent of Singapore's population is, in fact, Malaysian.

Yet Malaysia is a much bigger, more diverse land. Though the country's broad ethnic, religious and developmental diversity is apparent from afar, there are many smaller differences that emerge only upon close inspection. "You guys speak Malay right, but I tell you as you go up the coast, the language is going to change, even we don't understand," a Malay youth in Pahang told us. "Pahang is famous for *lepak*, relax, Kelantan is good for women, because they are mixed with Siam, they are beautiful up there, Terengganu is great for food and Johor is the place to look for work."

Nevertheless, Malaysia's and Singapore's shared histories, cultures, languages and place ensure that a familiar voice or recognisable sight is never far away. The experience of visiting some of Malaysia's small old towns is akin to stepping back in time, seeing what Singapore was like decades ago. Or at least that's what some older Singaporeans tell us, nostalgically, in those moments when they decry Singapore's rush to modernity.

If a Malaysian and Singaporean were travelling overseas, it would really be quite hard for the locals to tell us apart—our dress, appearance and accents are similar enough. When we've visited far off countries in Africa and Central America, some people there have given us puzzled looks when we've said, "We're from Singapore"— they may have heard of the place, but don't really know much about it. Many think we are a Chinese appendage, like Hong Kong and Macau. When we add "It's near Malaysia", most of them immediately get their bearings.

Our commonalities, then, are largely because of our proximity. Once we look past them, some startling differences emerge—most important, our political and socio-economic systems. Malaysia is a country where one ethno-religious group— the majority Malay Muslims, the so-called *bumiputeras*, sons of the land—is given preference over the others.[2] Singapore, which is majority Chinese, tries its best to run a race-neutral meritocracy. This difference in our worldview is the major reason our countries split apart in 1965.

Before we cycled through Malaysia, we had a feeling that Malaysia's system is inherently unfair. The Malays are given preference at the expense of the Chinese and Indians. The Malays, therefore, are lulled into complacency. The Chinese and Indians are aggrieved. Everybody is worse off.

What we did not expect, however, was for several Malaysians to complain about Singapore's system. Many of them believe that our exacting meritocracy is inherently unfair, because it allows the rich to get richer, and the poor to get poorer. It does not try to give a leg up to those at the bottom. According to this school of thought, Singapore is, at best, a tough place to live, and at worst, a Darwinian tragedy. Proud Singaporeans, we were shocked. We had not expected any Malaysian to trumpet their system over ours.

We think their system is unfair; they think our system is unfair. We remember feeling ignorant and sad. Our countries are farther apart than we had thought.

Although we listened to these diatribes against Singapore, we felt they were mostly poppycock, the indignant ramblings of residents from a poorer country. As the years passed, meanwhile, and as we found out more about Malaysia, I became even surer of our conviction—Malaysia's system is unjust, even racist.

Many Malaysians, of course, will shudder when reading that, all the more since it is coming from a Singaporean—anything that smacks of Singaporean superiority tends to evoke nausea in Malaysians. Still, that is no reason not to say it.

Through countless encounters with Malaysians all over the country, we have seen how the *bumiputera* affirmative action policies have created a culture of dependence amongst the Malays, sowed disharmony between the Malays and other groups, reduced economic efficiency and opened the door to mind-boggling corruption, cronyism and nepotism. The only people who have really benefitted from it, meanwhile, are the Malay aristocrats and politically-connected businessmen.

It is worth noting that the *bumiputera* policies, like so many other grand political ideologies, were born of noble ideals: eradicating poverty, economic empowerment, raising the dignity of the Malays. Some of its original proponents, such as Hussein Onn, are considered Malaysian heroes of impeccable character.[3]

Sadly, over the years—and most noticeably from the mid-1980s—the policy has been hijacked by vested interests. In other words, an idealistic but discriminatory philosophy has been completely undermined by corruption. Malaysians will never know what might have come of this grand experiment in social engineering.

In my opinion, Malaysia must dismantle these *bumiputera* policies. That is absolutely essential for social and economic progress. Some critics suggest switching the policy from pro-Malay to pro-poor. Though a noble idea, this could open up new channels of corruption and leakage. Malaysia needs to level the playing field as soon as possible (while providing highly targeted assistance to certain low-income groups).

The current prime minister, Najib Razak, seems to want change. It is unclear, however, if his mooted reforms signify a genuine shift or are more window dressing, in his bid to win domestic votes and attract foreign investment.

Sadly, serious reform appears far away, not least because of the powerful entrenched Malay interests in the country. Ultimately, there are still many Malays who believe that Malaysia's *raison d'être* is to protect Malay interests—not those of all Malaysians.

To my astonishment, we also met a fair number of Malaysian Chinese and Indians who believe that the *bumiputera* policies are essential—they have come to believe that Malays are so inherently handicapped that they will stutter unless given privileges and preferences. This, more than anything else, proves the absurdity of the policy.

The raft of privileges, preferences and exclusions has also sliced and diced Malaysian society, such that it has become extremely stratified. There is a bewildering array of honorifics and titles in use today. Malaysia's minions vie for these precious titles, some of which can open bountiful doors of opportunity.

Some might say that calling another person Datuk, Dato' or Datoh is just a form of respect. Well, maybe. All too often, however, I have seen bigwigs bossing people around, and cringed as underlings grovel at their feet. For all its egalitarian pretences, Malaysia can seem feudal, and much more classist than it was before independence.

Malaysia has, nevertheless, managed to bumble along, growing into a robust middle-income country with, amongst other things, strong agricultural and technology sectors. It is admired in many parts of the developing world.

With its rich resources and dynamic population, however, many Malaysians feel that their country should have achieved high-income status by now. Instead, it is stuck in the so-called middle-income trap, held back by, amongst other things, mismanagement, corruption, stagnant productivity, poor English standards, a shortage of management and presentation skills, a brain drain and economic inefficiencies—all in some way due to the *bumiputera* policy, and its philosophical father, *ketuanan Melayu*, literally Malay superiority, the idea that Malays deserve a special place in the land of Malaysia.

Rather than trying to emulate the likes of Hong Kong or Singapore, Malaysia is, therefore, constantly looking over its shoulder. Its neighbours have been busy building meritocratic, pro-business economies. Malaysia's policymakers might have once considered Indonesia and Vietnam as economic backwaters. Today, they worry about them winning foreign investment that might otherwise have gone to Malaysia.

There is little doubt that Singapore, on the other hand, is one of the 20th century's economic success stories. Amongst people I speak with—even some of his ardent critics—there is a general sense that Lee Kuan Yew, Singapore's first prime minister, deserves much credit for this. In a short span of time, following independence, he managed to root out corruption, strengthen the rule of law, foster administrative competence, instil a hardworking, disciplined ethos in Singaporeans, attract lots of foreign investment, and ultimately raise living standards. He also managed to build a party and government famed for its limitless ability to groom new leaders.

Much has been written about these successes, and there is little reason for me to harp on them here. What we did find far more arresting, throughout our conversations and travels, is the fact that there are some genuine problems brewing in Singapore. Most importantly, perhaps, is the fact that the Malaysians are right.

In 2004, as we cycled around Malaysia, many people lamented Singapore's cold capitalism, and predicted that income inequality would prove a big problem. Even back then, this was not really a new idea. Many Malaysians, including Mahathir Mohamad, a former prime minister, had made similar observations before.

In short, those predictions have come true. One of the biggest challenges in modern Singapore is the yawning gap between the haves and the have-nots. Singapore's Gini coefficient, a measure of income inequality, is higher than America's and China's.

A frequent complaint I've heard is that Singapore has become a place for the global rich, not the average Singaporean. These people frequently indulge in posh homes, luxury yachts, Cartier watches and foie gras. This group includes a small coterie of the richest Singaporeans, including—in many people's eyes—senior politicians, who are paid millions of dollars a year.

Below them on the income ladder sits a huge middle class—Singaporeans (and many foreigners) with enough money to afford an apartment, a car and a maid. Life is fairly comfortable, but certainly not as indulgent as one would expect for one of the richest countries in the world.

Right at the bottom, finally, are the people for whom the Singapore dream has become a nightmare. The real incomes of Singapore's bottom 30 per cent of earners stagnated from 1997 to 2007, a period during which Singapore's economy boomed.

One of the best descriptions I've heard for Singapore today is "a first world country with a third-world wage structure". If you are lucky enough to be a banker, consultant or some other senior executive, you will get paid handsomely and enjoy living in Singapore. Wages for lower-level jobs, however, have not kept pace with economic development.

Singapore offers cheaper food, haircuts, taxis and shop service than any other rich world city—only because the people at the bottom probably do not earn enough. At the risk of sounding simplistic, Singapore's poor people should earn more, and Singapore's rich people should pay them more for their work.

Income inequality, in a sense, should not come as a surprise—many developed countries grapple with the problem. What did strike us, however, was the fact that nobody talked about it much before 2007. While Malaysians warned us about it in 2004—even as we foolishly brushed them off—there was barely any mention in Singapore.

That speaks to another facet of life here—social, political and economic dialogue in Singapore is extremely shallow and narrow. Given the dominance of the People's Action Party (PAP), the government's control over the media, and a natural Singaporean deference to authority, there is precious little debate and discussion over many national issues. This reticence carries over to the workplace, where Singaporean workers, seeking refuge behind their fancy degrees, tend not to speak out much or challenge convention or authority.

In many other democratic countries, the problem of income inequality—or for that matter, any other contemporary challenge—would have been discussed extensively in the media, government and by citizens. In Singapore, it appears as if any topic has to receive an implicit nod from the government, before the public is allowed to discuss it. Once the green light is given, the media fall into line dutifully.

This, of course, has grave implications for Singapore's economy. Though a manufacturing and service success, Singapore has had trouble building a knowledge economy. No wonder. We Singaporeans are not trained to think or speak out.

That is one reason for the decline of Creative Technologies. In 1998, Creative Technologies was more valuable than Apple. Through its industry-standard computer sound cards, such as the Sound Blaster, Creative had established itself as a global leader in digital sound. It was in a perfect position to capitalise on the nascent MP3 industry.

Instead of bringing innovative new products to market, however, Creative dithered. Apple, with little prior experience in digital sound, released its iPod, which made Creative's players look like museum pieces. It quickly became apparent that while Creative is adept at building electronic cogs that work quietly within machines, it is hopelessly lost when it comes to design and marketing. In other words, excellent behind the scenes, stage fright in front.

Thus began Apple's resurgence. In 10 years, a Californian company had destroyed Singapore's pride and joy. Few people even remember that Creative once ruled the digital sound roost.

It is unsurprising that Apple is from California and Creative from Singapore. Singapore's inherent strengths are not creativity and dynamism. They are stability and rule of law. Given our current trajectory, therefore, it looks as if Singapore will not succeed in building a creative, knowledge economy so much as a safe financial centre and a corporate HQ. Switzerland of the East? Perhaps. But only the finance, please, not the watch-making.

How should Singapore change, then? The easy answer, in theory, is more social and political freedoms. In practice, though, this will prove tricky. Singaporeans have grown up knowing only one government, and one way of doing things. There is little impetus for change—for most of our history, the Singapore model has flourished economically while supposedly freer countries around us have floundered. If it wants to liberalise Singapore, the government has to simultaneously relax control over the country, while allowing independent institutions to grow. All along the way, naysayers will complain.

For Singapore has many sacred cows, certain fixed ideas and orthodoxies that nobody argues with. For instance, what if Lee Kuan Yew and the PAP were wrong? What if their plan of developing Singapore at breakneck speed, fuelled by foreign labour and foreign capital, was a mistake?

Imagine that development to a high-income knowledge economy is a 400-metre race. Singapore has sprinted the first 300 metres, exhausting itself, and now finds it difficult to complete the race. Perhaps it might have been better to run at a slower pace.

Some suggest that Singapore's economic model served it well only until the 1990s. It then should have been fundamentally retooled—rather than tweaked—to better prepare Singaporeans for life in a globalised knowledge economy. That would have helped lessen our dependence on foreign labour and capital.

What if Lee Kuan Yew was wrong? Many people in Singapore would consider me rude for even posing that question. That, quite frankly, is the problem.

Given our government's smugness, it is tempting to be overcritical of Singapore. Throughout my research, and during many conversations, I was reminded of the unbridled success of so many of Singapore's policies.

Even as Malaysians criticised our (supposedly) unfair system, they would heap praise on our effective, incorruptible administration and economic efficiencies. Despite a series of horrible gaffes recently—including letting a suspected terrorist, Mas Selamat, escape from a detention centre—Singapore's PAP-led government has, on the whole, done an exemplary job.

Are Singaporeans happy, though, with the country's success? From my anecdotal evidence, materialism has helped drive Singapore's economy, but it has not really led to that much happiness. In the land of the rich, many Singaporeans still feel relatively poor—we always want more. Those already with serious money, meanwhile, seem to be looking for something else in life. Oddly, we found many Malaysians, rich and poor, to be seemingly happier with their life.

Perhaps that reflects what we value in life. Malaysians, by and large, appear to place a greater importance on big families. We Singaporeans, meanwhile, are clearly more interested than Malaysians in making money.

Singapore's society has long pushed a materialistic definition of success, the so-called "5 C's"—Cash, Credit card, Car, Country Club, Condominium. Sadly, somebody forgot to include the most important one—Children.

When we Singaporeans say, "He/she is doing well", we are almost invariably talking about that person's material well-being. A good job, a high salary and possibly a killing in the property market.

If a Malaysian says, "He/she is doing well", we found them often talking about a person's health or family. Living well, perhaps, with many children.

More happiness could also be because Malaysia is a much bigger country, with many more places to go, jobs to do and activities to engage in. People have more options, avenues to explore and ways in which to be happy. Singapore, by contrast, is small, and people tend to do the same things. If you're not intent on making money, and racing your Ferrari from one traffic light to the next, then what exactly are you up to?

Happiness, of course, is relative and subjective. The Malaysians and Singaporeans we met are all somewhat happy, and yet still looking for happiness. Ultimately, that is because we are all unsure about who we really are.

What does it mean to be a Malaysian? What does it mean to be a Singaporean? What binds each country together? As we've traversed our countries, and asked hundreds of people, I've had trouble finding that common element, that special ingredient, in each country.

Both countries are still struggling to come to terms with their founding principles. Malaysia's constitution guarantees preeminence to Islam and Malays. What that means in practice is still a matter of great debate. Malaysians are genuinely torn between running a Malay country and a country for all Malaysians.

Singaporean identity, meanwhile, appears even more vacuous. We all grew up believing in a one-party system that delivers economic growth through a race-neutral meritocracy. All we had to do was keep quiet and work hard and we'd become rich. Cracks are appearing in that philosophy. And without hard work and lots of money, there seems precious little else to being a Singaporean.

As both countries search for meaning, our guiding philosophies are likely to converge. For most of its history, Malaysia has been guided by the desire for "equality of outcomes". It has been trying to redistribute the fruits of growth in a more equitable fashion by giving some people—the *bumiputeras*—more opportunities than others. Malaysians have been focused on the end result.

Singapore, meanwhile, has been guided by the desire for "equality of opportunities". We have been striving to provide every person with the same opportunities in life. But after that, we haven't really cared much about who becomes a millionaire and who a pauper. Singaporeans have been focused on the start.

Both countries have pursued their philosophies with a dogged determination. But both have realised that their systems are faltering. Malaysia's pursuit of "equality of outcomes" has created some serious problems, not least the ethnic tensions in society today.

Singapore's desire only for "equality of opportunities" has led to gross inequality—or very different "outcomes"—in the country. And with that, it has become harder and harder to guarantee "equality of opportunities"—a rich family's child will always be much better positioned for success than a poor family's child.

Hence, as Malaysia and Singapore embark on their next stage of development, they will have to become a bit more like each other. Malaysians will want more "equality of opportunities" and Singaporeans will want more "equality of outcomes".

This is not just theoretical fluff. These guiding philosophies have influenced how millions of Malaysians and Singaporeans think and interact with each other. In Malaysia, for instance, I have met Chinese and Indians who look down on the Malays around them because they are perceived as dependent on government help.

In Singapore, because of the assumption that everybody gets the same shot at life, those who ultimately do well are more prone to ignore—or even look down upon—those who don't. People are less aware that those at the bottom need extra help.

Therefore, this fundamental shift will dramatically change the way we think about ourselves and each other. It will shape the hearts, minds and souls of all Malayans. In many ways, this long transition has only just begun.

But these changes won't be smooth. In both countries, authoritarian states are slowly making way for more democratic societies. Ordinary people are only just finding out that their voices and votes do actually make a difference. Civil society is being forced to develop at warp speed. Private and public actors are having to adapt to new ways of communicating on a multitude of new platforms.

It is also worth noting that in terms of our guiding philosophies, Malaysia and Singapore are unique. We are probably the only two Asian countries where the original post-colonial movements still exert considerable influence over politics and broader societal mindsets. Almost every other country has seen some revolution or another—including China's opening up from 1978 to India's from 1991—that has effectively replaced the post-colonial philosophies with newer ones.

Not so here. For better or worse, the post-colonialists' ideas and fervour still hold great sway over society. Many of the younger politicians are cut from the same cloth. Malaysia's current prime minister is the son of the country's second prime minister. Singapore's current prime minister is the son of the country's first prime minister.

All that is, no doubt, largely a reflection of how economically and politically successful this generation has been. But it also points to a worrying fact—Malaysia and Singapore have never had to go through that process of broad political renewal and a reimagination of societal norms.

As the Malayan post-colonial generation nears its end, the coming changes are going to be turbulent, to say the least. Political players, mindsets and institutions have become so entrenched that they will not take kindly to being turfed out.

Malaya split apart 47 years ago. Our countries chose different paths, and went our separate ways. Both have developed tremendously since 9 August 1965. Neither, it seems, is much closer to finding its soul.

***

Going home. 13 August 2004.

They will tell you to never try and smuggle anything illegal into Singapore, whether it's heroin, contraband Marlboros or pirated DVDs. Security is tight and the penalties horrid.

But that's just what "they" say. Allow me to let you in on a little secret: to smuggle into Singapore, you don't need high-technology sleuths—just a plain old bicycle.

As we waited in the long, smoky, lung-gnarling motorcycle line to get checked by the meticulous Singaporean customs officers, we were filled with a sudden void. What were we to do now?

Sure, there were many things we were glad to be done with. The return home spelt the end of those daily insect-ridden "showers"—squatting below a dripping foot-high tap, sometimes right next to the potty, at another squalid Petronas station. On several occasions, in some of Malaysia's more rural towns, I had opened the toilet door only to be greeted by a wall of bugs, grasshoppers and spiders, flying right at my face, as if to thank me for freeing them from their aviary.

We were also relieved to be released from our RM10 per day spending limit. As noble an effort as we like to think it was, the truth is that austerity is tough. And painful. There were so many times we did not have ice in our drinks just to save an extra 20 cents. Perhaps austerity in an economic desert is easy, but in Malaysia, a thriving market economy, where all manner of goodies smile at you every hour, it is crushing. We would now finally be able to have that extra serving of meat.

Perhaps the most emotionally and psychologically draining part of the trip was not knowing where we were going to sleep. Almost every day, as dusk approached, we had to go look for a place to pitch our tent or sleep. Sometimes we would have to speak to more than ten people before we found a suitable spot, and even then all we got was a clearing in the gravel. The uncertainty, the sheer randomness of it all, had taken its toll on us.

It was the sort of intense experience that infuses your thoughts, dreams, memories, glands and heart. For weeks, every new sensory input would be interpreted in relation to that experience.

We had a lot of time for self-reflection, for the officer was fingering through each motorcycle like a dog in hunt of truffles. When we finally got to him, he looked at us, then at the huge bags saddled to the back of our bikes. He then smiled and waved us through, patting our backs instead of our bags. We still regret not having stuffed our bags full of rainbow-coloured chewing gum that day.

Fifteen minutes later we were guzzling down our first homecoming can of Tiger beer. It felt fantastic to have more than 10 ringgit a day to spend. But the decompression sickness had started, and we were wondering what to do. It was about 4 pm on Friday, 13 August 2004. Exactly 30 days since we had left Singapore.

And more than 62 years since the Fall of Singapore to the Japanese. They too had come storming down the Malay Peninsular on bicycles, entering Singapore over the same Johor Strait that we just had. What a cunning mode of transport, eh?

"From a very early age I've had to interrupt my education to go to school," George Bernard Shaw once said. We too had, from the age of six, suffered from the same interruption. This trip was our attempt at continuing education.

We had spent a month floating on a Malayan breeze. It felt strange to be back.

1
Forgotten histories

Betong, Thailand. 29 July 2004.

We should have given up two hours ago. In that time, we had travelled only five kilometres. We had started counting each push of the pedal, like dazed soldiers still mouthing a drill. The sun was scorching our skin, and a stream of sweat burning our eyes. Our water bottles felt like little radiators, the water inside too warm to drink. We eased around one bend only to find another steep slope staring down at us with indifference. We were tired by the slopes, angry at the sun, fed up with the countryside. Six months ago Sumana, my best friend, and I had decided to cycle around Malaysia. And now here we were, parched and punctured, in Thailand.

When we finally arrived at the peak—drained and soaked, our jerseys glued to our skin with sweat—we were greeted by a soothing breeze; but for its high-pitched whisper, the place was eerily silent. To get here, we had cycled on dusty roads that snaked through small villages and new rubber plantations, the incline getting worse by the minute. All those roving hills made the place inaccessible, and its inhabitants were grateful for that. Still, there was an expectation that once we reached the top of the hill, we would find something. It looked like disappointment lay ahead.

This isolated encampment, on the peak of a Thai mountain, several kilometres from the Malaysian border, had a lazy relationship with time. Things didn't just move slowly; they seemed to be slowing down, like a dying pendulum. There were few youngsters around. The place was like an ageing Japanese rural town, whose best years were behind it. As we strolled past two older residents, their worn faces aching to smile, we couldn't help wondering if they missed the buzz of yesteryears.

"So what are you doing in Betong? Came to see the tunnels?"

Robert, a leathery-faced, middle-aged Chinese man, had beckoned us in for a little chit-chat. We walked hesitantly into the makeshift zinc-roofed garage. He had an unspoken intensity about him.

"We might see the tunnels, but we want to talk to some communists as well."

"Speak to them? About what?"

"We interview people wherever we go. Ask them about their lives, their history, that kind of thing."

"But so, where are you guys from?"

"Err ... Singapore lah."

"Ya, I know, but I mean originally. What nationality are you?"

"Ya, we're Singaporeans."

"Really? You don't look like ... let me show you something."

Robert reached into the left pocket of his cargo pants, and pulled out a dirty, torn zip-lock bag. Inside was a little red book. We recognised it, and instantly felt our connection to Robert grow.

"You see this? I'm Singaporean too."

Robert, waving his passport, beckoned us towards him. He urged us to feel it, and leaf through it. We played the part, like sceptical immigration officers. We returned the favour, and showed him our passports. We smiled contentedly at each other, but the feel-goodness of our little nationality dance soon wore off. It was bizarre meeting a fellow countryman in this remote jungle hideaway. We thought the Singaporean would be a novelty item in Betong, but here was Robert, at place, and at ease, in this former communist enclave.

"But I am not a communist, ah," Robert asserted, "I am just here visiting some old friends." He gestured to the two other Chinese, one man and one lady, sitting next to him. They nodded and smiled, with a disarming warmth.

"Old friends? From where?"

"Oh just some friends. I've known them for a long time ... you might find some of the communists up there," pointing to the top of the hill we were on, "there are two villages further up."

"How do we know who the communists are?"

"Almost everybody there is a communist. Just ask around. But remember! I am not a communist, ah, I just know that they live there."

A skittishness about communist affiliations was hardly surprising, coming from somebody who carried our particular form of little red book. In Singapore, we grew up learning certain facts about the communist ideology: like "communist" is synonymous with "devil"; like communists are dangerous pariahs—first-order enemies of the state. Consigned to the footnotes of our history textbooks, the communist story did not deserve even a moment's attention. In any case, in school we had studied only topics we were going to be tested on—Communism wasn't on the list. And thus it was left covered by the veils of mystery and anarchy, aching to be unravelled just a hilltop away.

We were about to confront the evil we knew as youth. This was as daring as it got, the stuff of boys' dreams. So what if they had signed a peace treaty 15 years ago? So what if they had traded in their Kalashnikovs for Coca Colas? These geriatric terrorists had blood on their hands. We felt like Indiana Jones, swashbuckling warriors, boldly going where no Singaporean had ventured before.

When we got to the top of the hill however, we encountered neither fierce guerrilla nor Marxist literature. Instead, the philosophy on display was eerily familiar—a souvenir shop—and it quickly doused our brazenness. The things on sale weren't even communist merchandise. Had Che Guevara berets or bound Mao dictums been converted into capitalist expressions, we could have forgiven the situation. Not here. This shop, run by two dour ladies, was like any other Southeast Asian flea bazaar. Wooden Buddha statues jostled for space with Zodiac figurines, prayer beads and fake Adidas baseball caps. The only thing remotely "communist" about the goods was their "Made in China" stamp. Was this as close as we would get?

Across the road from the shop, there was an entrance. It sat there expectantly, beckoning visitors. A sign saying "10 ringgit per entry" lay at the front of an unmanned ticket booth. This was the entrance to the "Piyamit Tunnels". Once a clandestine underground bunker for the communists, it was now reduced to a tourist attraction. We weren't interested, being more bent on meeting the communists themselves rather than walking in their footsteps. We looked around the shop.

"Hello, can you speak Malay?"

"*Sikit sikit*, a little bit," answered one of the two ladies, without pausing from her task, polishing the head of a wooden Buddha.[1] The other did not even glance in our direction.

"What is this place?"

"Oh, the communist tunnels are over there. You can go and visit them. There is a souvenir shop here, and a medicine shop there. Feel free to look around."

She delivered her rehearsed greeting with a customary smile, and then returned to her monotonous task. Her thin black hair was tied in a neat bun, exposing smooth cheeks. She rounded off her polishing with a flurry of short, furious strokes, and then looked at her reflection in Buddha's glistening pate. She was admiring her work, not her looks. During our entire trip, she was the only person we met who did not ask who we were, where we were from or what we were doing cycling. It was as if the past did not matter to her, only the future.

"Erm, sorry to bother you again, but we were wondering if you could help us?"

"How?"

"We are actually looking for the communists."

"The communists? Why?"

"We'd like to meet some communists to find out about their life."

This time we got her attention. She looked us in the eye, and sized us up. Besides a little furrow of her brows and a slight pursing of her lips, her face betrayed no emotion. We felt naked, and guilty, as if we had said something wrong.

"Sure, you can talk to me. I was a communist," a fiery, indignant pride burning through her words, as she looked up at us.

"You?" we thought. We had not expected the fabled communist to come in the form of a diminutive Chinese woman.

"It's fine, don't worry," she said, sensing our doubt. "These days we are free to talk. The war is over. There is peace."

The Communist Party of Malaya (CPM) was founded at a congress in a rubber plantation near Kuala Pilah, Negri Sembilan, in late April 1930, according to Chin Peng, its leader.[2] That was a full 27 years before Malaysia gained independence from the British. Among the leftist luminaries in attendance that day was a certain Communist International (Comintern) representative, Nguyen Ai Quoc, later to become Ho Chi Minh.

The CPM's struggle was initially an anti-colonial one, against whoever stood in its way. First it fought the British, then the Japanese during the World War II occupation (1942–45). After the Japanese left, the CPM fought the British again, who had come riding back into Malaya after the war, unsure about the fate of their dwindling empire.

From 1945 to 1948 the British attempted to reel CPM members into the mainstream, in order to prevent the party from developing. Like many of the CPM's adversaries, the British did not know what to do with it, and their approach was decidedly schizophrenic. On the one hand, the British presented awards to the CPM, publicly acknowledging its role in ejecting the Japanese. However, the British simultaneously hammered down on the CPM or leftist activities they felt threatening: killing unarmed hungry demonstrators clamouring for food and money; shutting down leftist publications and prosecuting CPM members under dubious judicial procedures.[3]

After a few European planters and strike-breakers were killed on 16 June 1948, the British declared a state of emergency in Malaya. From that moment onwards, the CPM was pushed completely underground: offices were closed, its daily newspaper the *Min Sheng Pau* (Voice of the People) was shut down, and anybody having the faintest connection to it hauled in for questioning. The emergency lasted till 1960.

The period between 1948 and 1957 saw the CPM fighting a guerrilla war against the British. It received support and supplies from locals sympathetic to its cause, especially Chinese who were romanced by communist developments in the motherland. However, the British managed to successfully starve its supply lines and fight the communists off, pushing them northwards until they finally found refuge across the Thai border in Betong. Chin Peng reached Betong at the end of 1953. Betong proved a convenient nether region to operate from—outside Malaysia's territory, but too far south for Bangkok's elite to really bother.

While the communists waged a guerrilla war against the British, legendary Malayan nationalists such as David Marshall, Singapore's first chief minister; Lee Kuan Yew, Singapore's first prime minister; and Tunku Abdul Rahman, Malaysia's first prime minister, worked tirelessly within the system to get the British out. The CPM's contribution to Malaya's independence struggle is often downplayed. Still, even Mr Lee has admitted that without their armed resistance, his own constitutional methods of wresting power away from the British would have taken much longer to work.[4]

Nevertheless, following independence in 1957, the Malaysian and Singaporean governments, having no more need for the communists, cracked down on them, as an anti-communist wave swept across Southeast Asia.

"Tunku Abdul Rahman did not want to give us a chance to rise up. He wanted to capture us all and put us in jail! We were locked up straight away. Just for our beliefs!" wailed the little ex-communist lady whom we shall call Betty.

Betty said there was no acceptable legal way to practice communism in Malaysia. Prevented from political participation, the communists resorted to violence. At the height of the movement in 1975, the CPM consisted of a force of 3,500 guerrillas.[5]

"What else could we do? Once they started locking us up, we had no choice but to take up arms. Our comrades were spread out all over the country. We fled into the jungles and took up arms. Had we stayed in the towns, we would have been arrested. We had *no choice*." Not until the Peace Accords of 1989 would a CPM member be able to walk freely again.

The communist bug had first bitten Betty when she was in school in Selangor in the 1970s. At the time, Malaysian society seemed to be turning inwards, caught in the throes of pro-Malay nationalist policies. What hope then for the other races? To Betty and her would-be comrades, it appeared as though one colonial master was slowly being replaced by another.

Betty, faced with this perceived unjustness, found communism's theories liberating. She remembers the first time communism seduced her, at an underground meeting in Kuala Lumpur, where a party leader was making a speech. "He told us how we must make all the races equal. He told us how we must get rid of all the class distinctions in society. He told us about how each person should be the same as the next," said Betty, her face filled with dreamy nostalgia. "We were all inspired by this! I knew then that I must join the communist cause."

To some, this other system promised equality for all, and was worth fighting for. "Conversion to communism is as strong as a religious conversion," says Chin Peng. "It provides a faith and belief in a system which, at least to the convert, appears as the incontrovertible true path to what is right and fair among human beings."[6]

Betty was just 16 years old when she left her father's home in Selangor to join the guerrilla CPM army in 1978. "Yes, I ran away from my father's house. I remember the day. I was sad, but only for a while. I was really looking forward to entering the jungle! I was going to join the communist army!" she told us, her voice bursting with pride, as she reminisced about the day she eloped.

"Some comrades met us in the jungle. There were about six of us. We started trekking through the jungle towards Thailand. I was so happy. To be amongst fellow comrades. All along the way, they narrated communist stories and we spoke of our dreams for a communist Malaya. I was filled with pride."

Betty and her recruitment detail reached the border after about four weeks— the distance from Selangor to Betong is more than 350 km. "There, another senior comrade met us. He looked at me and then told me that I was too young and so I must return," says Betty. "I was devastated. I was scared to go back to my father. How could I? I had come all the way here. I was determined to join. This was what I had wanted to do."

Betty convinced them to let her stay by explaining her devotion to communism. "I was willing to kill, I was willing to die," she smiled, remembering her 16-year-old self. "I think my commander could tell I'd make a good soldier."

Betty and the rest of the posse were then marched up a hill. When she reached the lower camp, she was awestruck—before her was a phalanx of comrades, adults and kids, decked in crisp green uniforms, wearing fierce expressions on their creased faces, lining either side of the road, forming a victory tunnel to greet the new recruits. "That was the best moment. I was so impressed, so filled with pride."

Betty had arrived there a starry-eyed young damsel. While the kids she had grown up with were going to school in newly independent Malaysia, Betty was under a different kind of tutelage. She had swapped meek "Good mornings" for thunderous "Yes Sirs!" Instead of home economics, she was learning the trade of the jungle—including how to strip off a snake's skin using the branch of a tree, and then make medicine from it; how to carve up an elephant, and pluck out the tasty parts; and how to conceal the smoke from a fire.

She learned how to march and how to shoot. There was the brutal physical training, although, because of her small frame, Betty was rarely treated fairly. Male soldiers typically carried 80–90 kg loads, females 50–60 kg. "But they only let me carry 16 kg! I was very unhappy when they made it easier for me," says Betty. (By comparison, US soldiers in the Vietnam War carried a combat load of under 40 kg, while those operating in Afghanistan in 2003 carried up to 60 kg.)[7]

Classes were not confined to the physical. There was also training for the mind. Betty studied geography, military theory and communist philosophy. She even learned Higher Malay, in preparation for life in the young Malaysian nation. Each cadre maintained a journal which vividly documented observations, lessons learnt, and personal opinions and reflections. Instructors had access to each of the journals. Life in the jungle was an open book.

Cadres were all assigned to various specialisations—there were doctors, writers, dancers and technicians. These different roles would allow them to live as a community, but each role also offered skills that would come in handy during their struggle. "The doctors learned their trade in the camps mostly, studying with their own books. Some of them got sent to China for two years of study. Upon return, they held classes for others. We even got videos from China, brought by Chang Chung Ming, our leader.[8] Once a month, we got to watch a film about Malaysia."

"So you had enough time to relax then?"

"*Relax*?" Betty snapped, pouncing on our cheeky suggestion. "The television and radio were for educational purposes, for training. You have no idea how tough our life was."

"Well, we did serve in the Singapore Army for two and a half years."

Betty buckled over with laughter, as if we had just admitted to working as bell boys at the Ritz Carlton. We should have never thought there would be anything shared in Betty's experience in the jungle and our military service.

We served in a conscript army in a country that has never gone to war. Soldiers enjoy private canteens, duty-free beer and weekends off. Our army's finest hour was in early 2011, when a young Singaporean soldier was photographed strolling along the road in fatigues, with his Filipino maid two steps behind, carrying his backpack for him.

Betty, however, had volunteered for a daily armed struggle. She had probably marched more in 30 days than we'd managed in 30 months. She eventually managed to catch her breath.

"Do you know how strict our commanders were?" she continued. "If you stepped out of line, you would be punished and humiliated. For example, you cannot steal, go AWOL, talk too much or do anything bad to women. For the worst offences, they would just kill you. Right before I got here in 1979, three comrades were shot because they committed rape. In 1981, one of my good friends was accused of being a spy. Once convicted, they just pulled him aside and shot him."

They had to live under their own rules, under their own law. It could not possibly have been the same set of rules as on the outside. There was a code to live by, and that was honourable. But the severity of punishment took the gloss of purity off it.

Although Betty never shot anybody, she was part of the bomb squad, which laid traps for the Malaysian soldiers stationed south of the border. "We used to send troops out to hunt them." Betty's job on the front line was to prepare deadly traps. Once she laid the mines, her comrades would try and lure the soldiers to them.

They engaged the Malaysian troops in a game of cat and mouse. This war, however, was no great battle. It was an amalgamation of small encounters. Such were the margins that defeating a single Malaysian soldier amounted to a big victory. They would strip the soldier of his guns and bullets, and, if they were lucky, there were other supplies to be had. Food, drink, matches, boots— everything was a precious commodity.

"We could get 150 bullets from each soldier! The bullets could weigh up to 10 kg. And I was only 50 kg!" she laughed, a youthful, girlish laugh.

Inside this placid souvenir shop, it was impossible to imagine Betty as a communist guerrilla. We had expected to meet mysterious renegades who narrate gruesome stories with blood-shot eyes and smoke-scarred voices, punctuated by puffs of opium and sips of rice wine.

Instead, we got Betty. Had we cycled all the way here for this? It was difficult to reconcile it all. To think that somebody so innocent could have ever been moved to such violence. The way she candidly discussed killing suggested that all empathy had been drained from her being, rendering her incapable of feeling. She was personable yet distant. She was honest, but you still got the feeling you weren't getting the whole story. A human, who for a brief hiatus had been turned into an ideologue, a machine.

Compared to other communist struggles, this one seems rather forgettable. It didn't result in mass casualties. It has hardly affected towns and other urban centres. There were no major assassinations. It didn't dominate the imaginations of our countries. Post-independence, it has had hardly any impact on Malaysian and Singaporean politics. And it certainly didn't stymie our economies—people came and went, goods and services were traded, and huge amounts of capital flowed in.

Even as Betty and her buddies kept up their struggle, from deep in the Thai jungle, Malaysia and Singapore were growing at record rates. What a slap in the face. The countries they had been fighting for were doing quite nicely without them, thank you. The CPM was irritating but forgettable, like a receding pimple. After independence, the CPM's sole achievement was in getting Malaysia and Singapore to work together—against it.

Unless one has a very specific interest, I'm not even sure why anybody would bother visiting the "Piyamit Tunnels". They pale in comparison to Vietnam's Cu-Chi tunnels. Vietnam's are complex structures and symbolise one of the greatest guerrilla victories in history. The CPM's tunnels are small, of debatable historical value and, most jarringly, not even in the country that was being fought for. The tunnels are a theme park decorated with desperation. How rabidly un-communist.

Over the years, the communists here have also inevitably become less Malaysian and more Thai. For even as they fought a battle in Malaya, they enjoyed relative peace in Thailand. According to Betty, the villagers in Betong didn't mind them. "Chang Chung Ming, our leader, sent them a letter saying that 'we are just borrowing your jungle, not taking it over.'"

The communists, experts in extracting medicines from trees and animals, offered medical help to the villagers. They also provided them with protection. "There used to be some criminal gangs in the area. We defeated them all, and they left."

The CPM almost always shielded loyal locals from external threats. This civilian network, the Min Yuen, had been providing the communists with crucial supplies and finances throughout their struggle, both in Malaysia and Thailand. Not all locals were supporters though. Some needed a bit more persuasion.

"We would detonate a bomb near the village. After we detonated a bomb, we sent a letter to the *towkays*, businessman, asking for protection money. They would give three to ten thousand ringgit each."

Betty told us that the CPM now has great relations with the Thai government. After they signed an amnesty in 1989, the government helped them to develop their local economy. It gave each single adult and family six acres of land and 16,000 baht to build a house.[9] It also provided them with a RM330,000 grant to transform the area into a tourist attraction.[10]

Yet Betty wasn't sure if she preferred this new life. "It was hard to let go initially. That was our life, you know? But of course we are relieved there is peace. No more hiding away. No more sneaking around."

She seemed torn between the peace and stability of mainstream capitalist society, and the fervour and idealism their cocooned communist dreams had once offered. Her zest had been sapped away, rejuvenated on rare occasions when pesky strangers came calling.

"But are you still a communist?"

"Ha," she winced, reluctant to commit. "I do still believe in some of the communist teachings. You know, that all people should be equal. That a few people should not be able to control all the wealth and power. But I also know that communism has failed in many places. We all know that it has failed."

"But it finally worked in China. Look how well they're doing!"

"Ha. There aren't any communists left in China," Betty sighed.

Betty had long let go of her dreams for a communist party and state. "After all, I am part of this system now," she smiled, arms raised, gesturing at the wooden Buddhas for sale. Yet, though Betty had grown accustomed to the realities of life today, there was one thing that still bothered her. "I would like to see my family again," her voice trembled ever so slightly. Finally, a chink in her cold communist armour.

"I still don't understand why we can't go back. After the amnesty, we were given identity cards. But in order to visit Malaysia, we have to get a visa. That costs 380 ringgit. And we have to travel all the way to Bangkok to get it! What about the old people with us? Some are 70–80 years old. How are they supposed to get it?"[11]

In *I Love Malaya*, a 2006 documentary on the CPM, there is a scene showing some ageing former Malaysian communists receiving their residency permits, identity cards and citizenship applications from the Thai government.[12] Delighted at being recognised by a sovereign state, and finally having a formal identity—and thus a better chance of returning to Malaysia—some of the old Chinese ladies are wearing huge smiles while carrying around portraits of King Bhumibol Adulyadej. There is a delightful irony in watching former communists now submitting to a monarchy. This tiny community seems bound to become just another misplaced footnote in the annals of Southeast Asia's identity and nationhood struggles.

A few years before we met her, Betty had gone back to Malaysia. She had gotten a five-day visa, only enough for her to make the trip back to Selangor, say hello, and turn back. She was aching to return. "You know, my father died three years ago. I want to pay my respects at his grave." This was the 16-year-old Betty wondering how her life would be different had she not eloped with communism, wanting to atone for leaving her original family.

Betty's voice reflected a mixture of dogged persistence and immaculate patience. But the injustice was not lost on us. Here we were, a few miles away from the Malaysian border, in a mountainous Thai village inhabited by Malaysians and Singaporeans. They are leading a peaceful existence, in harmony with the Thai people.

Yet they are in exile, not welcome back in our country. In many ways, *their* country. We felt embarrassed. Some of these communists had done more for the independence and creation of our modern states than we could ever imagine. They had fought the British. Then the Japanese. Then the British again. They had fought for a free Malaya!

There we were, two jolly, pampered Singaporeans flippantly cycling by to visit them in their ostracised habitat, ignorant tourists dropping in to a cultural zoo. We felt we had no right to enjoy the fruits of their labour, while they suffer in ignominy, faceless, nameless outcasts high up on a Thai mountain. Many CPM guerrillas have already died in exile without getting a chance to visit the free land they spent years fighting for.

Assuming Betty's story is true, she was driven to the jungle and arms simply because she was not allowed to harbour communist beliefs. But surely these communists no longer pose a threat to our countries—why not let them back in?

I have struggled with this question since the day we met her. On the one hand, we end up romanticising the whole conflict if we view it through the prism of demure Betty. There is no doubt they engaged in terrorist activities from 1948 till the 1980s. It did not matter if one was a foreign aggressor or a fellow Malaysian. If you got in their way, you were subject to terror.

On the other hand, to simply call them terrorists is a biased reduction. Many of their original motives were noble, and their activities legal. Chin Peng's generation was struggling for an independent Malaya. Betty's generation was struggling for freedom of belief and political association.

Underlying this was a fundamental Marxist belief in the equality of all men and women, and a desire to divide wealth fairly. These are people who grew up in unequal societies. It is understandable how the allure of communism could grasp them so firmly. It is easy to see why they had so many sympathisers.

Theirs descended into an armed struggle for familiar reasons: the lack of a free, contestable political space; the inability to air their numerous grievances; the feeling of hopelessness; the use of clandestine supply lines; and, thanks initially to the British, the availability of arms.

Throughout history, and particularly from 1945–1970s, anti-colonial guerrillas have fought off foreigners and then subsequently been lauded. The problem with the CPM, of course, is that they were not just fighting foreigners (the British and the Japanese). They ultimately battled against the newly independent Malaysian and Singaporean states. In that tumultuous era of flimsy allegiances, the CPM even had Japanese (who had surrendered) and Thais fighting alongside them.

Many of the people they fought against—the Malayan Old Guard, so to speak—are still alive and around. To them, the suggestion that CPM members be allowed back in is tantamount to treason. Many remain deeply suspicious of Chin Peng, probably even after his apology in 2009 for the deaths of innocent people.[13]

Still, if truth and reconciliation commissions can heal scars in places such as Rwanda, why not in Malaysia and Singapore? Simply because there is no pragmatic need to. There is neither political will nor perceived economic or social need for it. The CPM has been silenced over there, and we can live peacefully over here. No further action necessary.

Occasionally, somebody speaks up for the CPM. In June 2011, Zabur Nawawi, a politician from Malaysia's PAS (Parti Islam Se-Malaysia, the Pan-Malaysian Islamic Party), suggested that the government should provide support to Malay members of the CPM. "They were not communist. They only worked together with three stars (i.e. CPM)," he said. Mr Nawawi regards them as independence heroes, much to the disgust of many older Malaysians.[14]

Throughout our conversation, Betty furiously denied that the communists engaged in anything illegal. "Our governments locked us up simply because of what we believed in! Who's the real terrorist?"

Time had passed effortlessly, as it does, presumably, when in the company of a captivating communist. She alerted us to the time, 4.30 pm, and said we better leave if we wanted to make it back to the border crossing before it closed in the evening.

"You should come back sometime! Stay a few days," Betty earnestly suggested. "And learn how to speak Mandarin too! Then I can tell you a lot more."

We promised her we would return, but probably without proper Mandarin skills. We also promised we would share her story, so that others would know how she got there.

It is unclear how history will remember Betty and her comrades. They probably won't ever get the intellectual luxury of a "Terrorist or Freedom fighter?" debate. Perhaps that's the way most people prefer it.

They are not alone. There are many others who our countries want to forget about. Chia Thye Poh, a Socialist Front member of parliament in Singapore from 1963 to 1966, was detained in 1966 under the Internal Security Act (ISA). The Singapore government accuses him of, amongst other things, having ties to the CPM (which he denies). Detained from 1966 to 1998, without having ever being charged, Mr Chia was one of the world's longest-serving political prisoners, locked up even longer than Nelson Mandela.[15]

All these people get little space in our history textbooks. History, after all, is written by the winners, and it is a peculiarly small group of winners who write the histories of Malaysia and Singapore. Despite being young—we recently celebrated 50 years of self-governance—the story of our countries, our national narratives, have long been scripted, co-opted and ingrained into our minds.

It is nigh well impossible to read an account of modern Malaysia that hasn't been influenced by Mahathir. Ditto Lee Kuan Yew in Singapore. In fact, if you want to learn about "Singapore", you'd likely read no less than Mr Lee's memoirs.

Which is, no doubt, an impressive work. Still, it is his view of things. There isn't much debate about these things. Can you imagine what would happen if, heaven forbid, somebody disputed something Mr Lee said? *They'd* be history.

Consider the roadblocks in front of Martyn See, a documentary filmmaker who persistently seeks to provide Singapore with alternative historical perspectives, by giving voice to forgotten souls. He has documented the struggles of, amongst others, Lim Hock Siew, a former PAP politician, and Said Zahari, a former editor-in-chief of *Utusan Malaysia*, a Malay newspaper.

Both Dr Lim and Mr Said were detained under the ISA in 1963 as part of Operation Coldstore, a government effort to weed out supposed communists. Dr Lim spent almost 20 years in jail without charge; Mr Said spent 17. In the past five years, Mr See has filmed both of them, separately, speaking about their experiences, providing first-hand accounts of seminal events during the time of Singapore's formation. It is humbling to watch these two old men as they share, without bitterness or remorse, their fascinating, insightful stories.

Singapore's Ministry of Information, Communications and the Arts (MICA) has banned both films,[16] alleging that they give distorted and misleading portrayals of the arrests and detentions.[17] In its statement on Dr Lim's film, it added that "The Singapore Government will not allow individuals who have posed a security threat to Singapore's interests in the past, to use media platforms such as films to make baseless accusations against the authorities, give a false portrayal of their previous activities in order to exculpate their guilt, and undermine public confidence in the Government in the process."[18]

What is most puzzling is that although neither of them was ever formally charged with anything, MICA suggests they are guilty of posing a threat to Singapore. How does it know? I suspect many Singaporeans would be interested in hearing the full story from MICA and Singapore's Ministry of Home Affairs.

Our governments have—from the first time they allowed us to vote them in—controlled the flow of information and decided what we can read, listen and watch. Government-sanctioned voices have been amplified. Others have been drowned out. Our histories are in our governments' hands.[19]

It seems unlikely that Malaysians and Singaporeans will ever get an exhaustive, broad account of our histories. As long as Mahathir, Lee Kuan Yew and their respective generations are around, few will dare venture there. And, by the time they are gone, so too will many of their peers who might be able to fill in the gaps.

Where does that leave the communists and everybody else who may not agree? Oblivion. They will watch helplessly from the sidelines of yesterday, their stars fading with each passing moment, their page in history edited out. Once labelled a great danger, they are now cast as an inconvenience in the path to nationhood.

While it may appear as if we are learning sharp, competent histories, it is really the shared perspective of a tiny group of like-minded individuals instead of a rich, broad spectrum of diverse views.

Where can one find those views, conspicuous only because of their absence? Do our government-controlled media channels present a fair and balanced picture, both of history, and of current affairs? What is life really like on the ground?

Those questions had been gnawing at us for years. Being inquisitive, 20-something-year-old Singaporeans, we felt unfulfilled, not knowing if everything is really as it seems.

Most of all, that would explain what we were doing there, high up on a remote mountain in Thailand, shooting the breeze with an ex-communist. We wanted to find out more about our neighbours—how they lead their lives; what they think about us; where they see the future taking them. We could not get the whole past from our history books. That made us wonder about how our governments presented current affairs, and where the future was heading.

At Singapore's Kranji War Memorial, a green, peaceful oasis, there are six simple words inscribed into a stone—"They died for all free men." The memorial is in honour of the soldiers who died in World War II, the brave men and women who gave their lives fighting for a free Malaya. There is no mention of the communists.

***

By sheer coincidence, our interest in cycling across the whole of Malaysia was sparked around the time of the US invasion of Iraq in March 2003. In any case, Operation Oust Saddam was of secondary importance to the average Malaysian and Singaporean.

We knew the US would do whatever it wanted to regardless of what our countries thought. We knew who our governments would support regardless of what we, the citizens, thought. In short, the average Malaysian and Singaporean was so far removed from the entire process that it quickly descended into another reality Hollywood blockbuster, narrated largely by Western experts.

On the other hand, something far more participatory was unfolding right before our eyes. Bilateral relations between Malaysia and Singapore had reached a nadir. On 6 February 2003, just one day after Colin Powell's UN audition, Mahathir, Malaysia's then prime minister, made a high-handed and volatile statement: "We," the Malaysian prime minister said, "gave Singapore its sovereignty. It was we who gave Singapore the status of a nation, a sovereign nation. Before it was just part of Malaysia."[20]

This statement came at the end of long and bitter negotiations between our two countries: negotiations that had dragged on for months; negotiations littered with mudslinging from government officials and their supporting cast of compliant journalists; negotiations that ultimately were a complete failure.

Nothing was resolved. The issues on the table were serious—Singapore's purchase of cheap water from Malaysia and the sale of the purified water back to Malaysia; the Republic of Singapore Air Force's (RSAF) use of Malaysian airspace; sovereignty over a disputed island, Pedra Branca (Malaysia calls it Pulau Batu Putih); the relocation of Malaysia's railway station from Tanjong Pagar, a valuable plot of real estate deep in downtown Singapore, in exchange for a plot of similar value nearby; the building of a new causeway over the Johor Straits; and the possible early withdrawal of Singapore Central Provident Fund (CPF) savings (pension funds) of West Malaysians who have left Singapore permanently.[21]

This time, the Malaysian and Singaporean governments were happy to see their people taking an active interest in politics. Traditionally reticent Malaysians and Singaporeans, energised by this international bickering, and cajoled by the flowery editorials in the papers, wrote droves of letters in the forum pages, slamming the other side.

It was incestuous commentary at its best, a pure inbreeding of opinion— Singaporean journalists, perfectionists of nationalist prose, would report proceedings to the Singaporean public, who would then respond with their best anti-Malaysian salvo, to the cheers of all around.

This ping-ponging was driving the country into a right frenzy. The Malaysians were doing the same. The irony is that we're not allowed to read each other's papers. To this day, Malaysians and Singaporeans cannot purchase each other's newspaper—it is easier for us to buy a copy of France's *Le Monde* than a copy of Malaysia's *New Straits Times*.

Worse, maybe inspired by George and Saddam, warmongers in our countries reared their head, including Malaysian ministers[22] and members of Singapore's People's Action Party (PAP) Youth Wing.[23] A war between Malaysia and Singapore was an unlikely scenario. But the fact that the "W" word had been whispered was enough to ruffle some feathers. There was talk of limiting travel to the other side. Age-old myths about dangerous, incompetent Malaysians and arrogant, insensitive Singaporeans were being tossed around.

There was nothing new about these problems, however. Ties between our countries have been edgy since 9 August 1965, the day Singapore gained her full independence.[24] Or rather the day when, in our first Prime Minister Lee Kuan Yew's words, "Singapore had independence thrust upon it."[25]

Separation was a bit of a shock. After all, Malaysia and Singapore share an ancient socio-cultural history, first through successions of kingdoms and sultanates and then later as part of British Malaya. Economic linkages, religious affiliations, kinship ties and business dealings bound Malaysians and Singaporeans together. The sudden divorce was an anomaly in a history of togetherness.[26]

It was a matter of race. Even before Malaya achieved independence from the British in 1957, there were signs Malay-dominated Malaysia would not get along well with Chinese-dominated Singapore. The divorce was largely the product of a single, fundamental dispute—nationalistic Malay leaders in Malaysia wanted to create a pro-Malay state while Chinese leaders in Singapore wanted to create a race-neutral state.

They differed in their opinion on how to create a flourishing and harmonious multi-ethnic society. In Malaysia, the Malays felt like they had been unjustly ruled by foreigners—the British then the Japanese—for long enough. Somehow they were now second-class citizens in their own home, economically weaker than the Chinese.

In *Among the Believers*, V. S. Naipaul recalls a discussion with two young Malay ladies:

> "The Chinese try to monopoly [*sic*] our economy. They are good businessmen. We are left behind. It isn't true what they say about Malays being lazy. We know it isn't true, but it hurts us to hear these things. If we don't have the Chinese we could be a good business people. If you look at history, in the time of the Malacca sultanate we Malays are very well known as the best business people."
>
> "Why do you worry so much about the Chinese?"
>
> "The Chinese have China, the Indian have India. We only have Malaysia."[27]

This need to reclaim Malaysia—what they consider their true homeland—has long guided Malay sentiment and policy. Therefore, special privileges had to be given to the Malays, in order to raise their living standards to that of the Chinese. Equality of outcomes was important.

In Singapore, Lee Kuan Yew and his cadres were much more interested in equality of opportunity and meritocracy. Why should any group of people be guaranteed quotas, or afforded special privileges? Instead, the market should have free reign to decide how the spoils are shared. Because of this worldview, most Singaporeans I know have always felt Malaysia has unfair, racist policies that give preference to Malays.

However, many Malaysians we met along the way—Chinese, Indian and Malay alike—told us that Malaysia is a fairer place, since it gives the poorer people in society a helping hand. Policies in Singapore, on the other hand, are unfair because they allow the rich to get richer while the poor get poorer.

We think their society is unfair, they think our society is unfair.

From that turbulent period, two political entities arose. In Malaysia, pro-Malay policies were slowly implemented—preferences given to Malays in different spheres of life; Islam established as the state religion, while protecting the religious rights of others; and Malay as the official language.

In Singapore, no preferences were afforded to any group; there was a clear separation of state from any religion; and four official languages were established— English, Malay, Mandarin and Tamil.

Whenever the governments or the people of Malaysia and Singapore interact with each other, these differences in our outlook guide our thoughts and actions. The ninth of August 1965 is our starting point, our Big Bang, if you will. For the people of Singapore, it was a shock to discover that we were not Malaysia's prized baby, but just the bathwater.

> Some countries are born independent. Some achieve independence. Singapore had independence thrust upon it. Some 45 British colonies had held colourful ceremonies to formalise and celebrate the transfer of sovereign power from imperial Britain to their indigenous governments. For Singapore, 9 August 1965 was no ceremonial occasion. We had never sought independence. In a referendum less than three years ago, we had persuaded 70 per cent of the electorate to vote in favour of merger with Malaya. Since then, Singapore's need to be part and parcel of the Federation in one political, economic, and social polity had not changed. Nothing had changed—except that we were out. We had said that an independent Singapore was simply not viable. Now it was our unenviable task to make it work. How were we to create a nation out of a polyglot collection of migrants from China, India, Malaysia, Indonesia and several other parts of Asia?
>
> —Lee Kuan Yew, in his memoirs[28]

Singapore suddenly had to find its place in this post-colonial Cold War world of shifting alliances and promiscuous bedfellows. We had no identity. We were nothing more than a trading port whose hinterland had just been cut off. Mr Lee had to find a way of galvanising his people into an imagined community.

As he says, most modern nation-states are the products of a drive to self-determination from a nation of people. In Singapore, the opposite happened. We were made a nation-state, and then had to create a nation of people.

This is an almighty difference. The process of creating a nation has one essential by-product: it creates the citizen through a mix of nationalist sentiment and the feeling that everybody is fighting for the same thing. It binds the collective psyche of a nation through the pursuit of a common goal, a pursuit usually long and fraught with danger. It's the sort of struggle that connects strangers, once they are victorious.

The Singaporean is an artificial construct. Created after the nation, the Singaporean does not have the common experience an organically driven nationalist process affords. We were completely at home in the place we lived, but out of place in our new nation. There was a need to anchor the Singaporean identity.

Amongst other things, the Singaporean was defined in opposition to the Malaysian. "We are Singaporean, they are Malaysian." The presence of a Malaysian other, against which Singaporeans could rally together, crystallised our identity.

How was this done? There were the frequent reminders about the nature of and reasons for our separation—we were differentiated from birth. Each side of course told its own story, through its own media, which in a matter of years was completely government controlled. To this day, save the Internet, everything Malaysians and Singaporeans read, listen and watch about each other comes from a government-sponsored outlet. Even if we could, the media buffer that has been built and ingrained will take some undoing—it will be a while before a Malaysian trusts Singapore's *Straits Times*, and a Singaporean Malaysia's *New Straits Times*. Why subscribe to the other side's nonsense?

Singapore's early identity crisis can be seen in our national flag, designed in 1959. Singapore is perhaps the only non-Muslim state in the world to have a crescent on its flag, there largely to please our Malay population. The flag is coloured red, and has stars on it, largely to satisfy the Chinese. But the flag's bottom half is white, and it has five rather than three stars, so as to differentiate it from the Communist Party of Malaya's flag. It is a flag of compromise.[29]

Lee Kuan Yew's realpolitik forte was his forging of bilateral relationships. He quickly snuggled up to the US, who used Singapore's naval bases as part of its war effort in Vietnam.

"Although American intervention failed in Vietnam, it bought time for the rest of Southeast Asia. In 1965, when the US military moved massively into South Vietnam, Thailand, Malaysia and the Philippines faced internal threats from armed communist insurgents and the communist underground was still active in Singapore," he writes in his memoirs. "Had there been no US intervention, the will of these countries to resist them would have melted and Southeast Asia would have most likely gone communist. The prosperous emerging market economies of ASEAN (Association of Southeast Asian Nations) were nurtured during the Vietnam War years."

Singapore quickly emerged as every capitalist's economic, military and political flagship in Southeast Asia. Mr Lee's strategic masterstroke was his choice of military advisors, a decision which placed Singapore firmly across the ideological divide from Malaysia. Following independence, Mr Lee looked across the world and realised there was one other state that had faced and repeatedly overcome a similar national security challenge—being "a tiny minority in an archipelago of 30,000 islands inhabited by more than 100 million Malay or Indonesian Muslims."[30]

And so in 1965, some 18 officers from the fearsome Israeli Defence Forces provided the spark for the Singapore Armed Forces, today the most advanced and well-trained military in Southeast Asia. In return, the Israelis consistently pushed for an embassy in Singapore, part of their ongoing struggle to earn recognition worldwide. Mr Lee was initially hesitant, unwilling to openly anger all the Muslims around, who were sympathetic to the plight of the Palestinians. However, by May 1969, Israel had an official embassy in Singapore. On the other hand, to this day, Israel does not have an embassy in Malaysia. The two country's peoples are barred from visiting each other.

Therefore, long before 9/11 and the supposed "clash of civilisations" was ever discussed, Malaysia and Singapore's lot was cast differently vis-à-vis Islam, the West and the Israel-Palestine question. Quite simply, when push has come to shove, we Singaporeans have gone the way of America and Israel. This basic difference in Malaysia's and Singapore's foreign policies has invariably influenced how we view and treat each other.

Over the years, our economies have grown at different rates—Singapore now firmly established in the developed world while Malaysia a middle-income country—and our countries have drifted apart. Niggling suspicions that existed when we separated have been periodically manipulated by opportunists wanting to score political points. Negative stereotypes and misconceptions have been created and accentuated by the border that divides us.

In Malaysia: The "ugly Singaporean" is materialistic, arrogant, insensitive, emotionless and overly pragmatic. Singapore, at worst, is an expensive, boring, soulless, artificial post-industrial construct.

In Singapore: The "ugly Malaysian" is lazy, inefficient, simplistic and governed by emotions rather than logic. Malaysia, at worst, is a cheap, dirty, dangerous, underdeveloped racist society.

An invisible political boundary can slowly transform into a veil of ignorance. Creating an opposition out of one another served both governments well. The Malaysians could justify their decision to kick Singapore out of the Federation, and this was an inherent affirmation of their own policies. Likewise, opposition to

Malaysia helped forge a Singaporean identity. Over time, differences on either side can become more pronounced, and the people on either side can forget that they were once one.

Singaporeans tend to look at Malaysia today and imagine what life was like before proper development. The whole notion of being transported back in time, while romantic, is often laced with condescension. "We've made it, and you haven't."

Ironically, Malaysia has been stuck in a middle-income trap, while for most Singaporeans, it might seem that we skipped the whole middle-income stage altogether. One minute we were poor, the next we are rich. Hence we have little economic empathy for Malaysians.

But as Singapore has developed rapidly, it has had its fair share of growing pains. Malaysians, therefore, generally look to Singapore as a guide to the future, with a mixture of admiration and caution. "Thanks for experimenting, and showing us what to do, and what not to do."

We were determined to explore the misconceptions and stereotypes bouncing around Malaysia and Singapore. We had been ignorant and daft for long enough. We'd also decided on a new way for us to travel. No guidebooks, no Internet searches. Just a map and a prayer. If we needed to find out something, we would have to talk to the nearest person. No cars or highways either. It was going to be bicycles and the snaky coastal roads. And no hotels. Just tents. Or if we asked sweetly enough, maybe someone would let us into their home. Would it work?

2
Two countries separated at birth

Malaya is the most vulnerable country in Asia today ... Its population is divided between Chinese who have recently overrun the peninsula and Malays who invaded it some thousand years ago. The indigenous Sakai have almost disappeared.

—James Michener, 1951[1]

Endau, Johor. 16 July 2004.

Waking up on Day 3 was easy. The whole night, mosquitoes had been whizzing around our faces, while an array of lights—yellow, white, fluorescent—strove to pierce our closed eyes. We had been trying to sleep on the hard concrete rows in the grandstand of the football stadium in Mersing, a sleepy fishing town on Malaysia's east coast, which is best known as a gateway to a number of holiday islands such as Rawa and Tioman.

Cycling out of Mersing at 9 am, we heard the familiar lyrics of an R&B song, blaring out of a boom box from inside a shoe store. "Yeah, yeah, yeah!" crooned, or rather, croaked, Usher. Whatever the case, it was a thankful respite from the night before, when someone in the *warung*, coffee shop, where we were eating had played an album on repeat the whole night. There seemed to be no obvious reason for this other than the torture of two innocent foreign cyclists—the cyclic crooning of Michael Learns to Rock can induce a state of traveller's despair.

For better or worse, our encounters with random pop music on the streets dwindled as we cycled further up Malaysia's east coast, towards the less developed and more conservative Northeast.

Highway 3 cut inland just north of Mersing, and we lost sight of the South China Sea. The sun's sweltering heat was tempered somewhat by the spatters of banana and coconut trees that accompanied us on either side, with the occasional wooden Malay house springing up, worn yet, almost always, still magnificent.

To ease his pain, Sumana had been chomping on Pontalons, a powerful analgesic, as if they were Mentos. Nevertheless, after about two hours on the mildly hilly road, his right knee gave out. We had to cut our trip short, and seek shelter and rest at a tiny *warung*. Looking like another forgotten stopover on a quiet highway stretch, it was unclear as to who actually patronised this place.

Like most people we encountered on our trip, the *warung* owner, Siti, stared at us as though we had dropped in from another planet. Wearing a splendid black Baju and Tudung, her eyes darted around, as if a million questions were racing through her mind. She restrained herself, more intent on serving us.

Tired and unsure, we forwent the usual banter up front. "*Coke satu, air kosong satu,*" we asked. She returned with a blue plastic cup of plain water, and a glass bottle of coke. After she laid the drinks down on the table, the straw in the Coke bottle started rising up to the top, and almost fell off. We gripped the cold bottle with nostalgic pleasure. Glass bottles are a rarity in Singapore today—replaced by cans and plastic—but we still find them in many parts of Malaysia.

We drank slowly—with our budget, Coke was something to be savoured—before turning our attention back to Siti. She was the only person in the *warung*, and had no choice but to face a barrage of questions from eager travellers with nowhere to go and time to waste.

The truth is that we were feeling quite down. We did not know how long we'd be there. Sumana's knee looked bad, and we worried that he might not be able to go any further—after all of three days! We tried to hide our anxiety by talking aimlessly.

Siti offered slow, reserved and often monosyllabic responses to our questions, a disposition we would encounter in many women along the way. The feeling was usually borne less out of unfriendliness than a simply shyness about chatting with strange men. Siti's husband would normally marshal such social encounters, but he was not around. "He's praying, he'll be back soon," she said, clearly a bit lost without him.

In a daze, it took us a while to even realise that the *warung* is located at the doorstep of a giant estate, the Kampung FELDA Endau. FELDA, the Malaysian Federal Land Development Authority, was established in 1956 as a national land settlement agency. It has been hugely successful in resettling thousands of landless, unemployed Malaysians, providing them with land and the technical know-how to engage in cash-crop cultivation.[2] By 2004, there were approximately 700,000 FELDA inhabitants, comprising 103,156 settlers and their dependants.[3]

Siti's little *warung* feeds the FELDA dwellers on their way in and out. There were only two white metal tables in the *warung,* both with a cracked red plastic covering. On the tables were clear plastic jars with red screw caps, each filled with a different delectable Malaysian snack, including *rempeyek*, a deep-fried peanut cracker, Pink & White "Love Letters", a biscuit made from rice flour, and *bahulu,* a cake made of egg, sugar and *tepung gandum*, wheat flour.

In the space between the doors and windows of the *warung*, Siti hung several decorations, a combination of advertising, officious notation and home improvement works. There was an ad for an instamix of Cenkudu Coffee, a local aphrodisiac. Beside that hung a Malaysian calendar and a tattered copy of their store license. Then, somewhat out of place, there was a chunky, black, retro electrical metre box, which somebody in a quirky Parisian antique shop might pay a fortune for; and a gold-framed painting of New York City's skyline, showing the World Trade Center. "I know about 9/11, but I didn't know *those* were the towers," Siti told us.

After about half an hour, a group of four teenagers walked into the *warung*, placed their orders and started chatting and giggling loudly. The two guys were wearing slacks with faded t-shirts. Both girls were wearing jeans, blouses and a fair dollop of make-up. One was wearing a white *tudung*, the other unveiled. Just like pop music, unveiled, dolled-up Malay girls would become less common the further north we cycled. After five minutes, the boys gingerly asked where we were from, but then subsequently limited interactions to the odd binary question.

At around 2 pm, a short, stocky man pulled up in his *kap-chye*, scooter. With his frame and his gait, he might have looked imposing, although his disarming smile put paid to that impression. Having seen our bikes and then looked for their owners, he walked towards us. His movements, though slow, betrayed his desire to find out more, to "get in on the game". He swivelled as he said a brief but polite hello to everybody else—the sort of all-encompassing single hello, directed at nobody in particular, but to all the same—before making his way unassumingly towards us.

As he approached us, his right hand shot out instinctively,

"Hello, hello."

"Selamat Petang!"

He was pleasantly surprised at our Malay.

Kamal, Siti's husband, pulled a chair near us, and seated himself down. He had unbelievably smooth, clean, chocolate skin. His jet black sideburns were thick, and were the only evidence of hair on offer— on his head sat a purplish *songkok*, the trademark boxy hat of Muslim men in much of Southeast Asia. His full-bodied blue shirt and plain black sarong were wrinkle-free. He was like a regal *bupati*, a regular regent, the kind of bridge-building Malay the British must have loved to deal with.

After the initial exploratory two minutes of conversation, and the surprise of being confronted by two cycling Singaporeans had sunk in, he succinctly described FELDA to us: A system whereby the government grants plots of land [about ten acres (4 ha)] to the *bumiputeras* for their own plantation, and gets them to pay back in monthly instalments until they own it.

"What happens if you can't pay back?"

"Nothing. Just wait till you can, lah."

Each family works hard towards the goal of full ownership, finally earning the property rights for their plot. It is a simple yet brilliant way of incentivising them, and certainly the bedrock of FELDA's astonishing success. Today, FELDA Holdings is a diversified conglomerate: it owns some 70 palm oil mills, 13 rubber factories, 7 refineries and 1 oleo chemical factory.

There are more than 50 subsidiaries under its umbrella—in supplies, research and development, farm management, milling, processing, transportation, shipping, bulking, engineering, property and construction, security, animal rearing, resorts and catering.

FELDA produced almost 8 per cent of the world's palm oil in 2009 and that year, its revenues reached RM11.8 billion (US$2 billion).[4] By 2011, the FELDA residents' average income was RM4,000 per month.[5]

FELDA is considered a pioneer in land reformation in the developing world. It currently exports its largely palm oil-based products to China, India, Pakistan, Sri Lanka and countries in the Middle East. It is constantly seeking new markets, notably in South Africa, Kenya, Nigeria, Japan and South Korea.[6]

Certain social challenges arise from FELDA's structure. For one, there are few non-Malays on the estate. As vehicles to increase land ownership amongst the *bumiputeras*, the FELDA Estates are giant ethnic Malay enclaves. We saw just two non-Malays during our time there. "We have some of *them* too," Kamal later confided.

As one of the flagships of the *bumiputera* affirmative action programme, many Malays feel very passionately about FELDA. At the United Malays National Organisation (UMNO) General Assembly 2004, Perak delegate Mohd Khusairi Abdul Talib commented, "Once you modernise FELDA, you modernise the Malays."[7] This statement implies FELDA and its inhabitants are a bit *ulu*, remote, like country bumpkins. That is certainly the sentiment of many Malay urbanites as well; FELDA is removed from the real, or important, progress of Malaysia. A Malaysian Chinese, writing in the *New Straits Times* about her experiences in National Service, said,

"My group is going to a FELDA settlement tomorrow. FELDA! What are we going to do there? You must excuse me if I have visions of being made to brave treacherous estates and harvest oil palm.

"Oh dear, aren't there snakes in the estate? They (trainers) are keeping mum about the plans since they want to prevent the trainees from playing hooky."[8]

Therefore, not only is there a distinct Malay-non-Malay divide that exists between the FELDA inhabitants and other Malaysians, there is also an undeveloped-developed divide, or at least the perception of one.

Drug trafficking and abuse is another problem. In a single operation in April 2005, police arrested 213 suspected addicts and 4 suspected traffickers in Pahang, confiscating more than 1,800 psychotropic pills, 34.2 grammes of heroin and 5 grammes of marijuana.[9] Social institutions such as village development and security committees, women and youth organisations, and mosque and *surau* committees, have been mobilized to help the addicted FELDA residents, who comprise about 0.27 per cent of the population.[10]

It is also difficult to keep the younger generations of FELDA inhabitants on the estate and interested in farm work, leading to a significant brain drain and exodus to urban centres. About 60 per cent of the children of settlers move out in search of jobs. To counter the trend, FELDA has been trying to encourage them to stay in the schemes and start-up small and medium businesses there, hoping to mould them into "young entrepreneurs of FELDA".

Increased development and better education has thus been a double-edged sword. While improving the lives and living conditions of the FELDA inhabitants, it also draws the younger generations away from the schemes, in search of established professions that want their expertise. FELDA may have to consider importing more landless willing farmers to work on their schemes, possibly buying back the land from the old, and mortgaging it to a whole new generation.

"So, why don't you guys buy a house in Johor? You know, one of those beautiful *kampung* houses?

"There's no way, we're still only students."

"Oh. What are you studying?"

"Government Studies."

"Oh, you want to become a civil servant?"

"Possibly."

"Ha, you'll have plenty of work and make lots of money. You can go to Iraq, to Afghanistan, places like that," he was chuckling before he even finished.

"But you know, the risk is high."

"I suppose. So what do you think of that Iraq war?"

"It's the same with everything else I told you. They're doing it for the money! They're doing it for the oil, for the power, for the money!"

"But don't worry, today might be the time of the West and America, just like once it was the time of Russia. But things will change ..."

On Kamal's radio, Peter Cetera was belting out "Glory of Love", sending nightmarish visions of Michael Learns to Rock through us.

"So, what do you think about your new Prime Minister, Encik?" Abdullah Badawi had been promoted just a few months prior.

"Well, he's good. Mahathir was good, he is good too. All Prime Ministers are smart right? They are the brightest and smartest people in the country. I really like Lee Kuan Yew, you know? He's a very smart leader."

"Ya, he is."

"But let me tell you something about him. Isn't it true, in Singapore, all guys have to serve in the army?"

"Ya, when we're 18, we have to go in for two and a half years."[11]

"And isn't it true that Malays are not allowed in some divisions of the army?"

"Ya, some of the 'high security' ones I think."

We did not like where this conversation was going. The last thing we wanted was a group of nationalistic Johorians demanding to know why there are no Malays in "high security" positions in the Singapore Armed Forces (SAF).

"Yes, but there's a reason for it, you know. Our army has always been worried about the fact that we are a tiny secular country flanked by two huge Muslim countries. And they fear that in times of war, some Muslims might switch sides, choosing their religion over their nationality."

We robotically spewed out our official government line, quickly, nervously, with the air of somebody unconvinced of a tenuous argument being put forth.

Kamal nodded his head, digesting the reasoning. He looked as though he was about to lambaste us for the discrimination.

"That's why Lee Kuan Yew is *bijak*, smart."

"Oh. Why is that?"

"Because he is right. We Malays *'tak boleh simpan rahsia'*, cannot keep a secret.

If a Malay in Singapore knows about high security state secrets, they will tell their relative or friend in Johor. Who will then tell his/her relative or friend in Kuala Lumpur (KL). And on and on. Soon our whole country will know your secrets. He made the right decision keeping Malays out of important departments."

We felt a mixture of relief and confusion, having never heard about the Malay inability to safeguard secrets.

"OK, OK, let me give you an example. You have travelled a bit around Malaysia. Have you seen Chinese people selling Nasi Lemak?"

"Ya. We've seen Chinese *and* Malays selling Nasi Lemak."

"How do you think the Chinese people learned how to make Nasi Lemak? It is a Malay recipe! We shared our secret with them. Then they marketed it, and now are making lots of money out of it! We Malays *tak boleh simpan rahsia*.

That's also why he was smart to get Singapore out of Malaysia. The Chinese in Singapore would not have gotten along with Malaysians."

"But didn't you see him crying on television when Singapore was kicked out of the Federation? He was sad!".

"Have you seen actors crying in movies? Do you think they mean it?"

I later wondered ... is it true that Lee Kuan Yew was happy "to get Singapore out of Malaysia"? That's not what he says. In his memoirs, Mr Lee states that Singapore—unlike most other newly independent nation-states—had independence thrust upon it. This saddened him immensely, because all his life, he "believed in merger and the unity of these two territories. It's a people connected by geography, economics, and ties of kinship". He broke down in the television studio shortly after uttering that line, on the morning of 9 August 1965.

Were they crocodile tears? Only a few Singaporeans I've spoken to think so. But, along our journey, we met many Malaysians, young and old, who do.

Amidst all the contemporary misunderstandings about airspace, water rights, railway land, second causeway bridges, and ethnic and religious policies, we often forget that "misunderstanding" was scripted into our national narratives right from day one.

To this day, many Malaysians and Singaporeans have different opinions on how and why our countries were split up. On this most fundamental of issues, we do not see eye-to-eye.

In Singapore, we grew up learning that a Chinese-dominated centre in Singapore which wanted to run a meritocracy could not get along with a Malay-dominated centre in KL which wanted to enshrine Malay rights above all others. And so, Tunku and his *kakis*, sidekicks, in KL decided to kick us out. Some Malaysians we met share this perception.

Many others, like Kamal, believe that Lee Kuan Yew had sneakily planned all along to get Singapore out. Why? Some say he's a dictator who wanted to run things his way. Others say he could never get along with Malays.

Some gave us the economic reason—he knew Singapore would be rich because of all the trade, so he wanted to get rid of its poorer, lumbering brother to the north. We even met Malaysians who speak of Singapore as a renegade state, which will one day return back to its rightful place in the Malay motherland—their Taiwan, if you will. Yikes.

Still others say Tunku kicked Lee Kuan Yew out because he wanted to run a Chinese kingdom in Singapore, with no regard for the economic malaise of the poorer classes. Malaysia was creating a "fair" society that looked after its poor, while Singapore wanted an "unfair" society where the rich get richer and the poor poorer.

If we can't even agree on how our countries were born, what chance for anything else?

"Hey, by the way, it's already 6 pm. Where are you two going to sleep tonight?" Kamal asked.

We had long given up hope of cycling more.

"Erm, we were thinking of putting up at that unfinished house over there, across the street."

"Why don't you come and sleep inside the *kampung*? You can sleep in our *surau*?

Perfect. Just what we had been hoping for. Our very first home invite. And to a prayer room no less, where we'd presumably hear chants from the Qu'ran. Definitely a step up from Michael Learns to Rock.

***

Singapore. 26 August 2011.

By August 2011, relations between Malaysia and Singapore had warmed considerably. This was partly due to Malaysian Prime Minister Najib Razak's efforts at improving the country's international relationships. With an eye on foreign investment, he has gone to considerable lengths to court, among others, investors from China, India and Singapore.

Wherever one looked, there was much evidence of improving Malaysia-Singapore ties. The long-standing railway dispute had been resolved in 2010, and July 2011 saw the last Malaysian train leaving downtown Singapore, as the station was moved from the middle of town to the Malaysian border. Singaporean businesses, meanwhile, were once again investing heavily in Malaysia and, in particular, in its Iskandar Development Region, a giant economic zone right on Singapore's doorstep.

Are Malaysia-Singapore relations on an upward trajectory? Without a doubt, says Idris Jala, the effervescent head of PEMANDU, the Performance Management & Delivery Unit in the Malaysian Prime Minister's office. He contends that as Malaysia strives to become a high-income country by 2020, the two countries will surely become more economically integrated.

I had first met Mr Jala in 2010, when he had come to speak to a group of senior executives working in Singapore. In August 2011 I again met him at a meeting when he had come to speak to a group of senior executives working in Singapore. He has become one of Malaysia's chief economic ambassadors, beating the country's drum wherever he goes.

By then, Singaporean firms had already invested over US$1.2 billion in Iskandar—more than 10 per cent of the total FDI into the region[12]—primarily in manufacturing, but also in the business services, education and healthcare sectors.[13]

The hope is that Iskandar will one day be like Shenzhen, complementing and collaborating with an economically advanced but land-poor neighbour.

"It is always difficult to find the right balance between competition and collaboration," he told us in his crisp but offbeat accent. "I know many Malaysians consider Singapore a competitor, but I think we can find a healthy balance. In the end, it doesn't really matter if Singapore benefits more than we do. As long as we both benefit."

Mr Jala delivers one of the grandest presentations one might ever see—it is more like an elaborate production than an economic briefing. He moves animatedly on stage, drawing one in to his narrative. He is geometrically proportioned, with a square head that sits on top of a rectangular, heavy-set frame, which might work for the front-row of a rugby scrum. As Mr Jala speaks, his two assistants—sharp, well-spoken young Malaysian Chinese men—sit at their computers and toggle furiously between four or five separate Powerpoint presentations.

This is necessary, one of them told me, because Mr Jala never delivers a linear presentation. Nobody, not even Mr Jala, apparently, really knows for sure what he might speak about next. He decides on the fly which intellectual tangent to run down. One minute he's discussing Malaysia's police force, the next he's on to Middle Eastern investors. As he speaks, his two assistants listen for any shift in emphasis that might require a sudden switch to another slide deck, where a golden nugget of supporting information lays waiting. They watch their computers intensely, like DJs who ponder their next MP3.

For the audience it can get slightly distracting, as there is constant motion on the screen. Any possible question is immediately answered both with Mr Jala's explanation, as well as a chart, or a series of numbers, flashed at you by his nimble elves.

Some people find it all a bit too pretentious. "Malaysia's problems can't be solved with Powerpoint," says one slightly cynical friend. Still, Mr Jala's straight-talking, hard-hitting style is like a breath of fresh air compared to many of Malaysia's typical politicians and bureaucrats, who tend to be pensive, reticent and inaccessible.

Among other things, Mr Jala spoke of the need for Malaysian businesses to be less insular, and more adventurous in exploiting foreign markets, including Singapore. Apparently there are many Malaysian firms who, after succeeding domestically, put their feet up.

"It reminds me of the time my nephew and I were line fishing off the beach in Australia," says Mr Jala. "Nothing was biting. There was an Australian man in the distance, however, who was amassing a big catch. So my nephew walks up to him and starts casting near him. Of course, after a few minutes their two lines had gotten entangled, and we had to stop and untangle them. The Australian man then turned to my nephew and said, 'It's a very big beach, mate.'"

With his incessant anecdotes and jokes, Mr Jala is like a cross between Robin Williams and a management consultant. What is curious, perhaps, is that he does not belong to any of Malaysia's favoured classes. He is a Christian from the Kelabit tribe, a tiny community in Sarawak. "There are only 5,000 of us," he says proudly.

Sabah and Sarawak, the two Malaysian states on the island of Borneo, have always had uncomfortable centre-periphery tensions with the Malaysian mainland, a few hundred kilometres away. Both states are physically—and in some ways culturally—closer to Brunei, Indonesia (Kalimantan) and the Philippines (Sulu archipelago) than to KL.

It is not even clear that Sabah and Sarawak should ever have been part of Malaysia. Over the past six centuries, several colonial powers, including the British, the Dutch, the Japanese, the Portuguese and the Spanish, have ruled over them. At no point during colonialism were Sabah and Sarawak politically connected to Malaya. The two states joined the Federation of Malaysia only in 1963, after a UN referendum whose legitimacy and results were disputed by Indonesia and pro-independence groups.

Along with places such as Aceh and Irian Jaya in Indonesia, and the southern provinces of the Philippines and Thailand, Sabah and Sarawak are states that got rolled up and absorbed into larger Southeast Asian post-colonial narratives. All these provinces have experienced occasional separatist urges.

Mr Jala has, therefore, always been an outsider. He grew up in a tiny rural village, surrounded by magnificent mountains and jungles. Mr Jala and his fellow students went to "primary school" in a tiny hut, where they used broken bits of chalk to write on the mud floor. KL was three days away, another universe altogether.

Put another way, Mr Jala's unlikely rise is analogous to somebody from Tibet growing up to become one of Beijing's most respected economic chiefs.

His star has shone brightly ever since he helped turn around Malaysian Airlines (MAS), the national carrier. Having risen up the ranks of Shell, where he worked for more than 20 years, he was headhunted in 2004 by the government. It was a very difficult decision, according to him. "I had to leave my lovely home in London, where I had manicured gardens, tended by an Italian gardener, to come back to live in Taman Tun," he says dryly, referring to one of KL's suburbs. "My wife wasn't pleased."

Upon his return, the national newspapers had a field day. "MAS—*Mati Anak Sarawak*, The Son of Sarawak will die," they declared, suggesting that Idris, the non-Malay, non-Muslim, East Malaysian, had been reeled in as the fall guy after years of mismanagement at MAS. "I immediately corrected them," says Mr Jala. "It's going to be 'MAS—*Masalah Akan Selesai*, the problems will be solved.'"

Within a couple of years, Mr Jala had turned a loss-making state behemoth into a lean, profitable carrier, even as budget airlines grew bigger and became stronger competitors. (After he left MAS, however, the airline again ran into difficulties, tarnishing his legacy somewhat.) He was then handpicked by Mr Najib to lead PEMANDU.

As an outsider in Malaysia's stratified society, Mr Jala's life has inevitably been more difficult, as he has had to face numerous biases— presumably he's been told *Mati Anak Sarawak* many times. But Mr Jala probably also enjoys an outsider's privilege—the ability to elevate himself above traditional ethnic tensions and other entrenched stereotypes. Unlike so many of Malaysia's other "Datuks" and politicians, he comes across as approachable and down-to-earth. He doesn't subscribe to, or need, the usual honorifics, platitudes, red carpets and minders (two Powerpoint chums aside).

It is this outsider's status that probably allowed him to parachute into MAS, and quickly embark on a massive cost-cutting and divestment programme. Similarly, today it enables him to motor around the country, relentlessly pushing through Mr Najib's Government Transformation Programme (GTP) and Economic Transformation Programme (ETP). Mr Jala does not bother himself with traditional hierarchies, processes or ways of doing things.

His achievements already look impressive. The GTP targets six areas: urban public transport, crime, rural basic infrastructure, education, low-income households, and corruption. The first time we met, he boasted of a 36.6 per cent drop in street crime in the first half of 2010, versus the same period a year before. The first half of 2011 saw a further 41.6 per cent year-on-year drop. Mr Jala says this is all the result of a series of simple initiatives by his "Crime Lab", including the redeployment of police to "hot-spots", community policing efforts and a ranking of police stations across the country.[14]

With his slick presentations and performance-based metrics, Mr Jala positions himself not as a government official, but a national business consultant. "Let's be clear, I'm one of you," he had told the Singaporean corporate audience in 2010. He does not hide his disdain for traditional government bureaucracy, regularly quoting Ronald Reagan, and quipping that "Government and speed do not sleep in the same bed."

Mr Jala seems to have a very clear and definitive vision of the new Malaysia—a harmonious multi-ethnic country, the so-called "1Malaysia", where old tensions and animosities will be managed; a business-friendly destination where foreign investment is welcome and corporations can become internationally competitive; and a beautiful land where many people can live together, enjoying nature's spoils.

If people such as Mr Jala can transform Malaysia's government and economy, then Malaysia-Singapore relations will surely keep improving. As Mr Jala points out, there are so many complementarities between the two countries. Economic cooperation and integration, in Iskandar and further afield, can serve as the bedrock of a golden era for both countries.

But one must take pause. Is it really so easy? Will historical suspicions simply evaporate if people do business together? If Malays *tak boleh simpan rahsia*, will they ever really trust the Chinese? Similarly, as long as Malaysia gives some sort of preference to Malay Muslims, can Chinese Singaporeans ever truly feel comfortable there? Lee Kuan Yew will one day be gone, but will Malaysians trust his son, current prime minister Lee Hsien Loong, anymore?

Mr Jala, for all his strengths, can sometimes sound a bit naïve. His outsider status might shelter him from some of the painful realities of life in Malaysia. For instance, Mr Jala frequently tries to downplay the importance of the *bumiputera* affirmative action policies to Malaysia's economy, and in particular to the ETP. But just five days before I met him in 2011, one of his colleagues, Muhyiddin Yassin, the deputy prime minister, reiterated that "assisting and safeguarding the interest and welfare of the Bumiputera remains the main agenda of leaders and the government today."[15]

There are, in essence, two competing visions for Malaysia. Mr Jala's dreams frequently run up against those of more inward-looking Malaysians, intent on maintaining the pro-Malay status quo. The future of Malaysia-Singapore relations hinges on this balancing act.

There is reason for hope, but we should also be cautious. We were once the same country, but that was a long time ago. Whatever its champions believe, Iskandar might actually never be as successful as Shenzhen. For although Mr Jala, the bright, spunky man from Sarawak, may not mind if Singapore benefits more than Malaysia, some of his countrymen might.

3
The end of dominance: Part I

"This is what it means to be a Malaysian!" Yap Mun Ching screamed, her voice swollen with pride. She was glowing, having finally found the answer that might shut us up. For days Sumana and I had teased her because she couldn't quite define what it meant "to be Malaysian". To be fair, we had the same problem with "Singaporean". But for some reason, the lack of clarity bothered her more.

We go back a long way. Short, sharp and defiant, Mun Ching stood out in junior college Malay class. Even before saying hello, we had suspected that she might be a Malaysian "ASEAN scholar". Except for the Indonesians, who had unique Dutch-Chinese-Malay hybrid names, the only Chinese in Malay class were the Malaysians, most of whom, like Mun Ching, were also ASEAN scholars.

The Singapore government gives out these scholarships to lure ASEAN's best students, in the hope that they will study and then stay. The policy is a recruitment masterstroke because the worst side effects are goodwill and an understanding of the country. Today, more than 200,000 Malaysians live and work in Singapore, and some of the most talented are former ASEAN scholars. Similar initiatives now try to attract young, smart folk from everywhere.

When we had started school in Singapore, students had only three choices of second language: Malay, Mandarin and Tamil. Malay class was a strange depository of uninterested students. There were the Singaporean Malays who were already too good at the subject. So were the bi- or trilingual Chinese from Malaysia or Indonesia, who were mostly bright ASEAN scholars. Last and most certainly least—in terms of Malay proficiency—were the displaced Eurasians and non-Tamil Indians, like us, who had no option to study our native tongue, and hence chose Malay, only because we were too scared to study curious Chinese characters or Tamil hieroglyphics.

Malay was, for us, the least bad option.

Moreover, in the mid-1980s, when nobody expected China to rise so quickly, many in Singapore also made a pragmatic argument for learning Malay—it would be the most useful given how close we are to Malaysia and Indonesia.

Today, anybody who can studies Mandarin. The era of non-Malays studying Malay in Singapore has ended. In other words, Singapore's attempt to ride the China wave has pulled us away from the Malay world, culturally and linguistically.

In terms of grades, our Malay class was suitably polarised. At the upper end were the Malays and foreign Chinese. At the bottom end were the Eurasians and Indians, who really didn't give a hoot. Malay class generated a wonderfully cosmopolitan apathy. It was a frustrating recipe for any teacher.

Therefore, since Mun Ching didn't have to study, and since we didn't care, we used to spend much of Malay class irritating the living daylights out of her, with our incessant chatter and general boisterousness. This was not what she had come to Singapore for. In the first few months, Mun Ching flashed only a stubborn pout at us. Despite being just a shade above four feet, she could look ferocious, her thick lips imposing enough to put off the most thick-skinned bloke. She was, in local parlance, a real *chilli padi* of a girl, in reference to the intensely hot, tiny Southeast Asian chilli.

It was only midway through the year, after the virginal thrill of junior college had died down, and the preconceived notions of character had given way to a more rational tolerance, that we got a glimpse of the loving girl, her tender, secret smile, and her undying compassion.

We had gone our separate ways: while we went off to the US for university, Mun Ching completed her degree in London. She later worked at *Malaysiakini*, an online newspaper that effectively broke the government's stranglehold on media. Mun Ching made a name for herself through rigorous investigative journalism, in particular her brilliant exposé on the plight of illegal Burmese migrants.

When we were looking for somebody to gallivant around Malaysia with in the lead-up to the 2008 general elections (GE 2008), Mun Ching was the natural choice. She translated weird-sounding northern Malay and Kelantanese for us, and got us long interviews with women young and old, two groups that, for obvious reasons, were never too chatty when we had approached them alone. Along the way, we relived the old JC days, ate a bit too much *roti canai*, and chatted about Malaysia, Singapore and all the space in between.

In some way, we got to know Mun Ching all over again. She told us how she was fiercely proud to be Malaysian, even though as a child she had been discriminated against because of her skin colour. She enjoyed telling us about her forgettable first encounters with stuck-up Singaporeans, and her hopes and dreams for a brighter future for Malaysia, and a fuller life for herself. Throughout the journey, however, there was one thing that bothered her. For all her pride, she could not explain what it meant *to be Malaysian*. That changed on 8 March 2008.

On the morning of the general election, Mun Ching joined us as we canvassed voting booths in Kota Bahru, Kelantan for interviews. She had been toying with the idea of hanging around, but in the end, she decided to fulfil her civic duty. A phone call later, she had booked a flight back to KL, just so she could vote in her district, Petaling Jaya Utara, where the three-term incumbent, Chew Mei Fun of the ruling Barisan Nasional (BN), was facing a fierce fight from a young upstart, Tony Pua of the opposition Democratic Action Party (DAP). All three of us had met him at a *ceramah*, public speech, just a few days before. Young, smart and articulate, Tony, himself a former ASEAN scholar, caused Mun Ching to gush and swoon and tiptoe. The pout was gone.

As she left us on Election Day, Mun Ching truly felt that her one vote would make a difference. Being Singaporean, we found this downright bizarre.

After casting her ballot, she returned to *Malaysiakini*'s newsroom, at the behest of her colleagues. When national media outlets kept suspiciously silent throughout the evening, Malaysians knew something was amiss. Starved of news, they turned to *Malaysiakini*. Hundreds of thousands of simultaneous hits caused the site to crash, leaving hungry election-watchers grasping at SMS updates.

Thankfully, as we roared over Genting Highlands on our way to KL, braving fierce rains, Mun Ching kept us up to date. Whenever an opposition MP gained a seat, she would send us a message, cheering each incumbent's fall, like frames at a bowling championship. She made sure we knew that her country was on the verge of a revolution. The phone rang. It was Mun Ching.

"Haha! It's unbelievable!" she screamed. "The opposition's won another one! I don't believe what's happening. They've won in Penang. They've won in Kelantan. They've won in Kedah. It's crazy!" We could hardly hear her; people in the background were shouting in chorus, like a troupe.

"So, tell me guys, is this possible in Singapore?" Mun Ching cried emphatically, happy that she could one-up us. "So there's your answer. This is what it means to be Malaysian! This is what it feels like to be Malaysian!"

Swept up by the political tsunami, we punched away at our handphones, sending messages back to Singapore. We were witnessing political history and it was exciting, but it was strange. We were like perverted voyeurs, dying to feel the emotion of the election. But not having cast a vote, no matter how much we felt like insiders, we were on the outside, looking in. This was Malaysia's moment, not ours. It was something neither of us had experienced in Singapore.

As the tropical rain beat down, we could barely hear her above the din of the engine and the water; but Mun Ching was on the brink of a fit, and we were sucked into the sheer excitement. As we approached KL, friends called and warned that rumours were spreading about sporadic rioting; apparently, tension was building in Bangsar, a rich suburb, where lots of people had gathered. Concerned friends and relatives chipped in with text messages to tell us to stay clear of Bangsar. And so, cursed by curiosity, we headed straight there. When we got to Bangsar, we found nothing. No drama. No outpouring of emotion. Bangsar was its normal self. Like disappointed addicts, we found a television to get our fix.

In the wee hours of that morning, watching sedate newscasters on RTM, the national television station, we got official confirmation of the results. They were being decidedly cautious in their announcements, not showing the same Mun Ching-esque kind of excitement when announcing opposition victories. But who could blame them? They were six hours behind. It was old news, cast against a new dawn for Malaysian politics.

***

At this point it's probably worth giving an overview of Malaysia's and Singapore's political systems. After all, I sometimes refer to our systems as democratic, other times we're authoritarian. It can all get a little confusing.

Nominally, both states are democracies, with British parliamentary systems. We hold free and fair elections every five years, choosing the leaders who will represent us in parliament. Whichever party forms the majority gets to choose the prime minister, who then chooses his cabinet of ministers. The prime minister nominates judges to the Supreme Court, which leads the judiciary, an independent body in theory.[1]

We also have two other executive leaders in the country. Malaysians have a king, and Singaporeans have a president. The Malaysian king is a rotating five-year chair, chosen from the nine state sultans (the other four states—Melaka, Penang, Sabah and Sarawak—do not have hereditary sultans). Singaporeans directly elect our president for six-year terms. Both roles are largely ceremonial.

However, in practice, our countries have always been authoritarian states. One party dominates parliament—the Barisan Nasional coalition (BN, the National Front) in Malaysia, and the People's Action Party (PAP) in Singapore. They have both been led by iron-fisted leaders, most notably Mahathir in Malaysia and Lee Kuan Yew in Singapore.

Their dominance is so utterly complete, that Singaporeans and—until the last elections—Malaysians have long equated the ruling party with the country. In other words, if you are loyal to the PAP, you are loyal to Singapore. On the other hand, if you are not loyal to the PAP, that means you are not loyal to Singapore. If you vote opposition, you are somehow being un-Singaporean. Many Singaporeans I meet have this marriage between party-country firmly planted in their minds, hence the fear of voting for the opposition.

Opposition parties have long been crippled by numerous hurdles, for example, a government-owned media that serves as its mouthpiece. What's more, the combination of a strong, fearsome leader and ruling party, and sustained economic prosperity, has made us wary of change. Most Singaporeans and—until the last elections—Malaysians, worry that if we vote opposition, our economic success will be under threat. And if there's one thing that scares the daylights out of us, it's the risk that our *nasi*, Nikes and Nokias might be taken away.

So, even though we are democratic by name, we are authoritarian by nature. How does this play out? Well, parliament is fiercely dominated by one party. Policy debate is conducted largely by one party. The mainstream media kowtows to one party. The judiciary is frequently accused of favouring one party.

We have enjoyed economic development without political development. This has led to much apathy. Why waste time thinking about politics when one can be outside making money?

***

For many years, many of us in Malaysia and Singapore have also been disillusioned by our neighbours' political evolutions. We are surrounded by giant democracies. There is Thailand to the north, the Philippines to the east, and Indonesia to the west and south. From our vantage point, "democracy" in these countries has been problematic.

Thailand seems to toggle between a smiling, peace-loving democracy and dictatorial—but rarely brutal—military rule. Above that tension sits the all-powerful monarchy, whose political role is often unclear. Worse, the country's current ideological rift is deep and seemingly unbridgeable. The Philippines is chaotic—caught between the oligarchic, power-hungry business elite; a population with a wavering faith in people power; and a volatile military.

Indonesia has known democracy only since 1998. Before that, it was run by an autocrat, General Suharto, who, while bringing impressive growth, also plundered the country, with the help of his family and a coterie of cronies. Indonesia's transition to democracy is proving messy. The media landscape is bewildering but starved of trust; legal uncertainty abounds; and money and power still seem entrenched in a tiny elite.

Then there is corruption. It sometimes seems farcical that all across Asia, democracy can sit so comfortably with corruption. Democracy in Asia has always lacked strong, independent institutions.

What's more, the rule of law is weak in these countries. Their judicial systems are overworked. Judges are underpaid and thus many can be easily bought. The Indian police force, for instance, often won't move without a little bit of "tea money". The Filipino army's allegiance seems to sway with the wind. Without these institutions, it is difficult to say that democracy is thriving.

From a pragmatic, and somewhat cynical, Singaporean point of view, what's the point of protest and "free speech" if all it leads to is hubris, and a new bunch of corrupt, inefficient leaders and administrators, who are going to sashay along and swindle some more?

Therefore, when one considers the workings of "democracy" on our doorsteps, it is understandable why many Malaysians and Singaporeans have long wanted no part of it. For years, our authoritarian countries have grown much faster than our neighbours, and we have enjoyed much more political stability.

As a further vote of confidence, foreign multinationals have gleefully invested in our countries. This has gone on for decades, exposing a contradiction: even as Western liberals trumpet human rights, their public corporations—often backed by their governments—turn a blind eye, embracing autocrats, voting with their pockets. At the end of the day, more than anything else, companies want a stable, business-friendly government which upholds the rule of law. In Southeast Asia, choosing stability has often meant choosing authoritarianism, not democracy.

Southeast Asia is thus less known for its democrats than its autocrats, such as Mahathir and Lee Kuan Yew. They are the ones who are idolised. In the late 1990s, the Cambodian leader, Hun Sen said, "I want to be a strongman and do something for my country ... I want to build our economy like other Southeast Asian strongmen did."

The point of all this is certainly not to apologise for our political immaturity or to one-up our neighbours. Quite the contrary, there are many aspects of our neighbouring societies—amongst other things the freedom of association and the presence of strong, credible alternative media channels—that I have long envied.

However, for many years in Malaysia and Singapore, peace, stability and economic progress have muffled the cries for political loosening up. To put it cynically, we have allowed ourselves to be bought: shut up, work hard, and you'll have money in your pocket and your streets will be safe.

Nevertheless, democratic pressures have been building for different reasons. Therefore, it doesn't really make much sense anymore to describe Malaysia as authoritarian; by March 2008, the impulse for change was so strong there that the ruling Barisan Nasional (BN) coalition suffered its worst ever electoral performance. The opposition took control of five of Malaysia's 13 states and won 82 of

222 federal parliamentary seats, denying the government the two-thirds majority it needs in order to change the constitution.[2]

When that happened, quite a few Malaysians I know—not just Mun Ching—jumped for joy.

Three years later, in May 2011, disgruntled Singaporeans perhaps took their cue from Malaysians, as close to 40 per cent of the country voted against the ruling People's Action Party (PAP), handing it its worst ever electoral result. For the first time in Singapore's history, the opposition won a Group Representation Constituency (GRC), one of the larger polling districts that were once considered unwinnable, due to the PAP's stranglehold over them.[3] Nevertheless, thanks to Singapore's first-past-the-post system, the PAP still secured 81 of the 87 elected parliamentary seats, guaranteeing the continuation of single-party rule in Singapore.

Still, just like in Malaysia, many in Singapore celebrate their newfound political voice. The political landscape in both countries has changed dramatically and, probably, irreversibly.

When I started research for this book, during our bicycle trip in 2004, Malaysians and Singaporeans alike appeared relatively content with their respective ruling parties, and were happy to live their lives quietly, under the democratic radar.

Since then, a combination of forces—including policy missteps by the ruling parties, the emergence of more credible opposition candidates, and the widening of political space through the Internet—has blown the lid off our hitherto politically apathetic countries.

Before, only taxi drivers would be willing to "talk politics" with strangers. Most others were always worried about "who might be listening". Today, the fear is gone: even civil servants are eager to share their points of view. Malaysia and Singapore are each in the midst of major political transitions, their first since the 1960s.

But what exactly are the reasons behind these political transitions? To understand why change has come to Malaysia, I recall a conversation we had with an opposition politician in Kedah, the Malay heartland, on 4 March 2008, four days before that seismic general election. Four days before Mun Ching realised what it means to be a Malaysian.

***

Kuala Kedah, Kedah. 4 March 2008.

We were approached by Mohammad, a dark, brawny bloke with a cherubic face, as we were chatting with a group of *nelayan*, fishermen, in Kuala Kedah, under the shade of their rickety boat shed. The shed, built of blackened wooden planks and a zinc roof, sits on the southern bank of the Kedah river's mouth. From the shed, we could see the open waters, the Malacca Straits, in the background. Different vessels were coming and going: some bigger ships, carrying wide-eyed tourist to islands such as Phuket and Langkawi; others *sampans*, tiny fishing boats, bringing blurry-eyed fishermen home after the morning catch.

They brought what fish they had into the shed, and placed them in Styrofoam boxes, awaiting purchase. Soon we had gathered a group of four, and were chatting away. While they loved the ocean, and their job, they were unhappy with a raft of issues. Amongst other things, the cost of living had spiked while fish stocks had declined, apparently because of both climate change and overfishing. "Large Thai trawlers sometimes sail here, and illegally catch our stocks. What can we do? They've paid off the Malaysian coast guard, so nobody really cares."

A few Malay villagers wandered in, picked out a few fish, and paid for them. Soon after, a Chinese man, wearing thin rimmed black glasses, a ragged white polo and white squash shorts, pulled up in a white pick-up. As he walked purposefully towards us, large Styrofoam boxes of his own in tow, the fishermen appeared stuck between routine and antipathy. Like a hungry shark, the Chinese man swept in to the shed, quickly chose what he wanted, and paid up. He drove off in a cloud of smoke, eager to carry on doing whatever he was doing. He was the first and only Chinese we met there. His impetuousness stood in stark contrast to the general laid-backness of Kuala Kedah. There were few fish left over.

"Our *towkay* lah," the youngest fisherman said. The Chinese middleman usually bought up all their stocks, delivering the fish to wet markets nearby. Even though the market price of fish had risen, along with most other foods, the dear *towkay*, businessman, still paid the Malay fishermen the same amount. "What to do? If he doesn't buy it, who will?"

The oldest of them, Roslan, was 75 years old, with dark chocolate skin, and a toned, youthful body. The leathery folds of skin on his neck, which flapped in an elephantine way, betrayed his age. He spoke slowly and deliberately, as though every word was a gift, offering more than the occasional smile. The rest kept quiet when he spoke. After all, for the past 60 years, he had worked the same routine, down the same river, towards the same fish, under the British, then the Japanese, then successive generations of Malaysian leaders.

Listening to Roslan lamenting about Mahathir, Abdullah Badawi, Khairy Jamaluddin and all the other "crooked politicians" who have apparently mismanaged Malaysia since the halcyon days of Abdul Rahman and Abdul Razak, the other fishermen sat there in silence, the balmy breeze stroking their hair, as they dreamed of leaders who could inspire once again. We empathised.

Mohammad, lurking in the shadows, seized the opportunity.

"You want to talk with Nasir Mustafa?"

"Who is that?"

"He is the PAS candidate for the district Dun Kubang Rotan."

A politician? We were much more interested in chatting with these *nelayan*, with the people on the ground.

"It will be good for you to meet him. He's a great guy. And the only free time on his schedule is the next hour."

In urban areas, we had to go around talking to people, actively seeking out interviews and people that we wished to talk to. In *kampungs*, interviews found us.

Mohammad had walked in to buy some fish, but within minutes of his arrival, we were sitting in his van, a crumbling, rusty old Toyota whose sliding door needed five attempts to close. His dashboard was emblazoned with PAS logos. Other party paraphernalia, including green baseball caps and smudgy newsletters, were scattered around. The inside was damp, and smelled of fish. None of the seats were actually securely fixed to the floorboard; while on the move, one actually bounced around *with* the seat. Tottering along in this stink-mobile, we had serious doubts about this expedition. Why bother chatting with PAS in Kedah? Nobody expected a strong showing from them, the fishermen's woes notwithstanding.

We drove for ten minutes, well out of the fishing community, to the main road, with *padi* fields around, and the ocean nowhere in sight. We pulled into a small, detached concrete house, newly built but simple. Mohammad scampered inside, all 500 pounds of him, and ushered a wiry, wispy young man out.

"Welcome, welcome, please come in." Mohammad Nasir Mustafa was dressed simply, in a green-and-white-checked shirt and thin white nylon pants. But for the gold pen in his left breast pocket and the PAS badge pinned over his right breast, he looked like any other rural resident. We felt immediately at ease.

There were a dozen slippers strewn outside the main door. We took ours off, and walked inside, to be greeted by a platoon of young men, sitting cross-legged on the living room floor, each with a humble, restrained smile across his face. They stood up, welcomed us, each shaking our hands softly, and then touching their chest.

They were comfortable with us, but not so much with Mun Ching. Luckily, she could sense this, and offered not her hand, but rather just a demure smile. The men bowed their heads slowly to acknowledge a greeting, but none of them shook hands with her. There were some women in the house, but they were all in the kitchen at the back. We could hear murmurs and the clanging of cups.

There was a soft comfortable sofa by the door, a settee opposite it, and a coffee table in between. Besides that, there was no other furniture in the hall. Nasir ushered us onto the sofa, and sat across from us, on one of the chairs. The other men all sat on a straw mat on the floor. Thick, sweet coffee was soon served.

"Democracy has been hijacked by Barisan Nasional," Nasir said, after we had done away with the opening pleasantries, and he had given us permission to record the conversation.

"This election is not fair. We have never had a fair election. BN has more money, they control the media, they spread lies about the opposition, they scare people into voting for them. There is no such thing as a fair election in Malaysia."

"That sounds a bit like what we have in Singapore," we said. "Except, probably, that the PAP doesn't spread lies about the opposition."

"That's because you don't have an opposition in Singapore," chuckled Mun Ching. The cheeky *chilli padi.*

Despite the hurdles, Nasir was certain this election was going to be different. The time was ripe for change, he insisted. The *rakyat*, the people, know what's going on, and have had enough.

"The other thing that has happened in Malaysia under BN's watch is the mixing of politics and business. This has led to 'Power Business'. It is like in the USA," he said carefully. "You may have different thoughts on this, but I feel that America's wealth is because of its power. It has become the global policeman. They go all over the world and do bad things in other countries for their own good. They create crises in other countries, and they gain from it. So, America does things in other countries for its own good. Barisan Nasional has taken this formula, and applied it *within* Malaysia—some BN leaders do corrupt things *inside our own country* for their own *perut*, stomach. This Power Business has made the whole political system corrupt."

Nasir cited three examples of this widespread corruption: the Bukit Aman incident, where RM27 million was swindled in a land-grab scandal; the Lingam tapes; and the high crime rate, which he said was proof that that the police could be bribed.

According to Nasir, Malaysia's resources and energy have not been committed towards the *rakyat,* but rather towards the preservation of BN. He cited Malaysia's police force as an example: "If BN wants to break up one of our political gatherings, no problem—the police are there immediately. On the other hand, the police can't even take care of basic security." Not for the first time, we were chatting with a Malaysian who was adamant that crooked politicians had been squeezing this rich country dry.

"But the *rakyat* is not stupid," Nasir smiled wryly, as he repeated his favourite refrain, "the *rakyat* knows all this."

"So, if the *rakyat* knows all this, then why does it still vote for BN?"

"People are scared to vote for the opposition. That's why. So they just go with the party that they know. They tolerate the corruption."

As Nasir spoke, the young men sitting on the floor looked on in admiration, like disciples, nodding their heads, hanging on his every word. It felt a bit like we were at some underground rebel gathering, all plotting against the establishment, with Nasir as our Malcolm X. It was exciting, no doubt, but also surreal; this group seemed somewhat detached from reality.

"The other BN tactic has been to divide and rule. Because of this, Malaysians have become suspicious of each other, we feel a lot of *curiga*, distrustfulness. When a Malay looks at an Indian he feels *curiga*. When an Indian looks at a Chinese, he feels *curiga*. And so on. That is because of the way politics is conducted in Barisan Nasional. UMNO asks MCA, 'How many Chinese can you bluff?' UMNO asks MIC, 'How many Indians can you bluff?' This has been going on for a long time. But the *rakyat* is aware of this now."

The game of politics in Malaysia has always been played with racial overtones. The ruling coalition, Barisan Nasional (BN), is dominated by three parties: the United Malays National Organisation (UMNO), the Malaysian Chinese Association (MCA), and the Malaysian Indian Congress (MIC). The three parties offer each ethnic group representation in government. In this way, ethnicity is enshrined in Malaysian society, as the most noble, and yet the most fundamental, of markers.[4] And so, from the street, all the way to high political office, Malaysians have been steeped in the art of race consciousness.

But there is a sense that this model has run its course. Why? The main reason, according to Nasir Mustafa, is that Malaysians are fed up with BN for practising "this race-based politics of divide and rule". The great irony, according to him, is that BN tries to portray itself as just and fair, while frequently slandering PAS as being a party that champions only Malay rights. Apparently Malaysians have woken up to this now. "The *rakyat* realises these are all lies. People can see the results of our 18-year rule in Kelantan, people can see how we treat Chinese and Indians and the Siamese people fairly."

Indeed, throughout my travels across Malaysia, I have encountered a hundred different opinions about PAS, ranging from the paranoid—"They want to create an Islamic State and start violent jihad against non-believers"—to the fiercely proud—"PAS is the best party to lead Malaysians, they are the only non-corrupt politicians out there." And, ever so often, the plain indifferent—"Bloody politicians. They're all the same."

What is most striking, perhaps, is that in Kelantan and Terengganu, the two states that had actually been governed by PAS recently, opinion about them tended to be generally favourable.[5] On the other hand, in other parts of Malaysia, particularly rich urban centres such as KL and Penang, many were fearful of them, and some harboured grave misconceptions.[6]

This was partly because of their fear of the unknown, of the nebulous force governing way out in the northeast. Some PAS firebrands have certainly fanned the flames in the past, spewing divisive sermons unashamedly. But it has also been the result of years of persistent media bias: Malaysian's mainstream media channels have done a fabulous job in painting PAS out to be radical and incompetent.

Another major hurdle for the opposition is "money politics". The system of patronage, fortified over the years with juicy government contracts, has led to much incestuous money sloshing around the ruling BN coalition, says Nasir. This creates two problems. First, it allows BN politicians to buy the loyalty of whoever they want, be it the voter on the street, or possibly even a judge. Since everybody's hands are in the cookie jar, the whole system gets legitimised: if you can't beat 'em, join 'em. Second, the honey pot pulls eager talented young politicians towards BN. This makes it all the more difficult for the opposition to attract them.

"Look at the current Kedah chief minister. He's been in office for four years, and already he's able to afford a big house. Everybody can see what's going on! His house is worth more than a million. His secretary's house is worth more than a million. People around him have gotten rich. That's how things work." Nothing riles an opposition politician the way "money politics" does. Nasir had grown much louder.

"This is the kind of money politics and Power Business that we have here today. But people are extremely upset with all this. Now the *rakyat* knows what's going on."

Partly because of all this cronyism, Nasir said that people had become distrustful of the government's grandiose development projects. "Do you know that the budget of the current National Development Plan (the 9th) is more than the combined budgets of all the previous ones? [Not true.] But the people know better, they know that this is all for publicity, the budget for this is going to be wasted, yet again."

According to Nasir, Malaysia's politicians had become quite adept at buying votes. "Every time there is an election, the government comes along with promises, and with *gula-gula pilihan*, election sweeteners. You'll notice, the government goes only to states where it is weak. Do you see the government making promises in the state of Johor [a government stronghold]? No."

"But they come here and offer to build roads. They offer to change street lamps. They offer gifts. They make promises. But only during election time! They do this to get votes. As soon as the election is over, they're gone. Next time there's an election coming up, they're back again with their promises. But think about it. This is the

12th election. This same thing has happened 11 times already. How many times can you bluff the people?"

Err, 11?

Nasir contended that there are, indeed, a lot of Malaysians who will vote for BN regardless of what happens. But he was also sure that there is a new generation of voters who have had enough, who realise that Malaysia needs "a good, clean government" in order to progress. "Can you imagine what would happen if we put this BN government in charge of Singapore? Within three months, you would be starving. You have no oil, you have no rubber, you have no oil palm. The only thing you have is seawater. They would run you into the ground."

In criticising the ruling BN, Nasir sounded at times like a demagogue. But a lot of what he said did not surprise us. We had heard similar things from scores of Malaysians ever since our bicycle trip in 2004. In fact, even some of BN's most ardent fans would grudgingly admit to us that the party is authoritarian, corrupt and inefficient. They still supported them because they were the best Malaysia had. "And at least they've brought development to our country," many would say.

But what good had PAS done? Besides fighting incessantly as an underdog, and governing the state of Kelantan—which has the lowest income per capita in Malaysia—has PAS actually achieved anything?[7] Has it played a beneficial role in the Malaysian story?

Its critics would argue that PAS, with its orthodox ideology and slightly wonky business sense, has only served to slow Kelantan's development, while not really having much of an impact on the rest of the country. Nasir, obviously, disagrees, pointing out that Malaysians do appreciate the role that PAS has played.

"We have been the opposition for 53 years, we have kept the government in check, we have ensured that any wrongdoing is highlighted, we have kept Malaysia running. Can you imagine how much worse things would have been without an opposition? People would have lived like they did in ancient times, under a king. If you challenged the king, you'd have your hand cut off, your head cut off."

Similarly, Nasir chafes at the suggestion, often made by UMNO members, that PAS has no track record. "That's really funny, because we have been around as a stable party for 53 years. UMNO, on the other hand, had a major crisis in 1988. UMNO is unstable, not us!"[8]

The constitutional crisis of 1988 had its roots in the 1987 UMNO elections. What was meant to be another run-of-the-mill photo opportunity was turned on its head when the incumbent president, Mahathir, was challenged by Razaleigh Hamzah, an outspoken prince from Kelantan, and his followers. The ensuing leadership battle was a bitter, drawn-out spat that cleaved the party in two.

Following arguments, disputes and a protracted legal wrangling, Mahathir and his supporters prevailed, forming UMNO Baru (New UMNO); Razaleigh and his supporters formed Semangat '46 (Spirit of 1946, the year UMNO was founded), a party that soon fizzled out. Nevertheless, Razaleigh, who is now the longest-serving parliamentarian in Malaysia, is still respected by many in Malaysia, BN and opposition alike, for his reformist ideas.

"So, if the opposition wins enough seats, do you think it can form the government? Is it ready and able to replace BN?"

"Definitely," Nasir answered.

"Really?"

"Definitely."

Hogwash, I thought.

"The reason is that the opposition will have the support of all the public servants and the military. The public servants are well aware that they have been made use of by the Barisan Nasional politicians for their own *perut*, stomach. If there is a clean, honest government, our public servants will be happy and motivated to work for it, to develop our country. Right now there is just way too much wastage. Morgan and Stanley [*sic*] said in a report that on average, for a project that costs only one dollar the Malaysian government spends four dollars. It's true. Go and check it." (I could not verify this.)

Nasir leaned his body backwards and clapped his hands sharply, a gesture he performed in synch with every triumphant point. As we listened to all this, we couldn't help feeling a bit sorry for him. Nasir really felt that this would be a watershed, that we were on the verge of a big change in Malaysia. We weren't so sure—why would there be change now? After all, the opposition did still face all the usual hurdles.

"Well, you're well aware that there are no real media freedoms here. BN controls the mainstream media. So, in order to spread the message, we have to find other ways, like giving lots of *ceramahs*. Do you know that there are days where I have given 16 *ceramahs*?" Nasir moaned. "Listen to my voice, it's disappearing!"

But there was no choice, he said. If the opposition relied on the mainstream media, the public would never hear its message. "When the media is restricted like this, the people's voice is never heard. This opens the door for corruption and for crime. We need a free, open media so that the people's voice can be heard, and only then can the country progress."

Although this was only the first time Nasir was standing for office, he had been involved with PAS full-time in some way or another for 13 odd years, during which time he had participated in four previous elections. ("That's how I know that this one is different.") He told us that he had joined the party because it is clean, honest, does good work in the community and is willing to champion the rights of all ordinary Malaysians.

He passed us a small publicity leaflet, written mostly in Malay, which documented his achievements and work for the party, complete with testimonials from party bigwigs and images of newspaper clippings. On the front cover there is a smiling Nasir and a greeting—"I am with you"—in Chinese, English, Malay and Tamil. On the back is a photo of his family: wife and four children, smiling, caring, supporting.

***

As compelling as Nasir was, when we drove out of Kuala Kedah that day, we were not convinced that Malaysia was on the brink of a political earthquake. How wrong we were.

Before 2008, Malaysia's opposition controlled only one of Malaysia's 13 states. But at GE 2008, voters in five Malaysian states—Kedah, Kelantan, Penang, Perak and Selangor—chose the opposition to lead them. Soon after the elections, the three opposition parties in power, DAP, PAS and *Parti Keadlian Rakyat* (PKR, the People's Justice Party), cobbled together an alliance, *Pakatan Rakyat* (PR, The People's Alliance). Although the ruling BN soon won back the state of Perak, Malaysians have had the chance to observe PR's performance in four states since 2008.

Its report card is mixed. By and large PR has done a decent job of governing. Some opposition state governments, most notably Penang's, have succeeded somewhat in making the government leaner and more transparent, and in attracting foreign investment. In both 2010 and 2011, Penang and Selangor recorded the two highest levels of approved manufacturing investment in the country.[9]

Whenever I have travelled across Malaysia, Penang is the place that has reminded me most of Singapore. This could be because it's Malaysia's richest state—going by per capita income—or because of its ethnic makeup, with more Chinese than Malays. Thus it just looks and feels closer to Singapore than do other parts of Malaysia. The two islands also share historical ties, both administered by the British as The Straits Settlements, along with Malacca.

When we cycled across Malaysia, Penang was also the first place where we had a guaranteed homestay: Uncle James and family live there. An evening with them recharged us. Superb hawker food, on-demand hot water, Aunty Leela Laundry Service, relaxed familial conversations, a cosy, snug sleep. And the freedom of being able to forget our bikes. It was all too good to be true, and we cycled off the next morning delirious, not wanting to wake from our Penang dream.

In fact, we felt so comfortable and relaxed that we decided to commit our most flagrant violation of Malaysia's traffic laws: we cycled across the Penang Bridge.

The spectacular Penang Bridge is the longest in Southeast Asia and one of the longest in the world. It is one of Malaysia's architectural wonders, and we were dead-set on crossing it.

Would we get caught? Well, we had our ignorant foreigner act down pat. Besides, how terrible can a *cycling* offence be? It's the sort of misdemeanour that one doesn't even feel bad about.

As we merged onto the bridge, we noticed three things. First was the sign telling us that bicycles are prohibited. Second, we detected a slight sway to the bridge, as the cross strait winds blew ferociously across it. More importantly, the shoulder lane, which would offer much protection against traffic coming from behind, seemed to be narrowing and slowly disappearing.

We were soon to be one with the permitted forms of transport on the bridge. The bridge sloped ever so slightly upward and we could not see over the centre of the bridge. The views on both sides were remarkable. Ships were gliding across the mirrory waters of the Straits and Georgetown sat quaintly to the left.

But who dared to look? There was an endless blur of gasoline-powered vehicles zooming by inches from us. Every time a truck, bus or even small Kancil—a tiny hatchback—passed us, we felt like we were being sucked towards them. The frenetic crosswinds made the cycle across the bridge somewhat tense, we felt like we could be easily carried off into the sea.

Outwards by the wind and inwards by the passing traffic. Out and in, out and in. On some occasions we had to wrench our bikes back into an upright position after a truck flew past. For the first time in our trip, our arms were working harder than our legs.

The combination of the traffic, crosswinds and the slight incline meant that we were cycling furiously but still at a sluggish pace. At times, the wind literally held us back, like a mystic force pushing against our shoulders, willing us to return to Penang.

Even though the bridge is only 13.5 kilometres long, it took us an hour to cross.* Each of the massive columns of the bridge stands at about 100 metres, although one will not notice this while on the bridge. When we finally made it past all the columns, we looked back at our conquest, said a silent good bye to Penang, and after a quick check that all limbs were in order, continued on towards Taiping.

Despite its successes in Penang, at a national level, PR has had to contend with sporadic disagreements and infighting. These partly stem from the fundamental

---

*   Our average speed for the whole journey was 20km/h.

ideological differences between its parties—in particular, secular, Chinese-dominated DAP does not make an easy bedfellow for Muslim, Malay-dominated PAS. Among other things, secular Malaysians worry about perceived creeping fundamentalism by sections of PAS, including suggestions to ban alcohol, gambling and pig-rearing in some or all of the PR-controlled states.

One person who is unbothered by all this is Nurul Izzah, vice-president of PKR, whose house we met at in September 2011. "The internal dynamics of PAS have always been greatly influenced by their performance in national polls," she says. Confident that PAS has become more moderate, she points to the rise of Mat Sabu, elected as PAS deputy president in 2011. "He is not even an *ulama*," she says, alluding to the fact that Mat Sabu is the first non-religious scholar to be elected to the party's leadership in 25 years.

She also believes that DAP and PAS have moved more to the centre over the years, and are now much more willing to make compromises for the sake of the alliance. Any conflict between the parties is simply a reflection of Malaysian society, says Nurul, and should not be swept under the carpet, the way BN has been doing for years. Instead there should be a constructive process of engagement that she believes will lead to some resolution. "Look at what happened in Kedah recently, where there was talk of banning entertainment outlets from operating during Ramadan. There were discussions and negotiations, and eventually the ban was revoked."

PR has created a common policy platform to use if it wins control of the Federal Government. Nurul says this serves as an assurance that the alliance will not be captured by special interests in any particular party.

When talking to her, it is easy to forget that Nurul is a seasoned politician. She has the young, innocent features of a five-year-old, and speaks in a gentle whisper, never raising her voice. It is as if a national Spelling Bee champion has been dressed up as a lady, and asked to govern.

But she is no novice. Thirty-year-old Nurul has been politically active for more than a decade. "During my summer breaks in university, I would travel in the country and abroad to speak on behalf of political prisoners." Articulate and measured, she seems polished in the art of quiet persuasion. Along with Tony Pua of the DAP, Nurul is one of the Malaysian opposition's starlets, and a leader of the *Reformasi* generation, the reform movement spawned in 1998 in the wake of the Asian financial crisis.

In conversation, Nurul seems to consciously avoid mention of her father, Anwar Ibrahim, who served as deputy prime minister under Mahathir, before falling out with him in 1998. Anwar was then convicted on trumped-up charges of sodomy, and was one of the "political prisoners" who inspired Nurul and the rest of the *Reformasi* generation.

In 2004, the charges against Anwar were overturned, and he was released from prison. He was not able to participate in the seminal March 2008 elections because he was banned from politics till April 2008. In August 2008, he finally rejoined parliament when he won a by-election in Permatang Pauh, after his wife, Wan Azizah, vacated her seat. Anwar, as the de facto leader of PR, is considered by his supporters as Malaysia's prime minister-in-waiting. In January 2012, he was acquitted of a second sodomy charge, after a two-year trial.

Though her father tends to grab much of the media spotlight, Nurul seems determined to carve out her own, independent political narrative. "Having Anwar Ibrahim as my father, his name can of course be beneficial, but it can also be a liability," Nurul says. "I love my father dearly, and he was one of the reasons I joined politics. Still, it was my decision, and I knew I could not blame him if I lost or won."

Nurul is convinced that ultimately voters will elect her based on how she performs, not because of her family ties. PKR's critics aren't so sure, and have lamented what they see as dynastic politics, particularly with Nurul's recent election to the party's vice-presidency. If one looks across Southeast Asia, there are no other political parties where father, mother and daughter all play such prominent roles.

Still Nurul is adamant that the decision to contest for the party vice-presidency was her own. She seems much less bothered by accusations of nepotism than she is by her own inability to fulfil her filial duties.

"My father's second sodomy case has come out, and I can no longer focus my attention on it," she says. "That saddens me because I was able to be there for him in 1998. But today I am also responsible to my constituents and to my own family. People voted for me, people trusted me. You have to be fair to everyone, equal time for my family, and for the voters."

With elections round the corner, Nurul also has to think about her own re-election campaign. Though she is confident that PR has done a good job governing, she worries about the broader political climate in the country.

"There is a concerted effort to make sure every opposition leader is vilified, and hence will be deemed unacceptable, especially by the Malay electorate," says Nurul. "My worry is that we are going to see one of the dirtiest elections ever, and it's going to cost us." Among her concerns are the electoral roll inconsistencies (many dead Malaysians are still registered as voters), the supposedly biased postal ballot and media, and "an election commission that is highly biased in favour of the government".

Nurul believes political and social freedoms have regressed over the past few years. "Malaysia under Najib reminds me of the Mahathir era," she says. "There are more efforts to silence dissent. The police force and the security apparatus are much more prominent now. It is a rather threatening environment for opposition lawmakers."

By contrast, says Nurul, the political climate was much more open under Abdullah Badawi, Malaysia's prime minister from 2004 to 2009. She compares the two demonstrations by Bersih, a non-governmental coalition for electoral reform, in Kuala Lumpur. The first demonstration, in 2007 during Abdullah's reign, carried on with little police disruption—"hardly 50 people were arrested." The second demonstration in 2011 resulted in almost 1,700 arrests. There were also 90 restraining orders imposed, preventing certain individuals from entering Kuala Lumpur that day. "Including me," says Nurul. It seems bizarre that the government would consider this meek lady a security threat to Malaysia.

Despite the harsh political climate, Nurul still sees the value of engaging directly with Najib. A few weeks before we met her, she had sent him an open letter listing eight demands regarding electoral reform. In it she refers to Najib with the standard honorific for a prime minister, Yang Amat Berhormat (YAB, The most respected).

"As a gentle and historical reminder YAB, the *rakyat* has never truly elected YAB as the prime minister of Malaysia," Nurul noted dryly, reminding Najib that he had yet to win an election. "Hence, let this opportunity to enact comprehensive electoral reforms present YAB with the opportunity to definitively receive the *rakyat's* mandate to govern."

"Why don't you eat," beckoned Nurul warmly, pointing at the lavish spread of cakes in front of us. "These homemade *kuih lapis* [layered cakes] are very nice and difficult to get." We had felt a bit bad meeting her on a Sunday morning, so much so that we had been speeding through the interview, ignoring the food. She put us at ease by revealing that she had other appointments that day. Such is the life of a politician. So we were not the only ones, but merely the first to interrupt her Sunday. We promptly wolfed down a few *kuihs*.

Beyond all the larger-than-life personalities, perhaps the biggest difference between PR and BN is PR's embrace of multi-racial politics versus BN's traditional race-based structure. "One of the main reasons I joined PKR is because we have a strong multicultural core," she says, "which is essential for Malaysia. We have to start ingraining that thought in many Malaysians so that we can progress."

Nurul is also confident that DAP and PAS are resolutely committed to becoming multicultural parties, moving away from their traditional focus on, respectively, the Chinese and Malay communities. After the 2008 elections, PAS created a non-Muslim membership wing, Kelab Penyokong PAS (KPP, the PAS Supporters Club). "Can you imagine an Islamic party doing this?" muses Nurul. DAP, meanwhile, has launched Roketkini, a Malay-language web portal, and is eager to field more Malay candidates. "All this is important because it helps the development of multi-racial politics."

I asked Nurul whether there was a risk that, in their efforts to broaden their appeal, DAP and PAS might lose support among their respective Chinese and Malay bases. "This has always been the justification by the younger generation of UMNO for the continuation of race-based politics," says Nurul. "Though everybody has the right to propagate the type of politics they see fit for this country, I don't think one should use positions of power to encourage right-wing extremist groups, such as Perkasa."

Many Malaysians I speak with lament Najib's tolerance of right-wing nationalists. Some suggest that he publicly denounces them while privately encouraging them. In early 2012, Najib's wife attended a Perkasa fund-raiser.

Whatever the case, these Malay nationalist voices won't go away. In February 2012, at the launch of Jati, a new Muslim NGO, Harussani Zakaria, the Perak Mufti, or religious leader, called on Malays to defend their land, saying "just forming groups and clapping your hands will get you nowhere."[10]

Still, Nurul is optimistic. "Younger Malaysians in particular will not be easily duped by the use of racial or religious fear-mongering tactics by the different parties," she says. Though Nurul still feels constrained, she is certainly a lot freer than she was a decade ago to do and say what she wants. When she was in university, no Malays wanted to hang out with her because the police had labelled her a subversive threat, she says. "All my friends were Chinese."

Nurul felt so beaten down that even on the day her father was convicted, she went to school, more determined than ever to study. "I knew that whatever they did to me, they could not take away my, ahem, 'stellar grades'," she told us, laughing at her own playfulness. University was her solace, and academic achievement fulfilled her. Through Nurul's life, one can see how the space for Malaysia's opposition has really opened up since she was in university, though evidently not nearly enough for them.

Despite her meteoric rise, Nurul seems to have remained fairly grounded. "Politics is a lifelong learning experience, the learning curve is so steep, and one has to try and master so many different skills, like public speaking."

She refuses to view her victory over Shahrizat Jalil, an UMNO stalwart, in the 2008 general elections as any sort of personal achievement. It was, she contends, more a victory for the Malaysians who voted for her, many of whom wanted change.

"One should never personalise politics," she argues. "It's not about me, or Shahrizat, or Anwar Ibrahim, it's about something much bigger than any one of us."

"My proudest moment, aside from having my two kids—without an epidural, mind you—was at a rally in Lucky Gardens, Bangsar," she says. "It was the night before the 2008 elections, and there was a completely multi-racial crowd there. I remember thinking that regardless of what happens in the elections, just the fact that we had succeeded in bringing all these people together, that was so inspiring."

Nevertheless, Nurul, prompted by her supporters, still has had to entertain thoughts of leading Malaysia. "Whenever somebody asks me about becoming prime minister one day, I always call it the Kiss of Death. One has to take it with a pinch of salt. You can be the darling of society one moment, and it could all end in the next."

Again stressing that individuals do not matter, Nurul argues that what Malaysia needs is a whole generation of reformers and progressive thinkers in order to succeed. "Even across the political divide, we need the reformers in UMNO to come to the fore. For a proper political transition, it can never be us against them. Nobody can claim ownership for reforms. It is a cause that should be embraced by everyone."

I asked Nurul who her favourite Malaysian prime minister of all time was. She gave us a mildly disapproving look. She then noted that it's difficult to assess the performance of prime ministers in Malaysia because, aside from a few notable scholarly works, the only commentary and news about them appears in the biased government-controlled media.

Still, she plumped for Hussein Onn, Malaysia's third prime minister, who is also known as *Bapa Perpaduan*, Father of Unity. "He was a visionary," she said. "He saw a possible future for multi-racial politics."

The truth is that, through Hussein Onn and many others, multi-racial agendas and ideas have bounced around Malaysia for decades, only to be undermined every time by nationalists. It is still unclear whether the *Reformasi* generation's efforts will be any more successful.

Indeed, it is easy to get caught up in Pakatan Rakyat's exhortations on electoral reform, multiculturalism and fighting corruption. It all sounds very liberating. There are many Malaysians, however, who have a highly cynical view of the opposition.

To his critics, Anwar is a conniving chameleon, somebody willing to sneakily do whatever it takes to get what he wants. All his talk about reforming Malaysia is to them simply a romantic political spin that masks a basic desire for power. His rhetoric is merely his vehicle.

Anwar's biggest miscalculation, perhaps, was his cack-handed attempt at winning control of Malaysia's Federal government in September 2008, shortly after he was elected. He had promised his supporters, his colleagues, his fellow parliamentarians, and even the rest of the world that he would have enough support to take over Malaysia's government on 16 September 2008. The day came and went with barely a whimper.

It later emerged, through WikiLeaks cables and other testimonies, that there were indeed BN MPs who were willing to cross over to Pakatan Rakyat. Nevertheless, the perception that Anwar had spun a quite elaborate web of deceit that might have seriously destabilised the country rankles many Malaysians.

His performance as PKR's head over the past three years has also been highly controversial. Amid accusations of nepotism, PKR has lost a fifth of its 31 parliamentary seats through defections and resignations. In an interview with the *New Straits Times*, N. Gobalakrishnan, an MP and PKR founder member, puts it bluntly, "Anwar may be God-given," he said, "but he thinks he is God."[11]

Therefore, though it may sometimes seem from the outside as if Malaysia is on the verge of an opposition revolution, I've met many Malaysians who still have firm faith in BN. They see the opposition more as a bunch of opportunists rather than the future leaders of Malaysia.

Nurul's confidence notwithstanding, PR probably remains one of the most unstable coalitions in the world. It is hard to imagine a more ideologically diverse grouping of people, including the Malay Muslim-dominated PAS, which for long wanted to create an Islamic state in Malaysia. In many ways, the only thing the three parties have in common is their opposition to BN.

Aside from its fragility, the other problem with the PR is that it is full of political greenhorns. Many of its politicians would never have dreamed of running for office five years ago. That doesn't mean they can't do it, but rather that there is a tremendous amount of learning-on-the-job going on.

PR's incessant infighting has left the door open for the ruling BN, which has been jolted into action by its poor performance in 2008. The prime minister, Najib, is leading a mini-revolution within BN as he prepares it for the next election. By purging the coalition's fat, he hopes to lead a fitter BN to victory. It will not be easy—BN is a coalition saddled with years of ethno-nationalism, racism, corruption, cronyism and nepotism.

In March 2012 the party was under the spotlight again, when Shahrizat Jalil, the minister for women, family and community development, announced that she will be leaving the cabinet when her term ends in April.[12] This came after months of public anger over accusations that Mohamad Salleh, Shahrizat's husband, had embezzled public money to purchase luxury apartments, including two in Singapore. He has denied the charges. At the time of writing, the corruption investigation was still ongoing. Whatever the outcome, the whole saga has undermined Najib's message of reform.

Nevertheless, Malaysia has begun its transition from an authoritarian state, rife with corruption, to a possible two-coalition, or multi-party democracy. This will prove long and turbulent. A political structure built on ethnic differences may have to eventually make way for a race-blind one.[13] The inefficient system of patronage politics is slowly being replaced by one based on old-fashioned values like honesty, integrity and responsibility. Entrenched corruption must ultimately be weeded out though progress here is especially slow. Meanwhile, it will take time to rebuild public faith in many of Malaysia's distrusted institutions, including the police force and judiciary.

Unsurprisingly, this transition is proving messy. The next election, due by 2013, will be as raucous and fractious as the last one, and with as many allegations of unfair tactics and rigging, such as the use of *pengundi hantu*, phantom voters.

It is difficult to tell who might win the election. If the ruling BN edges out PR again in a close fight, as seems likely, Malaysia will continue on the same reform road it has been on. If BN wins in a huge landslide, that might set the reform agenda back, as there will be less impetus for change within the ruling party. If the opposition PR wins the election, Malaysian politics and governance might be in disarray for a while, largely because more than half a century of rule would have come to an end—it will be a turbulent handover of power.

Perhaps the biggest worry, regardless of the outcome, is that politics might degenerate into squabbles along ethnic or religious lines. Even though many progressive Malaysian politicians speak about a new era of multicultural politics, it will take some time before societal attitudes and mindsets shift in that direction. If desperate, some politicians might be tempted to appeal to communal instincts. That would be a major setback for the country.

Nevertheless, at a broader level, the good news is that Malaysia's political transition is well underway, and there is no stopping it. The result of the GE 2008, where BN suffered its worst ever electoral performance, was the culmination of years of grievances and discontent brewing in Malaysian society. As the US was gripped by the audacity of hope, Malaysians finally found the audacity to vote. 2008 will be remembered as the year when ordinary Malaysians set in motion a chain of events that would one day lead to a stable democratic state.

The trouble is, "one day" could still be a decade or more away. As much as there is room for optimism about reform in Malaysia, there is also plenty of reason to worry—a generation of crooked politicians isn't just going to disappear. According to one senior Malaysian banker I know, there is a crop of emerging Malay wannabes who realise that their time in the sun may be coming to an end, and are determined to squeeze as much out of the system while they can—a philosophy known as *pukul habis*, or "hit it till the very end".

The political arena is not the only place where this contest of ideas will necessarily be settled. For once all the philosophising about race, religion and identity is over, it is also worth remembering that when voters go to the ballot box in Malaysia, just like everywhere else, they often vote on bread-and-butter issues.

"The first step is empathy. So many people are trapped in a cycle of poverty, they have more basic concerns than issues of identity. We need to empathise and then empower them," says Nurul.

The only thing that one can say for sure is that a political transition is underway. Instead of just listening to what Big Brother has to say, every Malaysian's search for meaning and identity has begun in earnest. Maybe that's what Mun Ching meant when she screamed at us, bursting with expectation, on 8 March 2008.

4
The end of dominance: Part II

Over the course of the past eight years, while shuttling between Malaysia and Singapore, one of the biggest differences I've noticed between people is in their willingness to speak up. Malaysians are generally much more eager to tell you exactly what they think, whether the topic of conversation is food, football or politics. I often had to pull myself away from chatty strangers, who had so much more to share.

We Singaporeans, on the other hand, are much more reserved. For a multitude of reasons, we tend to water down our opinions, or wrap them in a protective layer of waffle or anonymity. Many of us are simply afraid to let others know what we really think.

This feeds into our attitudes towards strangers. When you randomly stop somebody on the street in Singapore, just to ask a question, it feels like much more of an imposition to the person than it does in Malaysia. This probably stems not from any Singaporean unfriendliness, but rather just our natural shyness and reticence. Malaysians, by contrast, more often seem willing just to chat, even in the big cities. They seem more able to make time.

If this book had been published before 2011, I would have written all of the above on this page without reservation. It would have stood independently as a summary of Singaporean apathy and reticence.

But today it is woefully inadequate. Singapore's 2011 general elections (GE 2011) uncorked opinion in this country. It is still unclear if the PAP will continue to dominate politics in the decades ahead or, instead, if Singapore has taken its first step towards becoming a multi-party democracy. Still, irrespective of how our political landscape evolves, one thing is for sure—the myth of the apathetic Singaporean is dead. We have all found our voice.

During the 2006 general elections, I went around asking people who they were going to vote for. Although close friends and family shared their thoughts, no stranger would tell me.

By the time GE 2011 had come around, meanwhile, it seemed like everybody wanted to talk about it. People who had ignored politics their whole lives suddenly showed up for work with dissertations on individual candidates. This political awakening, perhaps, may be the most lasting impact of GE 2011.

But why were so many Singaporeans moved to speak up? Why was there such a seismic shift against the PAP, such that it won its lowest ever share of the vote? In the aftermath of GE 2011, analysts proposed many different narratives and theories, which together help to shed light on these complex developments.

Many people, after all, were surprised by the shift. Friends overseas called to ask why so many Singaporeans had lost faith in one of the most successful political parties in history. From the outside, Singapore appeared to have been performing brilliantly, with stellar headline economic growth, and a string of high-profile global developments, including two new casinos and the Formula 1 night race.

Most surprised of all, perhaps, were Singapore's new migrants, particularly those from other Asian countries. I met a Taiwanese lady who had become a Singapore citizen in the late 1990s, and was glad then to have swapped Taiwan's divisive politics for Singapore's "political stability". GE 2011 had left her in a bit of a funk.

Bobby Jay, one of my friends from India who became a Singapore citizen a few years ago, was even more aghast. Like so many new migrants, Bobby is a fervent PAP fan, and has sung its praises whenever we've discussed politics over beers. Just a few months before the elections, Bobby simply could not foresee the PAP suffering any major losses. "If the PAP ever loses power, I am leaving this country for sure," he told me.

***

Before discussing GE 2011, and Singapore's current transitional political landscape, it is worth touching on the atmosphere that has prevailed for most of our history.

First, how and why did the PAP achieve such an elevated stature in the minds of so many? There are two broad underlying reasons. First, the ruling party has been so overwhelmingly successful in delivering economic progress that Singaporeans, by and large, have happily subscribed to the notion of a one-party state. Second, the PAP has done a masterly job in fending off and discrediting its opponents, such that most would-be politicians either join the PAP, or stay out of politics completely.

The PAP's success must be couched not only in terms of economic development, but also mind control. While incessant growth has kept Singaporeans materially happy and comfortable, mind control has allowed the party to manage and dictate ideology and opinion in the country. Who feels that guys should not keep long hair? Why is nudity in film offensive? Should homosexuality be a punishable offence? Is average GDP/capita the best measure of economic progress? And after all the rhetoric decrying casinos in the 1970s, how come it is now all right to gamble in a casino?

These deep moral dilemmas, and many others, surface, are discussed and debated, and then opinion about them formulated, amongst an incestuous cocoon of commentators, under the watchful eyes of the PAP. Most Singaporeans are not fortunate enough to hear a plurality of opinions from a multitude of viewpoints. Rather, for the most part, we hear different sides to a story from the government, mostly through its compliant media. Any alternative views simply do not get the same air time.

This way, the PAP has not only been able to deliver economic success, it has also been able to define what "success" is. For instance, in an article in *The Straits Times Review*, senior writer Ong Soh Chin, gushing about Singapore, writes,

> There are few places in the world where the things that matter—transport, education, housing, healthcare—work as efficiently without having to pay an arm and a leg.[1]

She is correct that the government does provide those things relatively cheaply (though costs have risen recently). But—how did Ms Ong decide what "the things that matter" in this world are? Is that her opinion? Her friends'? Our government's?

Surely for some people, there are many other "things that matter". Perhaps cheap land, on which to build a house and grow your own vegetables. Or a thriving arts scene. Or tolerance for alternative careers. Or maybe friendly, spontaneous neighbours, who bake you a cake to welcome you. Or talk shows, where journalists constructively criticise government policy.

In short, there are many other things that a human might derive pleasure and satisfaction from which are not available in Singapore. Economists like to differentiate between known and unknown preferences. In a vibrant democracy, where competing viewpoints and voices are heard, we can easily learn about varying preferences.

But in an authoritarian state with a government media monopoly, it is almost impossible. Unknown preferences will remain, well, unknown. The government decides what is important. Journalists like Ms Ong tell us what is important. And hopefully, over time, all Singaporean people will come to believe this, our minds dissolving into an ocean of uniformity.

But what do Singaporeans really think? That has long been a mystery. Few opinion polls are ever conducted. When they are, one of the government agencies or media outlets is almost always behind them. "The data show that public opinion surveys in Singapore are fraught with theoretical and methodological problems and that their reporting in the news media leaves much to be desired," says Tsan-Kuo Chang, in a paper entitled "Reporting public opinion in Singapore".[2]

Whenever the opinion of ordinary Singaporeans is published in the mainstream media, there is a good chance it's been filtered, one way or another, by the government. There are no independent pollsters here.

With no independent gauge of what Singaporeans really think, the PAP has had full latitude to make sweeping statements like, "Most Singaporeans support the death penalty" or "Most Singaporeans are uncomfortable with homosexuality". With no evidence to the contrary, how can one disagree?

In any case, even if polls were conducted, there is a high chance that a majority of Singaporeans will agree with the ruling party's opinion, philosophies and dictum. After all, we've been drinking the same Kool Aid for years.

Meanwhile, Singapore cherry-picks from international surveys, opinion pieces and polls. If an international body gives us a thumbs-up, we wallow and bask in its glory. On the other hand, if it dares say anything bad about our system, rather than accept the criticism and try and learn from it, we heap scorn on it.

The best proof of this is our schizophrenic attitude towards the London-based International Bar Association (IBA). First, our country held them up as first-class examiners. This came after testimony by Lee Kuan Yew in May 2008 in the trial of Chee Soon Juan, the leader of the Singapore Democratic Party (SDP), and his sister, Chee Siok Chin, for defaming Mr Lee and his son, Prime Minister Lee Hsien Loong.

Mr Lee had said that after the IBA held its annual conference in Singapore in October 2007, its president sent a letter to the Law Society of Singapore praising the country's justice system.[3] A mention from Mr Lee himself! The IBA had garnered the ultimate accolade in Singaporean society.

Two months later, on 9 July, a report by the IBA's Human Rights Institute criticised the use of defamation suits by the PAP to silence the opposition and the press, and expressed concerns about the independence and impartiality of Singapore's judges. Singapore's law ministry quickly rejected the IBA's report and our media channels discredited it. As quickly as the Singapore government had put IBA on a pedestal, it had now knocked it off, and we the citizens never heard of it again.

Repeat the good news, banish the bad. In this way, the Singapore government bullet-proofs "the Singapore model", hoping that all of us continue to believe that we're living in la-la land. While most countries do this to some extent, Singapore pushes it much further than one would expect of a democratic first-world country.

In many ways, Singaporean *exceptionalism*—the idea that we are different and so should not feel a need to subscribe to global norms—is much more virulent than the oft-mocked American version. Singaporean exceptionalism has been buttressed by the notion of Asian Values, a cultural relativist theory that can inspire ardent devotion—"We are Asian, we are different, don't tell us what to do."

Therefore, by defining what "success" is, and then by consistently over delivering on that very definition, the PAP has built up a fabulous brand. What about its political opponents? With a few notable exceptions, they have been vanquished.

To understand the evolution of Singapore's opposition, it is worth noting that the PAP appears to regard them at best as noisy nuisances, and at worst as seditious anarchists who will ruin Singapore if they ever got the chance.

> If I want to fix you, do I need the Chief Justice to fix you? Everybody knows that in my bag I have a hatchet, and a very sharp one. You take me on, I take my hatchet, we meet in the cul-de-sac.
>
> —Lee Kuan Yew in 1997[4]

> Suppose you had 10, 15, 20 opposition members in Parliament. Instead of spending my time thinking what is the right policy for Singapore, I'm going to spend all my time thinking what's the right way to fix them, to buy my supporters votes.
>
> —Lee Hsien Loong in 2006[5]

By repeating these mantras, Singapore's leaders inevitably influence ordinary citizens into believing that opposition politicians are useless, and that opposition politics is, in general, a complete waste of time.

If you are an ambitious youth in Singapore today and you want to cause your mother to suffer a cardiac arrest, just tell her that you've decided to join the opposition. No other career choice will guarantee as much derision and social exclusion. Even though the opposition performed remarkably well in the last elections, many Singaporeans I meet still have a reflexive fear about being directly involved with the opposition.

It is a chicken and egg issue, really. Many Singaporeans grow up with a poor perception of opposition politicians. As a result, few talented people gravitate towards them. They raise little money, and have difficulty elevating their public profile. Opposition parties here struggle to gain widespread acceptance and thus have to continually rely on a band of die-hard supporters.[6]

In this suffocating environment, with little leverage, opposition parties perhaps feel they have to somehow challenge the government's authority. And so they criticise it, and sometimes say things that, according to *The Economist*, "would be normal in any other democracy".[7] In Singapore, however, our leaders have little appetite for perceived unjust criticism. If they smell even a whiff of libel, they will sue.

So, before long, some opposition member finds him or herself in court, facing huge punitive penalties. Many of them are bankrupted by this.

And of course, while all this is happening, some eager seven-year-old somewhere in Singapore is reading all about it in *The Straits Times*, and is probably wondering— "Why is it that every time I hear about an opposition politician they are doing something bad?"

This vicious cycle breeds a brand of adversarial politics that often seems myopic, petty and opportunistic. According to Human Right Watch's 2009 report, "Opposition politicians and their supporters are at constant risk of prison and substantial fines for simply expressing their views."

Another major obstacle for opposition parties is the system of Group Representation Constituencies (GRC). In Singapore, for the longest time, ethnicity played no role in politics. That changed in 1988 when the GRC system was introduced "to ensure the representation in Parliament of Members from the Malay, Indian and other minority communities".[8] The system effectively clobbered together adjacent single-seat districts into one greater multiple-seat GRC. So, instead of fielding one candidate in a small district, parties would have to field a team of candidates, one of whom had to be from a minority group.

The official rationale, then and now, is that with the GRC system, Singapore avoids the possibility of ever electing a purely Chinese parliament. If we want Indian and Malay representation, so the argument goes, then we need GRCs.

"It is make believe to pretend that race does not affect voting patterns," said Goh Chok Tong, then deputy prime minister. Curiously, at the time it was introduced, there was nary any evidence that Singaporeans had been voting along racial lines.

Consider what had happened seven years before, in 1981, when Joshua Benjamin Jeyaretnam, an Indian lawyer who rapidly became Lee Kuan Yew's nemesis, won a by-election in Anson, against, lo and behold, a Chinese man. If anything, it appears as though Singaporeans have long chosen purely on merit.[9]

In practice, the GRC system favours the ruling party in two ways. First it is harder for the opposition to contest and win any constituency, as they need to field a team of good candidates, as opposed to just one. In GE 2011, the Workers Party (WP) finally managed to win a GRC, the first ever for any opposition party, only by fielding an all-star team.

Second, the GRC system allows the PAP to blood new young candidates, who may not have the support of many Singaporeans, but who ride into parliament on the coat-tails of more experienced politicians as part of their GRC team. In GE 2011, for instance, many Singaporeans were outraged that Tin Pei Ling, a 27-year-old who came across as inexperienced and clumsy in the campaign, managed to win a seat in parliament as part of Goh Chok Tong's team.

Over time, the GRC system has been expanded to now include more than 85 per cent of Singapore's electorate.[10] Interestingly therefore, Singapore's political system started off a pure meritocracy, and was racialised, so to speak, in 1988. On the other hand, Malaysia had race built into politics early on, but many now feel the need to move away from it.

Due to Singapore's first-past-the-post electoral system and the effects of gerry-mandering, in GE 2011 the opposition's almost two-fifths share of the vote equated to just 6 of the 87 elected parliamentary seats. In other words, 39.86 per cent of the vote translated into only 6.9 per cent of the seats. By comparison, in the UK's last election, the Liberal Democrats' 23 per cent of the vote translated into 8.8 per cent of seats.

Aside from the these limits, other challenges that opposition politicians in Singapore face include social exclusion and electoral threats: before every general election, the PAP promises to reward any district that votes for the opposition by delaying public works and estate upgrades in the area.

And so that has been the PAP's two-pronged strategy for success. First, the party has been fabulously successful. This includes both *real* achievements, for instance in governance and economic development, supplemented with *perceived* achievements in a range of other areas, by controlling and manufacturing consent.

Second, it has vanquished its opponents. Many Singaporeans are convinced that if the opposition ever comes to power, the country will go to the dogs.

***

Against that backdrop, the slow, steady rise of Singapore's opposition in 2011 caught everybody off guard. In 2010, there were small signs that the ground was shifting. New opposition parties, such as the Reform Party, had been formed early. Opposition parties had also started to attract more "conventional" candidates— former government scholars and civil servants—who had once been the preserve of the PAP. Oddly, the opposition were also getting fairly decent coverage in the mainstream media. Still, there was a limit to the breadth of viewpoints that surfaced here.

The independent online media, meanwhile, had emerged as an alternative to the mainstream press. Facebook, Twitter and other social media sites have been recognised internationally for their roles in the Arab Spring and other authoritarian states. Less known is their impact on Singapore's GE 2011. Though the majority of Singaporeans still got their news from the mainstream media, these Internet sites became the central news portals for thousands of Singaporeans. Many people I know regarded Facebook as their first port-of-call for elections updates and chatter.

For a traditionally reticent, shy society, social media offered safety in numbers. Risk-averse Singaporeans drew great comfort from seeing friends reading, sharing and "Like"ing alternative news and viewpoints, and promptly followed suit. Overnight it became acceptable, even hip, to embrace non-establishment opinion. For some older Singaporeans, unversed in tweeting and poking, e-mail forwarding of articles became the norm.

In other words, in the lead-up to GE 2011, for the first time in Singapore's history, minority voices got a decent hearing, thanks largely to the Internet.

All this activity unnerved the PAP. In the previous election in 2006, Internet discourse probably ruffled the PAP's feathers, but the PAP nonetheless remained in control of the national discussion. Not this time.

Moreover, the PAP's usual scare tactics seemed to be backfiring. Before the election, Lee Kuan Yew said that Aljunied residents would have "five years to live and repent" if it decided to elect the opposition. Rather than pressuring voters to get in line, that statement ended up annoying many of them.

A few days before the election, Prime Minister Lee issued a stunning apology to the country. "If we didn't get it right, I'm sorry. But we will try better the next time." For a party that is used to domineering and dictating, this rare admission struck a chord with many Singaporeans.

Cynics invariably saw it as insincere politicking by a canny prime minister. Nurul Izzah, the Malaysian politician, was suitably impressed. "It shows that despite being in power for so long, there is still a strain of humility running through them," she said.

Tactically, it is unclear how much the apology helped. A few days later, the PAP turned in its worst ever electoral performance, winning just above 60 per cent of the vote. For the first time in history, it lost a GRC, in Aljunied.

Shortly after that, Goh Chok Tong and Lee Kuan Yew, two former prime ministers, resigned from their ministerial posts—Mr Lee, modern Singapore's founding father, had been a minister since 1959. Prime Minister Lee was forced into a major reshuffle of his cabinet.

Within the space of a few months, Singaporean politics had changed completely. The era of PAP dominance had come to an end.

***

When one talks about politics or governance or the systems we live in, it can sometimes get rather theoretical and distant. We can lose sight of the fact that ultimately it is ordinary people like you and me whose lives are profoundly affected by our countries' political decisions.

When Sumana and I bicycled around Malaysia, there was only one "appointment" that we had. John and Dianne—junior college sweethearts whose courtship we had been privy to—had decided to tie their blissful wedding knot in Kuala Lumpur on 7 August, two days before Singapore's National Day, and a very amenable Day 25 of the trip. If one examined the chronological schematics of the journey, one would see that this wedding was the single, central organisational factor behind them, the trip's North Star, the only guiding light in an otherwise Malayan sea of spontaneity.

We set out from Singapore on 14 July 2004 knowing that whatever happens, whoever we meet, however many times we fall from our bikes, we had 25 days to reach KL. And we also knew that if politics in our countries were different, this marriage would never have been.

John Devaraj Solomon grew up in Selangor and was sent to study in Singapore when he was 14. His father had been dissatisfied with Malaysia's ethnic and educational policies, and admired Singapore's. A few years later, he met Singaporean Dianne Lim in junior college. Ten years on, they were about to get married.

As we cycled across the country, moving from one town to the next, never knowing where our next bath or bed might be, the attraction of this one, single appointment grew. A truckload of our friends was going to be there, clothes and snacks in tow. We had given them detailed instructions and made arrangements, wanting to ensure that our arrival, the two Saddhus on two wheelers, would not be greeted with tepidity.

Arrangements. Good Times.

Not that the trip hadn't been fun, but simply that KL would be a different sort of a Good Time, with different pecuniary limits and the comfort of being in familiar territory, not having to think of where to sleep, what was cheap enough to eat, whom to talk to.

In KL we would be rid of the persistent niggling uncertainty that had gnawed at us throughout. Familiarity had its charm.

The week before the wedding, from the moment we hit Perlis, Malaysia's northernmost state, KL had become our beacon of probity. Each time the cycling got to us or the roughness of the trip became slightly too much to bear, we just looked at each other and counted down the days till Kuala Lumpur, when we could immerse ourselves in wedding bliss and the accompanying festivities.

"Eh, shack lah, I think better rest for a while".

"Seven days bro, *seven days* … "

"Wey, my stomach don't feel so good, better pull up for a rester's."

"Six days, only *six days* …"

KL exerted a magnetic pull on our bikes. Good times. Here we come.

And so John the Malaysian married Dianne the Singaporean that fateful day. And I suspect that when one examines the what, how and why of their coming together, politics probably had something to do with it.

***

Today John and Dianne live happily in Singapore with their three beautiful children. But though Singapore may still appear somewhat appealing from the outside, many Singaporeans have gotten increasingly dissatisfied with PAP rule. The first and possibly most important reason for this concerns basic material wealth. Many Singaporeans' standards of living have not risen much in the past decade.

Although Singapore has continued to record strong headline economic growth, the share of those spoils have not been distributed evenly. In the decade to 2007, the bottom 30 per cent of households saw their real incomes stagnate, even as Singapore continued to churn out millionaires. By some measures, Singapore today is more unequal than China and the US. Economic growth has not benefitted all.

The cost of living, meanwhile, has spiralled, particularly for housing. The government is not entirely to blame for all this. Singapore is subject to the same disruptive economic forces that affect other countries, including globalisation and resource shortages. Nevertheless, some policies, such as promoting high immigration, have certainly accentuated their impact.

Part of the reason for high immigration is that the PAP has been pursuing a high-growth economic growth strategy that involves feeding greater quantities of "inputs", such as low-cost labour, into the system, rather than focusing on improving the productivity of existing workers.

This depresses low-end wages—the median salary in Singapore was S$2,400 in 2010. In other words, 50 per cent of Singaporeans earn, at most, only as much as a university grad's first pay check. The most poignant description I've heard of Singapore today is a "first-world country with a third-world wage structure".

The building of the two new casinos and the staging of the Formula 1 race, far from winning over ordinary Singaporeans, only served to distance them from government policies. These developments contributed to the sense that the government is more concerned with attracting the global elite than with pleasing the average citizen.

The PAP's historical success has been based on a social compact with Singaporeans, which equated unquestioned electoral support for the party in return for continued rises in living standards.

This compact has slowly eroded over the past decade. Singaporeans have been disillusioned by the combination of rising inequality, income stagnation, and high immigration. For many people living here, the Singapore dream has turned into a bit of a nightmare. Transport, education, housing and healthcare are no longer as cheap or efficient as they once were. That is the most fundamental explanation behind the PAP's loss of support.

Many Singaporeans also believe that the government is responsible for a number of terrible gaffes, including security lapses that allowed Mas Selamat, a suspected terrorist, to escape from detention in 2008, and huge budget overruns on the Youth Olympic Games (YOG) in 2010, where the organising committee forecasted an expenditure of S$104 million. The YOG eventually cost the country S$387 million.

The PAP's critics argue that these two incidents show that the party is failing at its traditional strengths—providing water-tight security and impeccable economic planning. "If I had blown my budget by more than three times, I'd surely be out of a job," says a friend who is a senior banker.

According to Donald Low, a former officer in Singapore's Administrative Service, all that only explains part of the story. He believes that GE 2011 also saw a huge shift in the middle-class vote towards the opposition. This segment of Singaporeans, though materially well-off, has grown tired of the PAP's long-held mantras on growth and vulnerability, says Donald.

"The vulnerability mantra suggests that Singapore is a small, vulnerable country that can ill afford to accommodate new ideas or take risks," he says. "The growth fetish suggests that Singapore must consistently aim for economic growth at all costs." He believes these ideas have run their course. "Quite a few people no longer believe in the direction the PAP is taking this country."

Donald says that over the past decade, the Singapore government's growth fetish led it to pursue economic policies that boosted growth but did so with "an unusually high number of negative externalities", such as public transport congestion and housing shortages. As these externalities were initially ignored, "the policies aimed at sustaining growth were not sufficiently accompanied by policies that sought to ensure an even distribution of the fruits of growth".

Singapore's economic philosophy has long been dominated by a belief in the market and trickle-down economics. As long as we keep growing the pie, it doesn't matter if some people are getting an ever bigger slice. For many years now, Singapore civil servants' bonuses have been directly tied to Singapore's overall GDP growth rate. Policymakers have thereby been incentivised to boost headline growth—not, say, median wages or, heaven forbid, anything fluffy like citizen welfare or happiness.

(Following much public dissatisfaction with political compensation structures, the performance framework was broadened in early 2012.)

Donald has an intimate knowledge of the Singapore government, having worked there for 14 years. He was a director at the Ministry of Finance, then a director at the Strategic Policy Office in the Prime Minister's Office, and then head of the newly established Centre for Public Economics at the Civil Service College (CSC) from 2008 to 2011.

Like so many other talented Singaporeans, Donald was born in Malaysia. "My father moved our family to Singapore when I was eight," he says. "He felt that my brother and I would have more opportunities here than in Malaysia, where the Malays were getting preferential treatment."

Despite already being in Singapore, Donald managed to later win an ASEAN scholarship. He later became a Singaporean, completed his National Service and then won a government scholarship to study at Oxford and then at Johns Hopkins. He got married to a Singaporean, and they live here with their one son.

During his time in the government, Donald developed a reputation as a brilliant but unusually outspoken officer—being outspoken, of course, is not really a compliment for a Singapore government official.

For somebody so forceful and opinionated, Donald has a very relaxed demeanour. He is tall and lean, and walks lazily, his legs flopping forwards seemingly against his body's wishes. His face is very wide, as if to signal a natural, broad receptiveness to all around him. On it sits a rather dominant nose, and below that a mouth that is given to smiling. And talking.

"Every Admin Officer is opinionated. Some choose to shut up. Others choose to gently voice their opinions within the system. Some of us just say what we want," he admits. "I was not very smart about it."

Donald must have felt frustrated by the gag order placed on civil servants. In a bid to get a message through to the government, in 2007 Donald penned a letter to *The Straits Times*' Forum pages using an alias. It is quite admirable that somebody in his position—drawing a salary of more than a quarter of a million dollars a year—would risk it just to try to alert the government to flaws in the system. It is also telling that Donald, one of Singapore's elite civil servants, felt that in order to voice his opinion, he had to go down that route—other channels seemed shut.

That signalled the end of his Administrative Service career. Donald was shipped off to the CSC, presumably in the belief that, marooned there, he would be too isolated to poke his pesky nose around. It turned out to be one of the most productive stints of his life. "I was able to take a step back from day-to-day policy execution and really analyse the implications of our policies," he says. He found time to focus on policy-relevant fields, including behavioural economics and cognitive psychology.

Donald became a mini Internet sensation around the time of GE 2011, because of several articulate, lucid essays analysing the PAP's performance that he published on his Facebook page, *Donald Low's FC*. ("No, no, FC is not my Chinese name, it just means Fan Club.")

By then, many political analyses had identified the symptoms of the PAP's decline, including the fact that it had lost touch with the ground, and had become somewhat desensitised to resentment over issues such as wage stagnation and high immigration.

Drawing on his recent experience and research, Donald sought to explain "*why* the PAP lost touch with the ground, *why* it ignored public unhappiness and resentment for so long, and *why* the government pursued the policies it did despite more than sufficient evidence that they were flawed and deeply unpopular".

According to Donald, the PAP's errors in the past decade are due not to bad intentions or incompetence. Rather, Singapore's senior policymakers tend to have deeply held ideological assumptions and decision-making models. Like all people, they "suffer from cognitive biases, blinkers and blindsides".

These biases have an even stronger grip over the PAP, given their historical dominance. Ideas have become entrenched. The PAP's relentless success has, in other words, bred a certain mental and philosophical complacency. "PAP ministers are therefore less likely to subject their assumptions and worldviews to serious scrutiny," says Donald.

Perhaps, drunk off its own success, the PAP remains oblivious to the rapidly changing world around it. Policymaking in Singapore has become a lot more complex and uncertain, says Donald. This is partly because Singapore has moved rapidly from low- to high-income status, and "most of the low-hanging fruit in terms of economic governance have already been picked up".

The broader macroeconomic environment has also become a lot more volatile, partly because of the wrenching changes brought about by globalisation and technology. At the same time, Singapore's citizens have become "less tolerant of mistakes, less likely to trust government by default".

In this unpredictable environment, where new economic and social policies were needed, the PAP instead retreated into its shell, and found comfort in "tried-and-tested solutions that worked in the past". Because of Singapore's historical success, and the groupthink prevalent in the PAP, the space for policy innovation and experimentation has narrowed dramatically.

Singapore has transformed rapidly from a lowly educated, export-oriented manufacturing economy into a highly educated, knowledge-based economy. The PAP's approach to governance, policymaking and citizen engagement, however, has not evolved much. This disjoint partly explains its recent stumbles.

Many PAP supporters, including Bobby Jay, would disagree with this reading of recent history. According to Bobby, the PAP has consistently adapted its policies in order to steer Singapore through choppy economic waters. He believes that income inequality is inevitable in any open economy. "We shouldn't worry too much about the median wage level," he says. "It is far more important that the government has maintained a low unemployment rate. Other countries can't even create enough jobs!"

Judging by its new candidates, the PAP also continues to prefer people with similar worldviews. This is exemplified by Tin Pei Ling's views on income inequality. In a 2007 speech, she makes it a point to state that while the rich have gotten richer, "the poor have NOT gotten poorer" (her emphasis).

From a corporate point of view, it seems like the PAP can do no wrong. Many senior executives I speak with have nothing but praise for the government's performance over the past ten years. More and more global companies and jobs have been relocated to Singapore. The problem, of course, is that what is good for corporations isn't always good for ordinary people—many citizens have not benefitted enough from Singapore's rising stature in the corporate world.

Its own election post-mortem suggests that the PAP does not believe it made many policy mistakes. "The election has been a good learning journey and at the strategic level, many PAP policies are right but their implementation and communication can be improved," Dr Vivian Balakrishnan said in an interview.

Going by all that, it would appear that the problem has not been with the direction and substance of policies, but rather with the communication of these policies, and with the (lack of) ongoing engagement with a more demanding, vocal citizenry. This suggests that the PAP is going to focus more on its PR skills. Politics in Singapore is going to become more about politicking.

Many commentators, including Catherine Lim, a Singaporean author, do not believe that the PAP can renew itself fast enough to keep up with citizen's changing demands. Blogger Alex Au believes the party is too set in its ways to ever change sufficiently. He blames this on what he calls the PAP's "universality complex—a belief that what one believes and what one does is universally true and right for everybody else".[11]

Even if the PAP does not change enough for some Singaporeans, those people should at least have even more electoral choice by the time of the next elections in 2016. GE 2011 not only sanitised alternative views, it also brought many of Singapore's opposition leaders into the mainstream.[12]

Much will depend on the performance of the seven opposition politicians in parliament.[13] They all seem articulate, smart and reasoned—not the loony scoundrels that Singapore's opposition leaders have traditionally been portrayed as. All of them have the respect, if not the admiration, of most Singaporeans I speak with. (In February 2012, an opposition politician was expelled from the WP and subsequently fled Singapore amid allegations of sexual impropriety. This cast a shadow over the party, and led some to question the opposition's recruitment processes. Nevertheless, in May 2012 the WP's new candidate won a by-election against the PAP's candidate with a resounding, albeit reduced, majority.)

Parliamentary discussions are thus bound to incorporate a wider spectrum of views than ever before. The WP has already called for Singapore to adopt a more balanced immigration policy, and to reduce its reliance on government-linked companies (GLCs) and MNCs, partly because that will spur job creation in our small and medium enterprises (SME) sector. It recently also proposed that Singapore consider nationalising its public transportation system.

Going by the first few parliamentary sessions, it appears as if PAP politicians have also been jolted into airing more non-traditional opinions. In early 2012 Denise Phua even suggested taxing the rich more in order to fund social spending—a rather leftist proposal that just a year or two ago might have been considered heresy by the PAP.

In addition to new views in parliament, Singapore will surely also now benefit from more alternative, diverse views from individual analysts, commentators and other non-governmental sources. All this should improve the quality of discourse, leading ultimately to better policies.

The downside, say fans of Singapore's one-party model, is that administrative efficiency will be sacrificed, as the PAP has to spend more time arguing for and defending its policies. Former PAP chairman Lim Boon Heng worries about what might happen if politicians engage in "negative politics", as opposed to "constructive politics". "If negative politics prevail, and our younger leaders become reluctant to introduce right but unpopular policies, we will lose a strength of the past—that of being able to look long-term, to shape our future," he said in a speech to current and retired MPs in July 2011.[14]

Still, it must be a good thing that space has opened up for people such as Donald to air their views. Even after he left the Administrative Service, Donald remained as outspoken as ever, and in 2011, his contract with the CSC was not renewed. After 14 years in a dependable government job, Donald found himself out on his own. He soon started writing on his Facebook page.

The first time we met, in May 2011, Donald had just taken up a Corporate Planning position with Resorts World Sentosa (RWS). It seemed like a huge departure for a policy wonk. "It's the only one that could match my Singapore government salary," he explained.

But running resorts was not his thing. After four months with RWS, he assumed the position of director of the new Healthcare Leadership College at MOH Holdings, the holding company for Singapore's public healthcare institutions. He seemed quite pleased about being closer to the policy world again.

***

What next?

In many ways, Singapore faces a much more nuanced challenge than Malaysia. How do you convince a country that has enjoyed 45 years of stable government and fabulous growth that it needs to reform for future success?

Singapore has thrived on a system where discussion, debate and policy formulation are carried out by a small cabal of revered folk. Challenging the prevailing orthodoxy is frowned upon. Criticism is muffled and any opposition is co-opted or extinguished.

The top-down approach has provided an orderly, stable base for growth. Unencumbered by the short-term demands of electoral politics, the ruling PAP has been able to chart out a long-term roadmap for Singapore's economy. Through a rigorous process of talent-spotting and renewal, the PAP has also continually nurtured good, solid politicians.

Nowhere else in the world is policy so efficiently implemented. Government is lean, responsive and forward-thinking. This model is so successful that it is being replicated by a number of other states, including China and Russia, says John Kampfner, in his book *Freedom for Sale*. According to him, citizens in these authoritarian states are willingly giving up democratic rights and civil liberties in exchange for security and prosperity.

In fact, a good argument can be made that benevolent authoritarianism is the best system for a country as it moves from a primary economy to an industrial one, Michael Porter, a professor at Harvard Business School, told me in 2004. A benevolent authoritarian state, supported by strong institutional pillars, allows swift decision making, effective policy and rapid implementation, and does away with some of the time-consuming ordeals of a nascent democracy, like petty politicking and populist grandstanding.

However, Mr Porter also stressed that when a country develops into a more service-oriented and knowledge-based economy, freedom of thought and expression become crucial. In my opinion, the system that has served Singapore so well through its early stages of development is now proving inadequate. It has failed to foster the active, engaged citizenry that is the lifeblood of a knowledge society.

The state is still too heavy-handed. A robust knowledge society has to actively encourage diversions, disagreements and dilettantes; instead, we still frown upon them. That has to change. Only by harnessing opinion from every corner of society, and by allowing every type of personality to grow, will Singapore's economy be able to thrive.

However, Singaporeans are incredibly resistant to change because we are afraid that it will all fall apart. For years we have thumbed our noses at all those idealistic liberal democracy advocates and in the process built up one of the richest countries on earth. Don't change a winning formula, as a football coach might say.

Thus, many Singaporeans I speak to, particularly in the older generation, have an extremely fatalistic view of any liberalisation. Allow a freer media, for instance, and before you know it, there will be major ethnic conflict. Talk about human rights, and before you know it, society will crumble at the hands of fanatic individuals. Allow opposition parties more space, and before you know it, our Singaporean women will be working as maids in other countries.

Much of this poppycock is built on our sheer overdependence on the PAP. Singaporeans are odd in that in some respects we are independent of the state, but in others we are completely dependent on the state.

Consider employment, where the PAP has instilled in the population a hard-working ethos of self-help. Most Singaporeans find the notion of a welfare state parasitic. If out of a job, many Singaporeans might rather struggle than look for handouts or help.

When it comes to things like politics, policy, economic development, education, and healthcare, however, Singaporeans are extremely dependent on the government for guidance and support. And since dependence translates into votes, the PAP has been quite happy all these years to play the role of the benefactor. In recent times, however, this overdependence has also become a bit of a liability, as the PAP has found it harder and harder to satisfy all the electorate's needs.

As the population has become more politically engaged, particularly over the past few years, there are signs that people want much more of a say in all those policies. After more than 40 years of doing things their own way, it is doubtful if many civil servants really know how to engage citizens productively.

Singapore is therefore in the midst of a major renegotiation of the relationship and space between government and the citizens. Society is rethinking the role of public and private actors. This process could take many years.

The electorate is also trying to figure out how much of an opposition voice it wants in parliament. The PAP will probably remain the dominant party for the next decade. By then, the opposition may be in a position to pose a serious threat. That said, some speculate that the only conceivable major political development is for the PAP to split in two.

When Lee Kuan Yew is no longer in a position of influence, there will surely be some soul-searching within the PAP. Some older Singaporeans have told me they will never vote against the PAP as long as he is alive—both out of fear and respect. Many others believe that Prime Minister Lee's political influence and power flow partly from his father. If he is no longer around, dissenting voices within the PAP might emerge stronger.

GE 2011 crystallised the clear political divide in the country. I first had an inkling of it in 1990, when I was 13. Singapore's first ever stored-value card had just been introduced for use on public buses and trains. Unlike the contactless cards of today, which can activate a sensor just through proximity, the original "farecards" of 1990 had to be inserted into a machine, processed and then collected by the commuter.[15]

Today it might sound archaic but back then, for young, geeky students, this was all pretty cool stuff. After all, it was Singapore's first step towards becoming a cashless society. No more standing in front of the bus driver and fiddling around with change! I was thrilled. Many people saw this development as a victory for the government—another demonstration of Singaporean efficiency.

However, almost as soon as the farecard was introduced, I also started hearing rumours from people suspicious of the farecard. According to this group, the Singapore government was linking each farecard to individual identity card numbers in order to track the movements of every Singaporean.

Every time the PAP has initiated and implemented a new idea, there is one group of Singaporeans that sees only the efficiency. To them, it is inconceivable that the PAP might have anything but the purest of intentions and the best of ideas.

The group on the other side sees only Big Brother. To them, every new policy is primarily a nail to strengthen the edifice of PAP rule. Any benefit to Singapore is nice, but secondary.

Finally, there are people in the middle who might think that farecards are efficient, but that without proper safeguards, they may also be used for nefarious political purposes. Many may also believe that while the farecard system is good, it may not be the best out there—somebody outside the establishment may have had a better idea.

This, in essence, is Singapore's political spectrum. The last election saw people in the second and third groups gaining ground. In other words, the proportion of the electorate that believes the PAP has only the purest of intentions and the best of ideas is dwindling.

In terms of political influencers, this election also saw a marked inter-generational turnaround. "This time younger Singaporeans conveyed to their parents what transpired in the social media," says Lim Boon Heng. "In the past, parents had advised their children who to vote for; this time, the children were advising their parents."

A couple of things are clear. The PAP is finding it harder to deliver a perfect system for all Singaporeans. Meanwhile, as the electorate matures, more citizens are demanding greater political plurality. Therefore, whatever else happens, Singapore's opposition is likely to become much stronger, which would be good, as it would enhance the diversity of opinions in Singapore.

We should not expect the PAP, as a self-interested monopolist, to readily accommodate the opposition. For all its talk about embracing alternative viewpoints, the PAP will likely continue disparaging opinions at odds with its own. Prime Minister Lee has never really seen the point of an opposition.

> As long as the PAP changes itself, and continues to provide clean and good government, and the lives of Singaporeans improve, the country is much better off with one dominant, strong, clean, good party.
> —Lee Hsien Loong, November 2008

Nevertheless, many Singaporeans will cheer the opposition's growth, partly because competition can be inherently good. In this exacting meritocracy, citizens are taught the virtues of competition from the time we are toddlers. Primary school students fight it out for the highest grades. Our open, free, market-based economy is lauded for promoting the fittest companies.

However, when it comes to politics, Singaporeans are suddenly told that we should forget competition, and subject ourselves to a monopoly.

The model has worked, and there is no reason why the model cannot continue to work—with some tweaks. Democracy advocates around the world often assume that authoritarian states will naturally become more democratic as their citizens' incomes grow and they read, travel, and just generally experience more of the outside world.

Going by the Singapore example, it does seem like citizens will clamour for some aspects of democracy, such as a more active civil society and greater political participation. But it is not at all certain that people want to eschew the one-party state model for a multi-party democracy.

An effective political monopoly—which governed with nary any opposition or civil society—has built Singapore into a developed economy. Perhaps the next stage of our political evolution will involve one majority party in government, which is kept on its toes by an active opposition and vocal citizenry.

With more than half the seats in parliament, the PAP can continue to legislate and run Singapore efficiently, avoiding the gridlock that undermines policy implementation in some other countries. But it will have to listen more attentively to the alternative opinions and views of the opposition and ordinary citizens, who will together contribute to and improve policymaking.

If that works, Singapore will have once again thrown out the political scientist's rule book, and forged its own path. It might also set an example for other countries transitioning from single-party rule, such as China (notwithstanding the numerous differences between city-state Singapore and almost every other country).

In order for that to happen—and this is the big "If"—the PAP will have to change. First, it will have to recruit politicians who are representative of the wide spectrum of Singaporeans, rather than just continuing as a grouping of like-minded elites. On a related note, the party will have to become much more consultative and open to alternative viewpoints.

If the PAP can do all that, it might very well go down as one of the most successful parties anywhere in the world. If not, it might be remembered simply as a highly competent, efficient and ruthless machine—a dramatic experiment that worked in a unique place at a very specific point in history.

***

Malaya's political awakening

Even though Malaysia and Singapore are becoming more democratic, vestiges of authoritarianism will live long. Nurul Izzah shared an anecdote from the Pematang Pauh by-election in 2008. When Wan Azizah, the opposition leader who had just stepped down (and Nurul's mother), entered the police station, she got stopped by the police and treated very rudely. Moments later, Khairy Jamaludin—a BN politician who had no formal role in Pematang Pauh—entered the station, and instantly all the policemen were "oohing and aahing" and paying obeisance to Mr Khairy.

"This is a case of power being vested in one political party for so long that all the security apparatus and government agencies automatically associate any party member with power," says Nurul.

It is tempting to look for parallels between the political awakenings that Malaysia and Singapore have experienced over the past few years. Immediately after Malaysia's general election in 2008, many people in Malaysia and Singapore wondered if the revolutionary spirit would diffuse across the border. Given the close relationship between the two countries, it is highly likely that the results of Malaysia's GE 2008 did, to some degree, influence and embolden Singaporean voters ahead of their GE 2011.

But there are some key differences between the two countries. Most important is the credibility of the ruling parties. In Malaysia, Barisan Nasional (BN) appears to have permanently lost the support of a sizeable chunk of the electorate. They accuse it of being corrupt and incompetent. Even if BN changes its policy direction, there are many Malaysians who will never again vote for it.

In Singapore, on the other hand, it seems like many opposition voters are fed up with the government's policies, rather than the PAP itself. Only a few extreme critics believe that the PAP is actually crooked or incompetent. The majority of critics will contend that, at worst, the PAP has been misguided by its orthodoxy—the growth and vulnerability fetishes that Donald speaks about.

Malaysia's opposition supporters are all looking for a change of government. A fair number of Singapore's opposition voters, meanwhile, are looking for a change *within* the PAP. It appears as if few really want the opposition in power (at the time of writing).

Therefore, while the BN brand name has been irreparably tarnished amongst many Malaysians, it appears as if the PAP brand still has some cachet, even amongst its critics.

In that sense, Malaysians seem more convinced than Singaporeans that multi-party democracy is the way to go. In Singapore, anecdotal evidence suggests that the vast majority of people—much more than its 60 per cent vote share suggests—do want the PAP in power. Some want a bigger opposition voice, others a smaller. But Singaporeans are certainly happier than Malaysians, it seems, with having one dominant party. The model has worked better here.

If the PAP does not or cannot change, however, then Singapore may indeed witness the sort of electoral turnaround that Malaysia has, and muddle its way towards a multi-party democracy.

At a more philosophical level, the awakenings reflect Malaysians and Singaporeans starting to question the basic ideologies our countries have been built on—ideologies that most took for granted all these years.

In Malaysia, the long-held ideology is that the country has to be run by a race-based system where the *bumiputeras* are afforded preferences. This is being challenged by a competing vision that promotes race-blind multiculturalism.

In Singapore, the political paradigm that has established itself—after more than 50 years of PAP rule—prizes meritocracy and strong economic growth as prerequisites to success. Everything else takes a backseat. This is today being challenged by a competing vision that promotes inclusiveness and equality, even at the expense of meritocracy or economic growth.

Is it coincidental that both our countries are experiencing these awakenings at around the same time, 40 odd years after our separation? Probably not. External forces, such as globalisation, have in the past decade worsened the lot of Malaysians and Singaporeans at the bottom of the income ladder. Meanwhile, domestic developments, such as growing Internet usage and the emergence of more credible opposition figures, have greased the wheels of change.

Hence both countries are experiencing existential crises. These crises have revealed a curious difference in our countries' respective psychological makeups.

Malaysia has existed as it has because of a kind of "tyranny of the minority"— the small group of people who have relentlessly pushed a Malay nationalist agenda. Anybody who dares question the pre-eminence of Malays in the country, and the battery of special rights that are afforded to them, is portrayed as a traitor.

Singapore, conversely, has existed as it has because of a kind of "tyranny of the majority"—the PAP and its supporters have sidelined all other viewpoints. Anybody who suggests that there may be an alternative approach to development or personal fulfilment is very quickly drowned out.

Of course, in both countries, these groups will contend that their tyrannies have been for the better. It will be interesting to see how long they last.

5
Not civil enough

The International Monetary Fund (IMF) and the World Bank (WB) decided to hold their annual 2006 meeting in Singapore. For Singapore, it was a thrilling coming out party, seen as another step in our bid to become a truly important global city. For the two multilateral institutions, it was a perfectly executed event—and the first time they did not have to worry about kooky anti-globalisation protestors.

A few months before the meeting, Singapore suggested that it would not allow any sort of protest. We also said that we are ready to cane or imprison any protestors who engage in violent crimes. We later then agreed to the protests, but with a few caveats: only demonstrations by accredited activists, and they must be in a designated indoor space. No locals allowed, lest we get brainwashed.

A few weeks before the meeting, Singapore banned 27 accredited activists from attending the meeting, saying they had been part of "disruptive protests" in other countries. This drew a sharp rebuke from then WB chief Paul Wolfowitz, who said that "The most unfortunate thing is what appears to be a going-back on an explicit agreement."

Under pressure, the Singapore government relented, allowing 22 of the 27 into the country. By that time, hundreds of activists and organisations had registered their displeasure. Some speculated that the IMF and WB had chosen Singapore precisely so they could keep them away. Perhaps out of spite, a bunch of groups decided to protest on Batam, a nearby Indonesian island. The Indonesian authorities quickly snuffed out that plan.

Nevertheless, some activists still came to Singapore, determined to speak up. "We work with these representatives of civil societies, and we value their role—even when we disagree with what they say," said the WB in a statement.

However, it later emerged that the indoor space, for all of the protestors, was eight-by-eight metres big—one-eighth the size of a penalty box on a football field. "They were packed like sheep in a corner where nobody would notice," says a friend who attended.

And so it was. Singapore left a distinctly local mark on the global gathering. It wasn't the first time that Western democratic traditions have rubbed up against Asian authoritarianism, and it certainly won't be the last. (That said, given Asia's growing economic power, and the perceived flaws in Western governance that the recent financial crisis has exposed, any criticism of Asia has become a lot more muted.)

Many Malaysians and Singaporeans just shrugged. We are used to these restrictions. Democratic pillars that are taken for granted elsewhere—an independent media and judiciary, civil society organisations and grassroots activism—are still very much works-in-progress here. Given our addiction to authoritarianism, not everybody, anyway, believes in their value.

***

Gerik, Perak. 27 July 2004.

Sometime in the middle of our one-month cycling trip, Sumana and I found ourselves in Gerik, a tiny Malaysian town whose only purpose, it seemed, is as a stopover for tired travellers. We were exhausted, having just cycled across the East-West highway, a gorgeous but punishing two-day climb over the country's mountainous spine.

Coasting into Gerik, we passed a *Shariah* Court, another reminder of how far we were from home. The town was eerily quiet. From 1948 to 1989, this part of Malaysia, just south of the Thai border, had been engulfed in violent clashes between the government and the communist insurgents. Betty, the former guerrilla we met in Betong, must have been planting bombs around Gerik. The conflict had stunted development—a sense of aimlessness and yesterday-ness still hung in the air of this frontier town.

We stumbled into the first coffee shop we found. Before long, we had for company two milky ice teas and Rahman, a disgruntled Malay man. He droned on for half an hour, decrying everything Singaporean: Lee Kuan Yew, our government, our success, our arrogance, the fact that "the Chinese own everything".

Rahman spoke softly, with a certain subdued menace, his thin lips pursing with every denunciation. Half-expecting him to thump us simply because of our nationality, we stayed alert, and tried to reason with him, telling him why Singapore isn't such a bad place. He was having none of it. "We know exactly what goes on in your country," he insisted, "because we read about you in our newspapers."

Oh boy, here we go. Over the years, we have met many people in Malaysia and Singapore who regard their national newspapers as scripture, ordained from the heavens above, never to be doubted.

Of course, this religious devotion makes for a wonderful publishing business. Every year, *The Straits Times*, the newspaper with the highest readership in

Singapore, gives itself an almighty pat on the back. In a glowing editorial, it tells it readers how it has once again maintained its perch at the top of the local news business. If one were to read only *The Straits Times*—as, presumably, is the case for many Singaporeans—one may conclude that it is one of the few worthy survivors in a dying global newsprint industry.

What isn't immediately apparent is that *The Straits Times* operates in a virtual monopoly, shielded from competition by some of the tightest media regulations anywhere in the democratic world. Singapore has two big media groups, Mediacorp and SPH. They are controlled by the government, both in terms of ownership and management: their boards are stuffed with diplomats, retired politicians and former spooks from Singapore's Internal Security Department (our FBI).

Things in Malaysia aren't too different. After all, the government also owns and controls all mainstream media channels. During the last election, we kept track of their reportage on the parties. There were more than three times as many articles about the ruling BN coalition as there were the opposition. Proportionally, there were four times as many negative stories about the opposition than BN.[1]

"Lee Kuan Yew is corrupt. Of course he is corrupt! He has run Singapore like a dictator. Only he and his friends have gotten rich. The Chinese have all the money."[2]

"That's not true. There are rich Indians and Malays too."

"How many? How many? Just a few. Most Indians and Malays have a difficult time."

Rahman spoke at us with an irritable petulance, like an old sage fed up with having to justify himself to impish youths.

"OK, perhaps the Chinese have more money now, but anybody can grow up to be rich. A poor Indian or Malay can study hard, work hard, and earn lots of money."

"Rubbish. The rich will get richer. Singapore will always be a Chinese country."

"That's not true, really, it's not true. Have you even visited our country?"

"No."

"Then how do you know all this?"

"Do I need to visit a country before I know something about it?"

"Well, it helps."

"Come on. You guys are young. You know there are newspapers, television, Internet. I don't want to visit your country. But I know a lot about it."

"But what do you watch and what do you read? The Malaysian papers love to bash Singapore."

"Our papers tell the truth. If they wrote lies they would get into trouble, they w-..."

"Get into trouble? How?"

"Our government would scold them ..."

"Haha, right."

"Well what about your Singapore newspapers? Ah? You think they are so good? They always write bad things about Malaysia."

"Nonsense. They are fairly balanced."

Rahman laughed, perhaps sensing our doubt.

The problem is that we couldn't really prove the point; we couldn't buy *The Straits Times* here. Even though one can purchase newspapers from all over the world in Malaysia and Singapore, you cannot buy the other country's national newspaper.

Malaysians and Singaporeans do not get to read what the other side's media is saying.[3] We hear only from our own government channels. This anachronistic law is at the heart of all modern misunderstanding.

We left the coffee shop a little while later, Rahman still trying to ram his views down our throat. "Remember what I said!" We were fed up—with Rahman, with this whole trip, and mostly with ourselves, because we had dragged ourselves into a cockamamie exchange of nationalistic barbs.

Why, when confronted with accusations against our country, do we instinctively dig our heels in, sharpen our claws, and throw objectivity out the window?

We quickly forgot about Rahman, but were still annoyed at ourselves.

***

International press freedom rankings tell a dire story. The 2011 Freedom of the Press ranking by Freedom House, an NGO, puts Malaysia at 143rd in the world, tied with Cameroon, Qatar and Zambia. Singapore comes in at 150th, behind places such as the Ivory Coast, Iraq and Moldova.

With such a moribund domestic media scene, one might expect large international news organisations to fill the gap, particularly since Malaysia and Singapore are such important cogs in the global economy.

That hasn't really happened, largely because our governments have bludgeoned international news outfits into silence: foreign editors and journalists have been dragged through our courts so many times that most prefer not to discuss "sensitive" issues, such as politics.

Our countries despise it when commentators in the West implore us to live up to Western ideals of democracy or freedom. For example, in a speech in May 2008, Singapore's Attorney General, Walter Woon, berated human-rights "fanatics", who he claimed, "display all the hypocrisy and zealotry of religious bigots".

According to him, the discussion about human rights in Singapore "is a debate for us, not for those who know nothing of our history, culture or values and who do not have our interests at heart".

That sums up the Singapore establishment's position—foreigners should keep their noses out of our business, unless they have something nice to say. Just in the past few years, *The Economist*, the *Financial Times* and the *Wall Street Journal* have had to pay hefty settlements for things they wrote. No other democracy in the world so routinely cracks down on the foreign press.

But it's not just people outside who dislike our media system. In junior college, our football team was coached by one of our English teachers, Mr David Whitehead, a cynical, sarcastic geezer who was always ready to chew off somebody's head. One Saturday morning, when a new player showed up for practice without shin guards, Whitehead mocked him for his stupidity before finishing, "Sonny, why don't you roll up your *Straits Times* and stuff it in your socks? There's no better use for it."

Over the years, I have discovered that many teachers, professors, analysts and commentators share Whitehead's opinion of *The Straits Times*. Even some fans see it as a paper that does a decent job with regional news, but is woefully narrow in its local coverage.

But then again, the national media in Malaysia and Singapore are not meant to comment, give opinion or criticise. The Singapore media's job, according to PM Lee, is to "inform the population accurately about events at home and abroad ... from a definite Singapore perspective".[4] Shielded from competition, and given this narrow mandate, the quality of thought, analysis and writing invariably suffers.

Everything that Malaysians and Singaporeans read, hear and watch through our national media channels has been censored and sanitised for the ruling party.

Our system therefore clips the wings of our journalists. They tend to shy away from writing anything bold. That is a shame. By neutering them, we are depriving our society of their insights. In every other knowledge economy, journalists are thought leaders and opinion formers. In Singapore they are, for the most part, mere news reporters.

"Reporters have to be careful in their coverage of local news, as Singapore's leaders will likely come down hard on anyone who reports negative stories about the government or its leadership," a Singaporean journalist told the US Ambassador in 2009, according to a WikiLeaks report released in 2011.

"The government exerts significant pressure on ST editors to ensure that published articles follow the government's line. In the past, the editors had to contend only with the opinions of former prime minister Lee Kuan Yew and former deputy prime minister Goh Chok Tong. However, a younger generation of government ministers is now vying for future leadership positions and one way for them to burnish their credentials with the old guard is to show they can be tough with the media."

Scary stuff. Therefore, Singaporeans have come to expect only mild musings on the mainstream media. We are unlikely to see too much critical discussion about, say, widening income gaps or ministerial salaries. Those sorts of seditious mumblings find sanctuary only in the dark recesses of the Internet.

***

For many years, the same was true of Malaysia. However, over the past few years, the mainstream media's bias has forced discourse onto the Internet, resulting in a maturing of online political journalism. The main progenitor of this is *Malaysiakini*, literally "Malaysia Now", the country's first online newspaper.

Malaysiakini attracted many new readers with its independent, left-leaning news coverage, analysis and opinion. After surviving a near-death experience in 2003— when Malaysian police, unsure about how to deal with the threat from new media, confiscated their computers—*Malaysiakini* has established itself as the country's *de facto* alternative voice. In the process, it has informed and emboldened other political commentators. Malaysia's blogosphere has mushroomed.

Steven Gan, the co-founder of *Malaysiakini*, has had a front-row seat on this new media roller-coaster. In the space of a decade, the newspaper has grown from obscurity to become one of the few sustainable online papers in the world. Though it has enjoyed only moderate commercial success, *Malaysiakini* is now hugely influential. Yahoo! Malaysia syndicates some of its content every day.

The first time I met Steven, at a roundtable discussion in KL in 2008, I was struck by how relaxed he appears for somebody so busy. He laughs a lot, often at his own misfortune. His perennial five-o-clock shadow and loosely tucked shirt suggest rushed mornings. He wears a mop of thin hair, which hides his forehead and the tops of his ears. Along with his thin, round spectacles, he appears like the quintessential intrepid reporter.

Together with Premesh Chandran, another Malaysian journalist, Steven started *Malaysiakini* in 1999 because he "wanted to influence a lot more people, and perhaps bring about change in Malaysia". At the time, many Malaysians were pining for reform.

"Anwar had just gotten sacked, the country was facing financial problems, and the *Reformasi* movement had emerged, influenced by the one in Indonesia," remembers Steven. In order to reach the Malaysian people, the two realised they would have to look outside the mainstream media.

They were well aware of the difficulties that Malaysian journalists faced. "I used to write a column for the *Sun*, and there were times my copy was changed so much I did not recognise it," Steven says. News editors would routinely be "invited" to roundtable meetings with the secretary-general of Malaysia's Ministry of Information, Communication and Culture. "The sec-gen would walk in with a dossier full of newspaper clippings, and go through them one by one," Steven says. Over time, editors would get accustomed to the kind of reporting the establishment favoured.

Thus while Premesh and Steven were keen on print publishing, they knew they had to steer clear of the major papers. They spent time looking for established magazines that they could reshape and write for, with little luck. Next they tried to get a license for a magazine, but also failed.

As a last resort, they decided to do something on the Internet. Although penetration was low and connection speeds were pathetic, they were pleased that there would be no censorship of their content—in a bid to promote Malaysia's high-tech industries, Mahathir's administration had promised in the mid-1990s that it would not censor the Internet.

Unlike most other authoritarian countries, which strictly police both traditional and new media outlets, Malaysia gave birth to this dual-track media system—a tightly controlled mainstream media alongside a relatively unfettered online media. Many Malaysians flocked to *Malaysiakini*'s site. A year after it started operations, it was receiving some 100,000 unique visitors a day. Staff headcount grew from 5 to 14.

Premesh and Steven quickly realised that in order to remain sustainable, they had to quickly diversify their revenue streams. They later put up a paywall and managed to get many loyal readers to subscribe. By 2008, *Malaysiakini*'s revenue stream was evenly split between advertising and subscriptions.

It has been a long and rather unlikely journey for Steven, the son of a bus conductor and primary school teacher in Bentong, a highland region 70 km from KL. "Bentong was a 'red' area during the Communist Era," says Steven. "It was considered rife with communists."

Worried that the Chinese rubber tappers there might be providing support to the communists, Malaysia's government rounded up all the residents and housed them in a "new village" 2 km away from their plantations. The village initially had barbed wire around it, and its residents' movements were tracked.

"It wasn't a concentration camp," says Steven, "but every time we went to the rubber plantations, we were checked to see if we were carrying rice or food for the communists." From the time he was young, Steven had to contend with daily restrictions on what he could do.

When he was a teenager, Steven ran away from home because of differences with his father. "Even though it was a small issue, I never wanted to go back, I was afraid of losing face," Steven said. He never returned. "I know many people run away for a few hours, not me," he laughed. "I'm a really, really stubborn guy. Just like my father. That's why we clashed."

Steven went to KL, then completed high school in Kuantan, with hopes of one day becoming an architect. An uncle living in Singapore then agreed to help sponsor in part his university education in Australia. Hence in the early 1980s, Steven enrolled in the architecture faculty at the University of New South Wales in Sydney. He was probably the first person from his village to get into university.

College life provided Steven with his first taste of activism. He had signed up for a course entitled "World Architecture". The entire course material was comprised of gothic, renaissance, neo-gothic and other forms of Western architecture. "There was nothing about Eastern architecture," cried Steven. "You can't call that 'World Architecture."

Steven promptly typed out a petition, got fellow students to sign it, and handed it to the Faculty Administration. "They changed the name to 'Western architecture', brought in a new course on 'Eastern architecture', and hired a lecturer from Hong Kong," Steven said triumphantly. "That's when I first realised the power of activism."

Steven got involved with many other civil society activities, including anti-racism campaigns; solidarity movements in support of democracy around Asia; and anti-Marcos, anti-Suharto and pro-East Timor independence protests. All this involved establishing ties with students in Asia, fund raising, and increasing awareness about these issues among Australians.

During that time, he also became disillusioned with architecture, as he felt it wasn't serving enough of a social purpose. "As architects, we need to produce low-cost housing that is liveable," he says. "Building huge glass towers is not so relevant."

He switched course to politics, philosophy and economics (PPE), and fell instantly in love. After finishing his degree, he moved to Hong Kong and began writing. "I was a backpack journalist," he says proudly. Among other things, he covered the first Gulf War, entering Iraq through Syria and Jordan.

After four years, Steven returned to KL, and got a job with *The Sun*. He soon tired of having his copy transformed, and decided to leave for Bangkok, and a job at *The Nation*, in early 1997. That would be the last time he worked for somebody else. He returned in 1999 to start *Malaysiakini*.

In September 2011, I met Steven again at a coffee shop near *Malaysiakini*'s new office in KL. It was then that I first noticed his habit of tapping the table regularly when chatting. Tap, tap, tap—like a metronome, whenever he was making a series of points. It gave our conversation an unusual rhythm.

Even though *Malaysiakini* is a well-established news brand in Malaysia, Steven admits that it still faces an uphill challenge finding a sustainable business model. Subscription growth has moderated, partly due to increased competition from a number of free online news sites, such as *Free Malaysia Today* and *Malaysian Insider.*

Still, *Malaysiakini* can attract more advertising money today than when it first started. Even though Mahathir's administration did not censor content, Steven laments that it "would threaten companies that wanted to advertise on *Malaysiakini*". Today, many firms are more comfortable having their logos on *Malaysiakini*. "Even CIMB," Steven laughs contentedly, referring to the bank led by Nazir Razak, PM Najib's brother.

Nevertheless, Steven remains a fierce critic of the cosy relationship between Malaysia's government, its government-linked companies (GLCs) and the mainstream media. The GLCs are some of the mainstream media's biggest advertisers, providing much of their lifeblood. "This nexus between business, government and media [tap, tap, tap] is not right," Steven argues. "It ends up essentially as a laundering of public money."

Worse, Steven believes that the media situation in Malaysia today "is much worse than during the Mahathir years". He claims that *Utusan Malaysia*, the most widely read Malay-language newspaper in Malaysia, has been spinning and concocting stories like never before. "For instance, it has written about how Malaysia's Christians want to set up a Christian state, and about how Christians want a Christian prime minister," he says.

Steven speculates that *Utusan Malaysia's* attempts to stoke up Malay Muslim nationalist sentiment have been ignored by PM Najib. "I think Najib is very worried about his own political survival," Steven says. "In the urban areas, he projects the ideals of "1Malaysia"; in the rural Malay heartlands, he feeds the siege mentality [tap, tap]." Steven suspects that these seemingly contradictory efforts—encouraging cohesion in the cities while deepening divisions in the villages—are part of Najib's electoral strategy to appeal to different kinds of voters.

Malaysia's media landscape today is perhaps more diverse than ever, with several players using different publishing formats in various languages to reach their audience. It is also constantly in flux. *Malaysiakini* has been around for more than a decade now, but it is far from certain that it will be one of the survivors a decade hence.

That shouldn't bother Steven too much though. He has already done so much to broaden national discourse in Malaysia, giving muzzled journalists an outlet for their views, and providing alternative opinions and views to ordinary Malaysians. *Malaysiakini* has inspired hundreds of other news sites, even in other countries.

"I think I can retire anytime," Steven contends. "*Malaysiakini* has made some impact, and I'm very happy about that. There are enough good people in *Malaysiakini* to keep it going."

Steven said that he might consider stepping down after the next general elections, to "lead a more quiet life", where he will hopefully have time to write longer pieces, perhaps even books.

He would also, of course, have more time to chat with his dad, with whom he mended ties several years ago. What does his dad think of *Malaysiakini*? "He knows I'm doing something that the government is not so happy about," Steven laughs. "I guess he must be proud of it. But I don't think it means that much to him. Politics is way, way above his head."

***

Over the past few years, as the mainstream media dithered, an entire generation of Malaysians turned to the Internet and SMS broadcasts for their "news"—facts, rumours, opinion, credible and incredulous, sometimes unclear which is which. The last general election was their coming-out party: not only did the Internet satiate an information-starved public; it also threw up the world's first blogger-turned-politician, Jeff Ooi.

Malaysia's bloggers are hugely influential. One need only consider the predicament of the current prime minister, Najib Razak. From 2007 onwards, Malaysian bloggers started circulating unsubstantiated rumours that Mr Najib had somehow been involved in the sensational murder of Altantuya Shaariibuu, a Mongolian model who was blown up by policemen using C4 explosives in a jungle outside KL. The rumours quickly spread from the internet to the coffee shops and taxi drivers. Do what he may, Mr Najib simply cannot shake off these allegations—some Malaysians still believe he is responsible.

Malaysia's media has bifurcated dramatically over the past ten years. At the end of the 1990s, most Malaysians were still faithfully reading their national newspapers, including *The New Straits Times* and *The Star*. Nevertheless, many Malaysians had, by that point, gotten weary of the media's pro-government stance. *Malaysiakini*, which was launched in 1999, changed everything.

Prominent political events of 2007 and 2008—including the rise of Hindraf (Hindu Rights Action Force), an Indian rights advocacy group; the rise of Bersih, a coalition that pushes for electoral reform; and the watershed 2008 general elections—crystallised the divide in Malaysian society.

On the one side there is the establishment, made up of Barisan Nasional, and generally supported by the mainstream media outlets. On the other side there is the non-establishment bloc, comprised of a hodge-podge of actors, including opposition parties and civil society groups, who converse mostly through the Internet or SMS. (This is, of course, a broad categorisation of a diverse media and society.)

Malaysians now have access to a whole range of credible and very readable online blogs and news sites, including *Malaysiakini* and the *Malaysian Insider*. I recently met a senior analyst at a government agency in Malaysia. This person gets daily news and analysis completely from these sites. It is a similar story for many Malaysians, who have altogether stopped listening to the mainstream media.

Could the same happen in Singapore? Just a few years ago, it might have seemed impossible. For even though the Internet has evolved into an alternative source of opinion, it is hardly a threat to the mainstream media, the way it is in Malaysia.

Many Malaysians lost faith in their national media channels and thus turned to alternative channels, like the Internet, and SMS for election updates. In Singapore, many more people are seemingly satisfied with our government media channels, despite their pro-PAP bias.

Recently, in separate conversations with me, a member of parliament and a senior journalist complained about the quality of online commentary. According to them, many comments are vile, misinformed and misguided. Furthermore, they asked, why do so many writers choose to remain anonymous?

Indeed, one has to sift through much chaff online to find nuggets of insight. However, this is largely a symptom of the system we have created. Singaporeans have not had the opportunity to hear articulate arguments that challenge the prevailing economic and political orthodoxy. Instead, we can read them only in the unregulated Internet bazaar. In addition, our system has bred a culture where people are afraid to speak out—hence the anonymity.

All that said, Singapore's alternative media channels have matured tremendously. Some of the country's best analysis can now be found online. This includes personal blogs, such as Alex Au's *Yawning Bread*, as well as online news portals and discussion forums, such as *The Online Citizen*.[5] Over the past few years, and particularly leading up to GE 2011, many Singaporeans, particularly the youth, have been shifting away from the pro-government mainstream media towards the more independent online news sources.

These online sources tend to start off with an anti-establishment, liberal bent, but then over time move more to the centre. Their emergence has partly forced mainstream outlets such as *The Straits Times* to become more balanced in their reporting, as seen during GE 2011, when opposition parties were, for the first time, offered some genuine real estate in our main national paper.

In other words, both the mainstream media and the alternative online media have slowly started to embrace opinions outside their usual remit. Nevertheless, just like in Malaysia, an unhealthy bifurcation has emerged: pro-establishment report-age in the mainstream media, and anti-establishment opinion on the Internet. This has polarised many people I know.

Followers of Singapore's mainstream media tend to be older and/or more con-servative. They are likely PAP-supporters. Conversely, followers of Singapore's alter-native media tend to be younger and/or more liberal. They are relatively more likely to support the opposition.

The recent general election only served to sharpen the divide. Some mainstream media fans were disgusted with what they saw as a chaotic, unsophisticated online dialogue: including perceived petty nit-picking, mudslinging and character assassi-nations, particularly involving Tin Pei Ling, a 27-year-old first-time politician.

In the run-up to the election, our pro-PAP friend Bobby Jay started writing a stream of letters to our Forum pages, partly to counter what he saw as the biased, unfounded viewpoints online. Shortly after GE 2011, a senior journalist I know completely ridiculed Singapore's alternative media.

Alternative media supporters, meanwhile, grew even more disillusioned with the mainstream media, believing that there was insufficient or biased coverage of the opposition. Several young people I speak with do not bother listening to the main-stream media anymore.

In all this there are echoes of Malaysia. By the time of our next election, which will be held by 2016, few will be surprised if Singapore is even more polarised than today—between the mainstream media/PAP and the alternative media/opposition.

At worst, opponents of the national media believe it is in cahoots with a narrow elite, whose interests they protect. At worst, opponents of the alternative media believe it is somehow anti-government.

In both Malaysia and Singapore, then, the national media has evolved in tandem with the ruling party. Largely due to its headstart, Malaysia's online news sites are much more developed—with wider readerships, more sustainable business models, and clearer editorial direction.

It remains to be seen, though, whether national media channels in both coun-tries can reinvent themselves enough to win back support from disenchanted citi-zens. In order to do so, they will surely have to ditch their old biased, sycophantic ways and embrace a more diverse brand of journalism, tolerant of non-establish-ment views.

Malaysians and Singaporeans, for so long dependent on the government for news, now have their eyes, ears and minds open. There is no going back.

***

So, what kind of media landscape should Malaysia and Singapore strive for? To be sure, few people I have met want the kind of liberal, free-wheeling environments that have taken shape in places such as Denmark, the US and India.

There was general disgust over the Danes' lampooning of the Prophet Muhammad in cartoons in 2007—such caricatures could easily tear the ethno-religious fabric of our countries.

The American model, for all its strengths, is viewed sceptically as a system where a multitude of partisan liberal and conservative outlets fight it out over the airwaves, preaching to their devout followers and polarising opinion.

India's unwieldy media competition, partly to blame for the theatrical, shambolic coverage of the Mumbai hostage crisis in November 2008, is also seen as undesirable.

No doubt, *some* change is needed. Our national media channels may have been sufficient during our early stages of development, but they are woefully inadequate now. At best, they are intelligent outfits whose wings have been clipped; at worst, mere lapdogs of the state.

Knowledge economies, which Malaysia and Singapore are trying to build, thrive on well-articulated opinion and free-flowing debate, not pro-government reportage. It is a great shame that some of the best political and economic analysts in this world do not write more about Malaysia and Singapore. Some simply can't be bothered. Others are too afraid of a backlash. It is in our interest to encourage them.

What is most worrying is that this need for media reform comes amidst one of the biggest crises the global media and publishing business has ever faced. It seems foolish to expect new media channels to suddenly flourish in Malaysia and Singapore when newspapers all over the world are floundering.

It is therefore unclear how the media outfits of tomorrow will earn their keep. Perhaps we do have some guidance from the relative success of *Malaysiakini*. For all we know, the best, most sustainable newspaper model for Malaysia and Singapore might be to have a single, independent, non-partisan, responsible broadsheet.

Nevertheless, though the business model may still be unclear, our countries need a conceptual change in how we deal with the media. We need to encourage an open, independent, responsible media sector, which will allow all voices in our societies to be heard, and which will promote creativity and freedom of thought in our economies.

This is one area where Malaysia has unwittingly stolen a march on Singapore. Malaysians are revelling in their newfound freedom, to the probable benefit of their society and economy. Meanwhile, a generation of Singaporean leaders has grown up believing that a state-controlled media is essential for stability and prosperity. Disabusing them of this notion will be tough.

***

On 26 September 2007, hundreds of spiffy lawyers gathered under the hot sun, on the wide boulevards of Putrajaya, Malaysia's new administrative capital which, like almost all the country's cities, is built on what used to be dense tropical rainforest. Today, without the protective foliage, the surface gets blisteringly hot—its fiery concrete roads are hardly the spot for an afternoon's palaver between suited attorneys.

But they weren't there for scones and tea. They had come to protest about the Malaysian judiciary's crumbling credibility, which had taken another hit with the release of a video that showed a senior Indian attorney, V. K. Lingam, boasting about his ability to influence judicial appointments. Mr Lingam, a close ally of senior UMNO officials and cronies, was unknowingly filmed in 2003 by Loh Gwo Burne, a Chinese businessman, using a camera phone. By 2007, the video had somehow found its way into the hands of a certain Malay politician, Anwar Ibrahim. Anwar, ever the wily strategist, released it with paparazzi-like chutzpah. The law fraternity was incensed.

The Lingam case was an inviting hook on which to hang long-held grievances. In truth, the reputation of Malaysia's judiciary had been on a long, slow decline.

It had all begun with the fallout from the UMNO leadership struggle in 1987 between Mahathir and Razaleigh Hamzah. In the aftermath, Mahathir consolidated his power, cuddling his supporters and cracking down on his perceived opponents, including Malaysia's judiciary, whose fierce independence throughout the crisis had irked him.

Over the course of the next year, a bitter battle involving Mahathir and several judges ended with some of them, including the Lord President of the Supreme Court, Salleh Abas, getting suspended. Mahathir also pushed through constitutional amendments that effectively reduced the judiciary's independence.

If the Lingam case is anything to go by, then the Malaysian legal system has never recovered from Mahathir's action. Still, things are looking a bit brighter these days. According to Fadha, a young Malaysian lawyer, this is partly because of the new spirit of openness that has engulfed the country since the 2008 General Election.

"Now that the opposition has more power, our work has really begun, our chance is now," she said over dinner. Unsure whether the chicken was *halal*, she skipped it, opting instead to eat just vegetables. "The elections have brought that change. Judges and lawyers are starting to feel more empowered."

Shortly after the elections, then prime minister Abdullah Badawi announced goodwill payments to the judges suspended twenty years before, in an effort at reconciliation. He also emphasised the need for judicial reform.

Still, change won't happen overnight. Gopal Sri Ram, a former Malaysian Federal Court judge, said in September 2010 that Malaysia's judiciary has become so "executive-minded" and "the judges have become creatures of the government".[6]

He also argued that the judiciary had failed to protect minority rights. Lawyers point specifically to cases involving religious conversion out of Islam, where the Federal Court has often shied away from making a potentially controversial ruling, instead dismissing the case on technicalities. According to Malaysia's Bar Council, "the Federal Court failed to be decisive and abdicated its role as the ultimate arbiter in disputes involving constitutional questions and jurisdictional conflict".[7]

In early 2012 many observers cheered the supposed independence of the judiciary, when Anwar Ibrahim was acquitted of his second sodomy charge after a two-year trial. But critics immediately suggested that the decision would only have been made with the blessings of the country's highest political figures.

The challenge for Malaysia's judiciary, then, is to operate independently without feeling beholden to vested political or nationalist interests. That will enable it to rule decisively in cases where minority rights are threatened. This is an issue close to Fadha's heart—she does pro-bono work at an NGO that advocates for women's rights.

What did she think about law in Singapore? "Lawyers make a lot of money," she said, smiling. "But they are a funny bunch. I was once at a conference with some Singaporean lawyers, and one of my Malaysian counterparts said that she had four children. Immediately, a female Singapore lawyer asked what the tax benefits were for that!"

No doubt, lawyers are supposed to be instinctively calculative. More worrying, says Fadha, is that many Singaporean lawyers do not even feel comfortable expressing their true opinions. "I met this other lawyer, who worked at a prominent law firm in Singapore. He was so convinced that the Singapore government was watching him because of his views that he would take a different route every day to get home. Isn't that funny?"

Surely no laughing matter for critics, who frequently suggest that Singapore's judiciary is subject to political interference and partial to Lee Kuan Yew and the ruling PAP. Just in the past few years, the *Far Eastern Economic Review* and the *Wall Street Journal* have been sued for supposedly suggesting that Singapore's judiciary is compliant and biased.

But why do smart commentators question the judiciary's independence? Singapore has never seen political interference of the kind that tarnished Malaysia in 1988. Singapore has the second best judicial system in Asia after Hong Kong, according to a survey by the Political and Economic Risk Consultancy (PERC) in 2008.[8] Malaysia, meanwhile, ranked seventh, behind the Philippines and just ahead of India.

Singapore's legal sector is held in high regard; some of the world's best law firms and most highly paid lawyers practise here. The World Bank ranks Singapore highly in its measure of legal systems and corruption. Foreign companies who choose to do business in Singapore frequently cite the strong rule of law as a major draw. Ordinary citizens feel completely protected by the law.

All that may well be true, say critics, but some worry about the high sums involved in political defamation suits in Singapore. In defamation cases, the average damages awarded to PAP litigants is some 30 times higher than to non-political litigants, according to analysis in a report by the International Bar Association (IBA):[9]

> ... it is evident that in just six cases, PAP officials have been awarded over S$9 million in damages ... Meanwhile, the total for all seven non-PAP litigant cases is just S$307,350. This disparity is of serious concern for the independence of the judiciary.

The government's argument is that these high sums are necessary to preserve the reputations of politicians. Perhaps. But these settlements have bankrupted several opposition leaders, preventing them from standing for election. They have also effectively silenced many media outfits, who are deterred from writing critically on Singapore. In other words, though the high sums help preserve reputations, they also inadvertently dampen critical dialogue.

In the same report, the IBA contends that Singapore's judiciary maintains high standards in commercial cases not involving the PAP, but in cases involving PAP litigants "there are concerns about an actual or apparent lack of impartiality".[10]

Some individual cases offer fascinating insights into the workings of Singapore's judiciary. In 1984, opposition parliamentarian Joshua Benjamin Jeyaretnam was accused of misusing party funds, in relation to three cheques that were written to the Worker's Party, for a grand total of S$2600.[11] Subordinate Court judge Michael Khoo acquitted him of two of the three charges, and fined him S$1,000—less than the S$2,000 minimum necessary to disqualify Mr Jeyaretnam from parliament.[12]

An appeal was upheld, and Mr Jeyaretnam was convicted at the retrial before a different judge at the District Court, and sentenced to one month's imprisonment and a fine of S$5,000.

Mr Jeyaretnam thus lost his seat in parliament, and was disbarred from the Singapore Law Society. At that point, Singapore law allowed him to appeal his disbarment to the Privy Council in London, which concluded that "by a series of misjudgements", Mr Jeyaretnam had "suffered a grievous injustice".

Soon after, appeals to the Privy Council were abolished in Singapore. And Justice Michael Khoo was transferred quickly to the Attorney-General's Chambers. Any judicial ambitions he harboured were snuffed out.

The Singapore government denies allegations that there was any executive interference in Mr Khoo's transfer. The IBA, meanwhile, suggests that "the circumstances surrounding the transfer of Judge Khoo remain suspect and cast doubt on the impartiality and independence of the judiciary in Singapore in cases involving opposition members."[13]

"If the PAP is so sure of itself, then why doesn't it pursue its cases overseas?" a septuagenarian friend asked. He was referring to the government's libel suit against the *Far Eastern Economic Review* (FEER) in 2006. The government had taken umbrage with FEER's interview of Chee Soon Juan, in which he suggests that a corruption scandal at the National Kidney Foundation may reflect a deeper malaise in the establishment.

The Singapore government sued FEER, which argued that since it did not have an office or staff in Singapore, it should not be subjected to local laws. FEER wanted the case brought in Hong Kong, where it is based. "They do not fight these libel cases overseas because they know that other courts do not see things the way our Singapore courts do," my elderly friend smiled.

Aside from opposition politicians and foreign publications, the punishment our judicial system metes out to ordinary Singaporeans who criticise the government can seem unusually harsh.

In 2008, Justice Judith Prakash sentenced two Singaporeans to seven days' jail for wearing t-shirts emblazoned with a logo of a kangaroo in a judge's gown, while attending a court hearing. In sentencing them, she argued that their t-shirts constituted the "worst form of insult possible against the court system here by calling it a 'kangaroo court'".

By contrast, a few months later, Michelle Lim, an executive editor at a government newspaper, was sentenced for her part in an accident in 2006, when she drove her SUV through a red light—while allegedly using her mobile phone—and mowed down a motorcycle, killing a 24-year-old Indonesian maid.

She faced up to seven years of jail. She was sentenced to 18 months in 2008. At her appeal in April 2009, her sentence was reduced to one day.

Though the two cases are infinitely different, society should question whether the punishments fit the crimes. If negligent motoring that kills a person warrants just one day in jail, does criticism—no matter how insulting—really deserve seven?

This is not a question about judicial bias. Rather, from a structural point of view, it is unclear if Singapore's legal system affords to government critics the same due process and resources—including access to good attorneys—that it does to those accused of any other crime.

In 2002, Subhas Anandan, the current president of the Association of Criminal Lawyers of Singapore, said that he would represent murderers, thieves and terror suspects but would not act for dissidents in Singapore.[14] Several lawyer friends have also told me they will never represent a government critic.

And so critics of Singapore's judicial system certainly have plenty of ammunition for their conjectures and conspiracy theories. However, they would do well to remember one fact—Singapore's judiciary has never been found to be compliant or biased. Until there is hard evidence supporting this claim, it is reckless of critics to suggest so. Those who do should, indeed, be held to account.

Malaysia and Singapore's judiciaries both face credibility issues. The difference is that in Malaysia, there is little doubt that the judiciary's independence has been compromised. It faces an uphill struggle to rebuild its reputation in the eyes of many citizens.

On the other hand, Singapore's judiciary faces only a perceptional challenge. These are not really concerns about political interference. Rather, some observers wonder if Singaporean justices *feel* they can really act and rule independently, as they so wish, without considering the political exigencies of the day.

***

Throughout my life in Singapore, and journeys in Malaysia, I have not interacted much with civil society. It isn't as visible or loud as the government or private sector, and tends to get drowned out.

That's not to say that there aren't any civil society actors—indeed, there are a plethora of non-governmental organisations, registered charities, community groups, professional associations, faith-based institutions and clubs. They represent a variety of interests and perform valuable work in our countries, from helping drug addicts recover to fighting for women's rights.

Nevertheless, civil society occupies a subordinate role in our countries. They operate with the permission of our governments, within neat boundaries of acceptable behaviour. Overreach and they risk being banned. Unlike in developed democracies, they do not have much power. Their ability to lobby and influence policy is limited. It is almost oxymoronic, activism by government decree. Some refer to them as GNGOs (government-backed NGOs).

Before Sumana and I left on our bicycle trip, we actually got a kind of "work approval" letter from *Yayasan Strategik Sosial* (YSS, the strategic social organisation), a Malaysian NGO. The letter said something to the effect of "Here are two Singaporean students on an educational trip around Malaysia and we support their endeavour."

We thought it gave us some legitimacy. Several individuals were impressed. But twice we were rebuffed: once in Pekan, when we tried to get admission to the Pahang Sultan's royal stable—the guard laughed us off—and once in Gerik, when a nutty policeman interrogated us as if we were Maoist guerrillas. "Who the heck is YSS?" he asked.

Later, on a separate trip, we had a chance to see what goes on at YSS, which calls itself "a social development centre for the Indian community". Amongst other things, YSS provides social services for low-income Indians. We visited a Tamil community living in temporary housing in Sunway, just outside KL.

The "temporary" homes were ramshackle wood and zinc units—clean, with running water and electricity—erected by the government to house these former slum dwellers, before they were moved into proper public housing. What was meant to be a one-year stay had become a five-year bloc of their lives, this project repeatedly bumped down the government's to-do list.

"Yes, our children have schools to go to, but often they have to leave school to work. If not, who will support their family? Who will support their siblings?" 32-year-old Rajan told us.

Rajan had spent time in the Simpang Renggam Detention Centre in Johor, one of many gang members arrested under the Emergency Ordinance. He had endured horrid living conditions, abusive prison guards and militant racism in the prison. He looked at least 10 years older than he was. Yet, there was a steely independence about him, and he refused to blame government policy for any of his personal woes.

"The problem here is not that there are no jobs. It's just that people are very selective about the jobs they want. Sure, if I just wanted any old job, I could find one. But we are selective. We want to earn more money. After all, a lot of the menial jobs can be done by the [often illegal] Indonesians."

Like most Indians in the community, Rajan was a descendant of estate workers. For decades, many Tamil estate workers had been affected by the rise of synthetic rubber and, more recently, the industrial world's thirst for palm oil—all over Malaysia, oil palm was replacing rubber tress.

Much of the refining on these new estates was capital intensive. Machinery was taking over the work of the Tamil rubber tappers, and forcing them from their cosy self-contained communities into the haphazard chaos of a developing Asian city. Disoriented and disadvantaged, many resort to crime and drugs.

YSS, underfunded and overworked, does its best to help them develop—worryingly, hundreds of these estate Indians have lived most of their life undocumented, without access to government services and support, like illegal immigrants in their own country. YSS helps them get identity cards, bringing them into the national fold.

But there is only so much a group like YSS can do. It simply does not have the resources or the mandate to help these disadvantaged Indians fight for greater rights. Instead, three years after our bicycle trip, we saw the emergence of a quasi-political organisation, Hindraf, which catapulted "the Indian issue" to national prominence.

For overstepping the bounds of civil society, a few of Hindraf's leaders were detained without charge for more than a year. By then they had done enough, though, to help plunge the ruling BN coalition to its poorest ever electoral performance, in GE 2008.

Building on its successes, Malaysian civil society has blossomed tremendously over the past few years. In particular, Malaysians now have an unprecedented ability and willingness to organise themselves around specific causes. In February 2012, more than 15,000 people around Malaysia joined environmental protests against Lynas, an Australian mining company, which has been building the world's largest refinery for rare earth metals near Kuantan, one of Malaysia's biggest cities.[15]

Aside from environmental concerns, the protestors allege that the government has not been completely transparent about the investment and operation—indeed, many Malaysians first found out about the plant from a *New York Times* article in March 2011. The "Stop Lynas!" campaign has succeeded in bringing all these issues to light. At the time of writing, the plant's fate is unclear.

Unlike many previous demonstrations in the country, these protests cut right across society, bringing together Malaysians from different ethnicities, income levels and political affiliations. Just a few years ago, such activism would have been unimaginable.

***

There is no such excitement in Singapore. Organisations here tend to keep their noses out of trouble (read: anything vaguely political). Even so, our usually sleepy NGO world was treated to a raucous spectacle in early 2009, when a group of conservative Christian ladies took over the reins of AWARE (the Association for Women's Action and Research), one of Singapore's most prominent NGOs.

The Christian group took control by winning AWARE's elections fair and square. Or so it seemed. In the months leading up to the elections, there had been an odd influx of new members. On election day, of the 102 people who showed up, 80 were new members. "It was so strange. Usually 30 people turn up to vote. We had never seen anything like it!" says Braema Mathi, a former AWARE president.

What was usually a perfunctory game of musical chairs amongst old friends had turned into a full-blown battle. Outnumbered, many incumbents lost. The new executive committee—"the new exco"—was made up of ten new members, and only two old ones. In one fell swoop, the complexion of AWARE's leadership had been transformed.

At first, AWARE's "old guard" must have been enthused by the spike in interest from a new generation of women. But they soon smelled a rat. For one, the new exco was opaque: when asked about their agendas, the women fudged. They treated the press with disdain. Nobody knew what they stood for. Even the two old members in the new exco were unsure what was going on. A mysterious aura soon surrounded AWARE.

The new exco also started to shake up the organisation. It decided not to renew the tenure of some of AWARE's research councils. It made redundant some volunteers and paid staff who had been with the organisation for years. From the outside, it appeared as if a Machiavellian revolution was underway.

This encouraged a few conspiracy theorists to dig around, and they soon discovered that 6 of the 12 new exco attend the same church. Journalists and members of the old guard started to pontificate about the new exco's motives. Faced with this growing suspicion, the chief puppeteer suddenly reared her head.

Thio Su-Mein, a 71-year-old lawyer, admitted that she had instigated several of her church members to get involved with AWARE. Her motive: to stem AWARE's alleged drift into a pro-gay organisation. Amongst other things, Ms Thio objected to AWARE's comprehensive sexual education (CSE) programme, which was being taught in some 10 schools to around 500 students in Singapore. She felt the CSE promoted homosexuality. "Are we going to have an entire generation of lesbians?" she wailed.

With her admission, the battle lines were drawn: Thio and her disciples were pitted against the more liberal old guard. Or, to look at it another way, a group of conservative Chinese Christian ladies were up against a multi-religious, multi-ethnic group of progressive ladies. With God, sex and children's education in the mix, we had all the ingredients for a titanic battle.

Most of the volunteers were there simply out of a sense of civic duty. Not all of them were from the Ulu Pandan constituency. Some came from far off. Perhaps they just liked working with Dr Vivian. (Joy, his beautiful wife, was also a draw for some. Whenever she showed up, slouching, tired uncles would suddenly jerk up, their hearts fluttering.)

Soon after I started volunteering, I joined the Young PAP. I wasn't forced to; it just seemed the natural thing to do. (My membership has long since lapsed.) Almost all the volunteers were Young PAP members. Some may have harboured political aspirations, but many didn't. They almost joined subconsciously.

And that, perhaps, is the one downside of MPS—it further entrenches the idea that serving your country is synonymous with serving the PAP. It may give some citizens the idea that when in need, only the PAP can help them.

For although the opposition conducts its own MPS, it suffers as the underdog—after all, how powerful is a letter written by an impotent opposition MP?

For much of Singapore's history, grassroots community activity has been politicised in some way. Government critics frequently lament the close ties between the PAP and the People's Association (PA), a statutory board that, among other things, organises community events and provides services such as free legal advice.

Still, Singapore is on the cusp of change. There are now many more MPS volunteers who will probably never join a political party. Meanwhile, the links between the PAP and the PA may be getting weaker. "The opposition supporters and non-PAP folk are now much more visible at the PA," says Bobby Jay, a friend who volunteers there.

As Singapore's democracy matures, the lines between politics and civil society are slowly becoming clearer. But there is still a long, long way to go.

***

Kota Bahru, Kelantan. 7 March 2008.

The night before the election, we were filling up at a petrol station, around 9 pm, when a convoy of about 15 motorbikes approached. Loud screams pierced the hum drumming of the 75 cc engines, together producing quite a commotion. It sounded like a gang. As they entered, we noticed that they were all carrying green PAS flags. Some wore green and white bandanas. They were tiny fellows, some probably no older than 12.

"I can't wait to vote!" shouted one of the kids even though he was two election cycles early. The group were temporarily mesmerised with Mun Ching, and gleefully posed for a picture for her, and then requested to be in a picture with her. It didn't seem very PAS-like to be salivating over a young Chinese lady, but Mun Ching was more than happy to oblige.

These convoys of cars and motorbikes, barrelling through to support their party, were a common sight in the cities. If you hung around long enough, you would eventually see the same bunch of adolescents dressed completely differently, wearing the colours of the other side. Political promiscuousness at its best. Apparently each mobile nuisance charged RM10/hour to don your colours and scream at the top of his voice.

It wasn't clear if this particular type of electoral spending boosted each party's chances. More than anything, these motley groups, as harmless as they were, seemed to be disrupting life. But since both sides were doing it, they effectively cancelled each other out; a rather annoying race to the bottom. Still, at least these youth were earning some money which, presumably, would be pumped back into *warungs*, Internet cafes and motorbike shops.

While all this was happening, Mun Ching spotted some girls in pink *tudungs* across the street. Puteri UMNO! We walked over expectantly. Puteri UMNO (literally "UMNO's princesses") was the women's youth wing of Malaysia's biggest political party.

Members of Puteri UMNO—known colloquially as *puteris*—had been elusive thus far. That was mostly because while we had been able to secure interviews with older women, young Malay girls had hitherto seemed out of reach to us, no matter how charming and deliberate our approach.

With Mun Ching by our side, they suddenly seemed accessible; we were credible reporters just trying to get a story. Mun Ching was our passport. The girls were coy at first, unsure if they, as junior members of the party, warranted all this attention from foreign journalists. The five of them, who looked between the ages of about 18 and 22, seemed shy but excited.

We were led up a narrow stairwell to a small conference room. Inside were stacks of pamphlets, cards and newsletters, and two big whiteboards on wheels. It was the office PR hub.

Coaxed on by Mun Ching, they soon opened up, and started telling us about how they spent much time organising youth social events, particularly sporting activities. They showed us newspaper clippings of a semi-annual futsal tournament which they organised. There were pictures of girls in *tudungs* and full-length pants, covered from head to toe, running around a small court chasing the ball. Four of the girls screamed ecstatically, pointing at a photo of the fifth, who was apparently a local futsal star. She was the least made up of the lot, and also the quietest. She brushed off the attention.

We wanted to know what had drawn them to Puteri UMNO in the first place. "We just liked it, you know. We find the activities fun," said Yati, the ringleader, checking around to confirm. Friends even before joining, they had now been part of the UMNO fold for two and a half years.

They were about to vote for the first time, and were clearly excited. The past month had been particularly busy, as they worked late nights, figuring out how best to help spread UMNO's message. Unlike *puteris* elsewhere in Malaysia, who had the benefit of the party's incumbency, these Kelantan *puteris* were the under-dog—UMNO was the opposition in Kelantan. This made their job all the more challenging.

For instance, one of the huge national successes of Puteri UMNO is their *anak angkat*, child adoption, rural outreach programme. The *puteris* visit villages, laden with baskets of goodies and party messages. They learn about the problems which the villagers face and they initiate social and sporting activities. In this way, Puteri UMNO has forged strong grassroots bonds across the country.

In Kelantan, however, the *puteris* elicit a lot of resentment through the *anak angkat* programme. When they venture into the rural areas, many villagers view them as symbols of the urbanised, liberal Malaysia that they want no part of. They perceive the *puteris* as encroaching upon their territory.

Yati admitted that they had even been threatened at knife point. "Many times," she said, with a mixture of sadness and hardiness. "Many of them, their minds are green, they will never be blue." (UMNO's party colour is blue. PAS's is green.) Yet amongst the rejections were a few conversions, which kept their spirits up.

So too did the support of their parents, who, by and large, supported UMNO. That gave them the strength and resolve to roam the streets with their party flags, despite being heckled at by men, old and young.

"They look at us as if we are different people. They think we are dressed inde-cently," she says. "They think just because their PAS women are wearing the tradi-tional dress, they are holy and don't do anything bad. That is so untrue. Anyway, a lot of PAS women dress sexily as well, but they never see that."

This reserved bunch of girls all wore *tudungs* and long-sleeved shirts, each so baggy you could fit two of them inside. And they, apparently, were the liberal ones. The PAS moralists would have a fit if they ever came to Singapore.

Despite all the discomfort of campaigning in Malaysia's ultra-conservative Islamic heartland, these "sexy" girls couldn't control their adolescent excitement. "This is the first time we can vote!" They had helped out in the last election but now, about to cast their first vote, felt truly engaged. Still, politics sometimes got in the way of life. "There is one thing I don't like," whispered Yati, her voice fading on the brink of her admission.

"What is it?"

"Er, we have had a lot of misunderstandings with our PAS friends during this election campaign, so we just don't meet up during this time."

"You think it is just political differences? Will everything be OK after the elections?"

"I don't know. We think differently from them. I was from an Islamic school and PAS would bring their political values to class. The class is no place for that. It's *tinur garik*, not nice."[16]

In the lead up to the elections, daily life was politicised. Apparently the PAS girls would vociferously voice their support for Nik Aziz, the party's spiritual leader, in class. Emboldened, they would also criticise the dress sense of the "sexy" UMNO girls. The girls looked despondent when recounting these stories. "*Tinur garik*." Nik Aziz poisoned the chalice further when he apparently called all UMNO people "*orang hutan*", people of the jungle.

The girls were well-trained, caring and demure. It is easy to see why the Puteri programme has been a success. In fact, perhaps a bit too successful—even within the party, there is some resentment towards the *puteris*. Wanita UMNO, the adult female wing, is not always comfortable with the level of success of their younger peers. The two groups dress different and so are easily distinguishable.

"Yah, the older UMNO ladies don't like *puteri*, they think we interfere with their job. They are very sensitive," Yati said. "We are all working towards the same goal in the end, I don't think it is important to consider who is more successful than who."

The girls then started asking us a few questions, curious to find out more about our country.

"Is there a lot of entertainment in Singapore?"

"Well, I think there is more than there is here," stating the painfully obvious again. "We have a lot of shopping centres, movie theatres and bars, it can also get boring, even though there are so many."

"Ha! We have a lot of entertainment here too, you know. It's not like what people say." Because of its high religiosity, social life in Kelantan is stricter than elsewhere. "There are some places that are underground. But we also go for a lot of *mesyuarat*, conventions. We like it, there is a lot of camaraderie and comradeship there."

They had two standard impressions of our country. The first was that it is really clean. The second impression was from a Singapore Tourism Board advertisement—they could sing the jingle from the "Uniquely Singapore" adverts. We cringed.

"You girls think you would like to stay here in Kelantan?"

"I don't know, I would like to move. Actually, a lot of us would like to move," Yati admitted. "There are few jobs here, if we get the chance we will move away. Apparently it was even harder for young men to find jobs. "That's why there is so much crime here." Yati said that drug offences and rape were not uncommon.

"There is a lot of AIDS. More than they tell you." According to Yati, many Kelantanese men visit the prostitutes in Sungai Golok, the Thai border town about an hour away. "Look what they bring back. PAS likes to keep this [AIDS] under wraps. But you know, *Puteri* UMNO has given us a chance to change things, and we want to give back as well."

Before we said our goodbyes, we remembered one last question. "What do you all think about Hindraf?" The demure footballer, subdued till now, spun around and stared us coldly in the eye. "*Benci*, hate," she said, slowly, softly, letting the word hang in the air. "*Benci*."

The rest of the girls, who 30 minutes earlier had raucously cheered her football skills, this time kept quiet, their heads facing down. Two of them nodded.

***

Though most of Malaysia's and Singapore's histories have been characterised by political apathy, docile media channels and subdued civil society organisations, things are changing rapidly. As the BN's and PAP's eras of dominance have come abruptly to an end, so citizens have been standing up and making themselves heard—sometimes randomly, sometimes in a highly coordinated fashion.

Ordinary people are keen to be more engaged in society. Democratic traditions common in other countries are finally taking root here. This will have a profound impact on identity. Malaysian and Singaporean identities have largely been government constructs. But the democratisation process will change this. Ordinary people will start to have a major impact on the shaping of identities and the reimagining of communities.

However, while there is tremendous pressure for change from below, it is unclear if the two countries' leaders have much appetite for change. There are still many archaic, draconian laws and regulations on our books that act as a drag on civil society development. These include strict regulations governing societies and the media; laws against public assembly; and the dreaded Internal Security Act (ISA) that allows for detention without trial.

Although Malaysia has passed a new public assembly law and has plans to repeal the ISA, some worry that the laws that replace them will be just as repressive. Meanwhile, though a good argument on anti-terrorism grounds could be made for the ISA, critics allege that both governments have been only too happy to use them against political opponents too. Hence there is the potential for abuse. That said, both countries' electorates will be far less forgiving today than in the past of any alleged abuse.

As Malaysia and Singapore transition from authoritarianism to democracy, there is a grand negotiation occurring in society, as new players emerge and jostle for space. Debates that were once conducted within the peaceful confines of one party have now been thrown out into the marketplace, where a cacophony of voices vie for mindshare on a multitude of new mediums.

From a governance standpoint, it is a multidimensional blur. A Singaporean minister today has to figure out how, for the first time, to engage with so many newly energised constituents—even as he discovers how to communicate on Facebook.

The worry, of course, is that both countries' ruling parties will close ranks and become ever more conservative and paranoid, in their bid to hold onto power. This is what some critics say has happened in Malaysia under PM Najib's administration. But if they persist on that path, they might be sacrificing their own parties' long-term sustainability for a bit of short-term gain. And that would be very un-Malayan indeed.

6
Alibaba and the thieves

Ipoh, Perak. 3 March 2008.

"Well, in a funny sort of way, I benefited so much from the oil crisis in the 1970s," Mohammad Zamin said.

Sumana and I were sitting in a small coffee shop in Silibin, a little neighbourhood on the outskirts of Ipoh. People kept shuffling in and out, some on tea break, others aimless; the hungry streamed towards the *prata* man in the corner for some of the dough he was twirling, theatrically, like a circus performer.

A fat lady in a pink *baju kurung* waddled towards us. She walked with her hips— they led, her feet merely followed. She stopped in front of us and wiped her brow with the back of her hand, then put her blunt pencil to a piece of scratch paper. It was time to order.

It seemed rather busy for 10.30 am on a Tuesday morning, four days before the 2008 general elections. That time should have been a dead zone for a coffee shop, too late for breakfast, but too soon for lunch. Then, in Malaysia, as in much of Asia, tea breaks are a crucial part of any workday.

We had accosted Mohammad moments earlier; he was standing outside a bank, squinting while checking his text messages. Despite having spoken to countless random Malaysians, we still had to pause and pluck up the courage to talk to him.

Taken slightly aback, Mohammad gave us the once over. Sensing he needed more convincing, we flashed our Singaporean identity cards. He looked stumped, just like every other Malaysian we did that to. Still, he agreed to an interview, smiling, "Oh, I see. You want my, how do you say it, 'two-cents worth'?" We were soon getting much more.

Mohammad had enjoyed two lucky breaks early in life, both because of *Insyah Allah*, Allah's grace. The first was winning a government scholarship in the early 1970s that allowed him to attend university in Australia. The second was the oil crisis. "When I returned from Australia in 1976, the world was entering a recession. My scholarship board MARA said they could not afford to hire me anymore, and so I was forced to make it on my own."

Many Malaysians pine for a position in the lucrative, stress-free government establishment; Mohammad was thankful that he had been booted out. He then worked in "odd jobs for six or seven years", before setting up his own engineering practice. Later on he entered into a partnership with a Chinese person. Crucially, theirs was "a genuine *bumi-non bumi* partnership".

"Genuine? What do you mean by that?"

"Ah, well, you know, in Malaysia, there are lots of these partnerships between *bumis* and *non-bumis*, the *Alibaba* businesses. They are only partnerships on paper. In truth, the Chinese does all the work, runs the whole business, just gives the Malay a small token sum in exchange for putting his name there."

From 1970, as part of its affirmative-action New Economic Policy (NEP), the government had tried to forcibly increase Malay shareholding in the private sector by mandating a minimum Malay equity requirement.[1] *Alibaba* business arrangements blossomed in response to this, and have since become an unofficially accepted part of Malaysia's economy.

"Ours was not like that. Ours was a genuine partnership. We both worked hard and we learned a lot from each other. And, the way things work in Malaysia, it is good to have active Chinese and Malay partners. The Chinese will help you get contracts from the private sector, and the Malay will help you get contracts from the government."

"Really? In the private sector they prefer Chinese?"

"Sure. Many of the big firms are Chinese. They prefer dealing with a Chinese."

This might be simply because of racism, according to Pak Zamin. Another reason could be evolutionary: over the years, having encountered and dealt with so many *Alibaba* businesses, it becomes a bit hard to tell which Malay partner is genuine, and which one merely a figurehead, pocketing cash while not knowing much about the business. And so the private sector prefers dealing with the Chinese, amongst whom there are fewer charlatans.

No matter. If all else fails, the *Alibaba* companies, meanwhile, can look to the government for business, says Pak Zamin. Therein lies the other split in Malaysia's private sector: between those with political connections and those without.

Companies with the connections are the ones who land the big government contracts. These relationships allow government officials to fatten their purses. Many of them have stakes in private companies. Every time Malaysia holds an election, the share prices of certain "politically-linked" companies move up or down, depending on the electoral fortunes of their governmental benefactors. To be sure, not all *Alibaba* companies have good political connections.

There are therefore two distinct cross-lines in Malaysia's private sector. Any given company is either a genuine partnership or an *Alibaba* business; and is either politically connected or not (though this is more a spectrum of the quality of one's political access). The success of any business in Malaysia depends much on where it sits on this matrix.

As we digested all this, Pak Zamin smiled, sinking further into his seat. His words had proven unexpectedly cathartic.

***

Malaysia and Singapore are developmental states, in which our authoritarian governments have often led the private sector in many facets of economic development. Our brand of state-led capitalism has involved specific industrial policies that pick and promote winners through incentives such as generous tax holidays, preferential land allotments, and recruitment help.

However, Malaysia's and Singapore's developmental states were born in very different circumstances. For Singapore, the stimulus for an economic action plan crystallised at the point of independence. The separation from Malaysia was not easy, and the future was unclear—we were a young nation under threat. The shared understanding was that rapid economic development was essential to ensure Singapore's survival. This is where our vulnerability mantra and growth fetish stem from.

What of the Malaysian developmental state? It probably really only took shape around 1970. After all, between independence from the British, in 1957, and the late 1960s, many politico-economic issues were in flux. Malaysia did not have a clear direction. For instance, in 1963, Singapore joined the Federation of Malaya. In 1965, it was thrown out. Around the time, Malaysia was also facing a *konfrontasi*, confrontation, with Indonesia, over, amongst other things, sovereignty over land on the island of Borneo.

Unlike Singapore, Malaysia certainly didn't feel a need to fight for its survival, given its size and bountiful natural resources. Singapore's separation did not force Malaysia to develop. Instead, Malaysia's developmental state emerged after the ethnic riots of 1969; it was shaped by a need to address racial imbalances.

That was the main difference between the two countries at the outset of their development. Singapore's developmental state was born with the psyche, "We have absolutely nothing; we are surrounded by powerful giants; we must do all we can to build this country. We need the government to lead us."

Malaysia's, on the other hand, went something like this, "We are a fairly rich country; but the Chinese, who are not really from this land, own a disproportionate share; in order to preserve racial harmony, we must do all we can to redistribute it."

Singapore, without any natural resources, was forced to invest heavily in human capital. Malaysia felt no such compunction. Pak Zamin doubted the effectiveness of the Malaysian model's redistribution.

"But that's the thing. I want you to write this down too," he said, tapping his finger on our notebooks, "there's all this talk about racial integration and multicultural Malaysia and all that. Well, if it's serious about integration, do you know what the government should do? It should award government contracts only to genuine *bumi-non bumi* partnerships. That's what it should do. That will bring people together, and teach them how to work and survive together. Through business, that's the way."

"But then you'd be discriminating against single-race businesses, no?"

Pak Zamin ignored us.

But what might have happened if there was no oil crisis in the 1970s, and he had been given a job at MARA? "Well, who knows … I suppose I would have risen slowly up the ladder, and gotten used to a cushy government job."

"Not too shabby then?"

"I would have had a good position, I would have had prestige, and I would have had enough money. That's true," he admitted. "But on the other hand, I wouldn't have learned as much. I wouldn't have been exposed to the real world. I wouldn't have learned how to live and work with somebody from another race."

He slumped back to his chair, but then lurched forward again, as if suddenly remembering he had more to say.

"And come on, let's face it, like I mentioned earlier, this world is increasingly globalised. We Malaysians—and Malays especially—have to stop relying on the government for everything. If not, how are we supposed to compete with the likes of Vietnam?"

Pak Zamin was a walking contradiction and he knew it. He had many doubts about the effectiveness of the NEP, admitting that it had enriched only a few Malays while not doing much for the masses; that it had made Malays dependent and lazy; that it had led to greater friction between Malaysia's different ethnic groups.

But on the other hand, over the years, he has basked in the NEP's sunshine. He was part of the first batch of *bumis* to be awarded scholarships to study abroad. After completing his secondary school in 1970 at the regal Malay College Kuala Kangsar (MCKK), he was sent to read Mechanical Engineering at the University of Western Australia.

"Yes, I had a good time in Perth, I was there for one plus four years. First year foundation, then four years degree." His son, meanwhile, is a current beneficiary. Just like his father, he had graduated from MCKK, and is now studying in Cologne in Germany, on a scholarship from the Jabatan Perkhidmatan Awam (JPA, the Public Service Commission).

Even as he wailed about the chasm between Chinese and Malays, and about how the private sector is dominated by the Chinese and the public sector by the Malays, he quite smartly teamed up with a Chinese in order to leverage their relative advantages in winning contracts.

It may seem hypocritical, but it is actually very human—and economically rational—to keep playing the game while trying to change the rules.

Still, I kept thinking about what he had said about society's dependence on the government. In our own unique ways, Malaysians and Singaporeans have become reliant on our governments, not simply for social and political direction, but for economic development too. Our governments play a huge role in our countries' economies, mostly through their government-linked corporations (GLCs). They've brought development, for sure, but, as Pak Zamin suggested, they've perhaps also crowded out others, stymieing the growth of local enterprise.

***

Malaysia and Singapore are developmental success stories. In 1965, at the time of independence, Malaysia's GDP per capita was US$335, and Singapore's was US$512.[2] By 2011, that had grown to respectively US$5,700 and US$35,163 —Malaysia had catapulted into the league of middle-income countries, while Singapore had planted itself firmly in the rich man's club. Government officials from emerging markets in Africa, Asia and Latin America visit frequently, braving the humidity and keeping quiet about the heat, to admire, solicit advice, take notes, and eat.

No doubt, our economies today are very different from each other. Malaysia is a resource-rich country, with bountiful supplies of oil, natural gas, minerals and huge expanses of fertile agricultural land, upon which locals have grown crops like *padi*, rubber and, more recently, oil palm. Malaysia is also a food processing hub, cooking up and exporting products as varied as freeze-dried Durian chips and Tongkat Ali coffee.

(Durian is a pungent tropical fruit with quite complex flavours. I love it. As we cycled around Malaysia, villagers showered us with endless durians; the fruit's size, colour, smell and taste seemed to vary with the *terroir*. Like drunk vinophiles on tour, we slurped our way around the country. Durians gave us lots of energy, and hours of horrid belches. The root of the Tongkat Ali plant, also known colloquially as the longjack, is famous as an old Malaysian cure for impotence. Nobody offered us any.)

The world's leading manufacturing firms are here too. Having long moved on from low-cost labour-intensive production, Malaysia currently churns out everything from oil rigs to computer chips. They are there because of, amongst other things, the skilled labour force, good infrastructure, business-friendly government policies and tax incentives. Oh, and of course, Penang's legendary cuisine, famous even *amongst* Malaysians.

Perhaps Malaysia's most well-known—and controversial—product is the Proton car. One of Mahathir's brainchilds, the national car company was founded to transport Malaysians around the country and to thrust Malaysia into the 21st century. What better national symbol than a car, that beacon of modernity. The best part about Proton: "developed" Singapore had no such industry. If Singaporeans wanted to buy the Proton Saga, the first model produced by the Malaysian motor industry, they had to pay much more.

Things went well initially. With Japanese money, technology and assistance, Proton started pumping out technically sound engines, each wrapped in what looked like recycled tuna can. They weren't the most beautiful cars on the road, but so what? They bore a Malaysian birth-mark. Government tariffs protected Proton from foreign imports; government subsidies made them affordable. At the same time, the government embarked on massive road development projects.

The first, Projek Lebuhraya Utara Selatan (PLUS, the North-South Highway Project), sliced through the spine of the country. Compared to the windy, coast-hugging, two-lane street that we cycled on, PLUS was a logistical dream, cutting the travel time from Singapore to KL from seven hours to four.

Thus began Malaysia's automobile revolution. In 1990, less than one in ten Malaysians owned cars. Today, one out of every four has one.[3] Malaysia, with a population of about 28 million people, has Southeast Asia's largest passenger car market—bigger than Indonesia's (population of 243 million) and Thailand's (68 million).[4]

Cars provided a wonderful newfound freedom. All of a sudden, it was much easier to visit far-away friends and relatives. It made sense to find work in another state. And it became possible to go eat at that restaurant in the next town that you had heard about. Proton cars empowered Malaysians, and they were more than just a status symbol. For the aspirational Malaysian, Proton was a ticket to "development", to the feeling that, finally, their country had arrived. Proton spawned others, such as Perodua and Kancil.

After a great start, Malaysia's car industry—and Proton, in particular—is struggling today. Being sheltered from foreign competition has bred complacency and inefficiency. Numerous scandals have plagued the industry. The Koreans and now the Chinese can make better cars for less money. There is constant speculation that

Malaysia's automobile assets will be gradually broken up and sold off to foreign manufacturers.

That shouldn't break Mahathir's heart, though. His automobile ambition did a lot for Malaysian mobility and pride. It also helped to integrate the country, allowing people to visit hitherto unreachable areas.

That said, without sufficient urban planning and road control, it has also led to some of the most horrendous traffic jams in Asia. Maybe Singapore, known for its smooth traffic flow, will have the last laugh. Tawfik Ismail, former Johor state parliamentarian and full-time joker, said that George Yeo, Singapore's former foreign minister, had once asked a question that stumped him: "Tawfik, tell me something. How does Malaysia control traffic jams while at the same time promoting a national car industry?"

Malaysia's service sector has also been garnering accolades of late. The much ballyhooed Multimedia Super Corridor, though less successful than intended, has still managed to attract attention and talent to Malaysia's nascent IT services sector, including in niches such as computer animation and design.

Tourism is booming, partly thanks to Malaysia's stunning natural beauty: be it the white sand beaches, gorgeous coral reefs, or lush, tropical rainforests, thousands of years old, home to all manner of animals, including charming *orang-utans*. Pair that with exceedingly humble, unfailingly polite, Malaysian hospitality, and you have a first-class tourist experience, much underrated.

To move you even faster around the country, you can hop on an Air Asia plane, one of the country's most recent business innovations. Tony Fernandes, the budget carrier's charismatic founder, has, according to *The Economist*, "done more to turn Southeast Asia into an integrated economic block than any ASEAN ministerial summit".[5]

Petronas, Malaysia's national oil producer, has gone from strength to strength, transforming itself into a fully-fledged energy services company, with interests across the world—it is often cited as a shining example of how to use and invest a country's natural resources wisely.

And so the country's economic landscape is dotted with a plethora of economic communities, from rice farmers to geeky cyberworkers. A Malaysian, given the right opportunities, can probably find employment in whatever vocation he or she wants to, right at home.

What's more—for better or for worse—chances are the job will be in a GLC. A whole slew of GLCs—either partially or wholly owned by the state—has grown up with the country. Most, like Sime Darby and UEM, are massive conglomerates. GLCs contribute about 17 per cent of Malaysia's gross fixed capital formation and account for almost 10 per cent of GDP. Many of them are subsidiaries of Khazanah, the state investment vehicle.

***

"The day of reckoning came. In 1998 you saw all the Malay giants, the tycoons, collapsing like a deck of cards. We spent massive amounts of public money in bailouts, inducing moral hazard."

Din Merican was struggling to hold back his anger. According to him, 1998 was the year when Malaysians could finally see the extent of corruption that had occurred on Mahathir's watch, as the taxpayer was forced to bailout inefficient, debt-laden firms run by crony capitalists. I listened intently, among a crowd of people at a post-elections pow-wow at Singapore's Institute of Southeast Asian Studies in 2008.

Articulate and blunt, Din, then the economic adviser to Anwar Ibrahim and the Parti Keadilan Rakyat (PKR), has a habit of working himself into a fury, before proclaiming that everything is okay, and that actually an old man like him is better off outside of politics. Today he is an independent commentator, best known for his popular blog, "the Malaysian DJ Blogger".

Din has had the privilege of an insider's perspective. In the 1950s he attended Penang Free School, and got to know a young, soft spoken Malay by the name of Abdullah Badawi, who was studying at the Methodist Boy's School there—"a nice guy, a really nice guy. But he has failed to deliver at the highest office."

In the 1970s, as a student at the George Washington University in the US, Din had the luxury of an international student's life: a good education, the chance to rub shoulders with would-be luminaries from back home, and an external perspective on what was going on in his newly independent, post-colonial homeland.

He later returned to Malaysia, and worked for a number of organisations, including Malaysia's central bank and Sime Darby. He says he sympathised with UMNO's goals, because "I generally shared what the founding fathers were trying to do." He got to know Mahathir and Anwar, leaders who were helping to build the new Malaysia: smart, developed, multi-ethnic. However, by the end of the 1980s, Din started getting disillusioned.

Many Malaysians point to this period, the late 1980s, as the time when corruption, cronyism and nepotism intensified in the country. In 1986–87, so the reasoning goes, Mahathir began to feel increasingly threatened by opponents within his party. In 1987, in the wake of a direct challenge to his leadership by Razaleigh Hamzah, Mahathir got UMNO to change its internal party rules so that a challenger needs to obtain nominations from at least 30 per cent of UMNO's 191 divisions to be eligible to contest the presidency (before only two were needed).

Meanwhile, Mahathir decided that he had to shore up his own base. This is apparently when the politics of patronage in Malaysia began to blossom. Mahathir started awarding government contracts to his cronies; their loyalty was bought, and Mahathir consolidated his position. Over time, these cronies became reliant on government work and handouts, and so the government had to keep dishing out contracts to them, instead of awarding them based on a normal public tender process. To this day, much internal jostling and bidding for contracts happens at UMNO general assemblies—hence Malaysia's reputation for "money politics". Since work is awarded not on merit, but on familiarity, there are huge efficiency losses.

This money politics racket is best described through this lovely anecdote I heard from a friend, whom I shall call Matthew. After leaving Penang some 30 years ago, Matthew went on to complete his PhD at Harvard, before becoming a scientist. He has worked as a consultant with many businesses around the world, including in his native country.

"Winning government contracts in Malaysia is quite simple, really, once you know how the system works," Matthew admitted matter-of-factly. "OK, let's say the government wants to award a contract for a new sewage system. The officer in charge of the tender will solicit bids from a couple of Malaysian companies who can do sewage work. He will ask for bids from a few of his buddies, guys who probably don't know anything about sewage work.

Suppose the genuine Malaysia company puts in a bid for RM12 million. One of the cronies will put in a low bid, say RM7 million. Another will put in a higher bid, say RM35 million. And the third will put in a ludicrously high one, say RM75 million.

The officer will dismiss the high one, on the grounds of being too expensive. And he will dismiss the two low ones, supposedly as underestimates. And so he will plump for the one in the middle—RM35 million—which seems to make sense on paper, if only for being in the middle.

The crony who submitted the winning bid will then simply walk over to the genuine company, and offer a sub-contract for RM12 million. He will then share the loot with the other cronies. At the end of the day, decent work still gets done, the genuine company makes a living, but the Malaysian taxpayer has overpaid by RM23 million."

As a result of these shenanigans, many people have a rather jaundiced view of Malaysian business. It is hard to measure exactly how much money has been drained from Malaysia through crony capitalism. Indeed, to get a full picture, one has to measure not just direct leakage, but indirect wastage and inefficiencies, like the long-term damage to productivity. Some of these may have a much longer-lasting effect.

According to Barry Wain, an author, up to RM100 billion may have been wasted during Mahathir's reign on grandiose projects and corruption. In some senses, the exact amount is irrelevant, says Din Merican—far more insidious is the fact that "all this is done under the banner of affirmative action. Corruption goes on freely under the mask of trying to help the poor Malays."

In the lead up to the UMNO elections in December 2008, the problem of money politics cropped up again. As Badawi's administration stepped aside, numerous political hopefuls started jostling vigorously, promising sweeteners to all and sundry. Apparently, each of the 2,500 delegates could expect up to RM20,000 for their vote.[6]

Ironically Mahathir, of all people, decide to rail against this. "Corruption in UMNO at all levels has become a talking point for everyone. They are sick and tired of UMNO, its members and leaders. The hatred towards the party that is immoral has spread wide," he wrote in his blog.

And yet Din, and most others I speak to, place the blame for money politics squarely on Mahathir's shoulders. Even if he didn't enrich himself, most contend that he oversaw the growth of money politics.

As he spoke, Din grew increasingly frustrated and disgusted with the state of affairs, with the system that he had been a part of, with himself. Before his eyes, the rot had set in, and had, by now, spread throughout the system.

"You know, when I look at UMNO today, and when I compare it to the 1970s, when I was a young man, looking forward to building a new independent country, I am so sad," mused Din. "Back then, UMNO was filled with men of the highest integrity and honour, fellows like Tunku Abdul Rahman and Tun Hussein Onn. Look at what it has become."

This rot coincided with a decline in education. "Some people say that Malaysia does not have enough universities, not enough private sector involvement in education. That is rubbish! The problem is that we have too much. We have quantity, but not quality. We have become degree dispensers—anybody can get one."

Din worried about all the big engineering projects in Malaysia. "I am scared our bridges will fall apart!" Apparently, many of the engineers working on them graduated without having really studied proper engineering. "When I think back to the high standards that we had to maintain back then, when I got my degree, and I compare it to the standards today, I am ashamed—my degree has been debased."

Nevertheless, many people, particularly BN supporters, would still argue that Malaysia has developed fairly well over the past 50 years, money politics or not. But Din is having none of it. According to him, Malaysia should have grown much faster, and in a more equitable fashion.

"We have grown way below potential. We are a very rich country! We have land, we have oil, we have beaches, we have mountains, we can grow rubber, we can grow oil palm, we are a very rich country!

So, you might look at our high growth rates and think that we've been growing well. But I say that we could have done so much more. You know in the 1960s, when I went to Singapore for a holiday, for every one Ringgit I brought to Singapore I could get one Singapore dollar in return. Today, I can't even get 50 cents. That's how far behind we've fallen."

Ah yes, the exchange rate. Malaysians love talking about the exchange rate. Singaporeans? We just like shopping—especially in Malaysia.

***

Alor Setar, Kedah. 5 March 2008.

Serendipitously, I got an insight into this cosy government-business relationship in Kedah's capital.

Kedah is a giant, diverse state. Its southern end touches Penang, and so is more industrialised and richer. Its northern end flanks Thailand and is dominated by acres of lush paddy fields, spread across the land like giant green carpets. Kedah is Malaysia's rice bowl. It is poor, with a per capita GDP in 2008 of RM13,301 (US$3,994), just half the national average, and higher only than Kelantan.

The state does have a rich history though: Bujang Valley, a sprawling archaeological goldmine one-third the size of Singapore, is recognised as the cradle of a Buddhist/Hindu civilisation that dates back 1,500 years. Not much is known about it, in part because of archaeology's immaturity in Malaysia, but partly also because of the establishment's fear of finding out anything that might rock the boat of Muslim Malay pre-eminence.

Alor Setar, with a population of around 300,000, is like any mid-sized Malaysian city: Proton cars zipping in and out; the odd traffic policeman in white, looking disenchanted, directing cars, buses and bicycles because a traffic light has broken down; a couple of multi-storeyed hotels with familiar names but in need of touch-up in the centre of town; on the outskirts, old-style *kampung* houses quickly being replaced by concrete monstrosities; and a big stadium, with a Muslim mosque, Hindu temple, Christian church, Buddhist temple and Sikh gurdwara not too far away.

And food. One thing though—the Alor Setarans are culinary agnostics, caught between Malay and Thai food. The result is a somewhat forgettable mishmash.

Sumana and I were drawn to Alor Setar's one star attraction: the cradle of modern Malaysia, Mahathir's birthplace. It is given a fair bit of prominence, so that

Malaysians who want to learn more about their great leader can do so. When we floated the idea of visiting the attraction, a fisherman in Kuala Kedah laughed us off.

"Visit Mahathir's birthplace? Why would you want to do that? It's so small! I've got a better idea—why don't you visit one of his other hundred houses, they're all bigger and more beautiful. Look, he even built one for his daughter Marina, right across the river over there."

When we visited in 2008, a few days before the general elections, we stayed in a lovely little homestay, where we paid RM96 for an air-conditioned room with attached bathroom. The common living room outside had a television—late that night, we sat cross-legged next to the "concierge", Amin, and his buddy who was bunking over, all four of us glued to the telly, as a young Arsenal team beat the reigning champions, an old Milan team, 2-0 in a UEFA Champions League match.

Before that we had met another young Kedahan, Wan, who was overflowing with ambition, and looked like he had grand plans.

It had all started when we tried to look for an UMNO *ceramah* at night. Fed up with having met only opposition candidates thus far, we wanted to join the ruling-party campaign trail. After getting rough directions from some hawkers outside the stadium, we found an UMNO party office: a house with just one large room (more of a hall), with a sort-of-mosque next door, both on a large plot of land.

It was past nine, yet there were still three boys outside the house, painstakingly pasting and preparing lines of triangular UMNO flags, under a flickering bright fluorescent light, while Islamic choruses bellowed out of the sort-of-mosque. Although visibly tired, they went about their work with a quiet intensity. They perked up when they saw us, and welcomed us in.

After a couple of minutes, we managed to convince one of the boys, the self-appointed leader, that we did indeed want to talk to him—plain, little, worthless him—rather than one of the senior Kedah UMNO officials.

"We are usually here every night, doing little things for the party. The elections are here! Very exciting time."

"Who do you think will win?"

"UMNO, of course, UMNO."

Wan smiled at the foolishness of our question, and for a moment seemed to be losing interest. We're not even sure why we kept asking that question. Wan had a handsome face below his thick, short black hair. His bluish contact lenses gave his eyes a surreal look, like a character in Avatar.

"So what do you do when there are no elections, then? Do you do anything else for UMNO?"

"Of course! One of the things I do is to try and help the Malay youth who have nothing better to do, who take part in illegal street races, the *mat rempit*."

"Is that a big problem here?"

"Yes. I know a lot of people who race. I know people who have died."

His glassy eyes stared at us, without emotion. Wan and his buddies helped racing addicts find other things to do. At the very least, they moved them on to legal race courses.

"Those are much safer, and they are under guidance. Much better than racing illegally on the streets, where they endanger so many lives."

"What else?"

"We also recently organised a trip to Cambodia for these guys. They really enjoyed it. We went there and helped unfortunate Cambodians, did some volunteer housing work."

"Is that why you joined UMNO? To help other Malay youth?"

"No, not really. I joined initially so I could improve my business network."

"What do you mean?"

"Improve my network. Make contacts. Learn how to do business, learn who the right people to be in business with are."

"How does UMNO help you with that?"

"A lot of the older UMNO people are very good businessmen. They win a lot of the government contracts, and do a lot of the work. So, by joining the party, I get to meet a lot of these people, I learn how to do business."

Just then Wan received a call on his Nokia. The person on the other line seemed to be asking about us: who we were, what we wanted, what we were up to. It was obvious that somebody else in the hall had informed a "party elder" that Wan was talking to some reporters.

Wan seemed a little aggrieved, as he muttered, "They just want to chat … OK, OK, I'll ask them." He had raised his voice a little, and seemed annoyed that he had to ask. This might have been a small party office, but Wan had relative authority here.

"That was my father. He wants you to go talk to him. Maybe it's better, because he knows much more than me, he will be better able to answer your questions. I may not have all the answers that you want."

"No, that's OK actually. We have spoken to a lot of older people, we actually want to speak to some young people. Like you."

Wan smiled, somewhat flattered, and rather vindicated, as he whipped out a *kretek* cigarette and started puffing.

"Go ahead then. Ask me."

Wan is 27, and three years ago started working with his father, doing "government work". He came from a family of UMNO businessmen. His grandfather
belonged to UMNO, and so did his father. Joining the party, and following in their
footsteps, was simply family duty. In any case, there weren't too many opportunities
in the regular workforce—low-paying clerical work was the most he could expect.
That wasn't enough.

"I want to make money, of course. I want to be successful."

"Just business, or politics as well."

"Ha, you never know. Definitely business. Maybe later if UMNO feels I have the
right qualities, then I can be a political leader too!"

"Prime Minister? Like Mahathir?"

"Ha, no. There's only one Mahathir."

In Wan's eyes, UMNO membership meant business first, and maybe, only maybe,
politics later. He had a deep interest in national and global affairs. He read *Utusan
Malaysia*, a government-owned Malay daily, and occasionally looked up what the
online community had to say at an Internet cafe. Like most Malaysians we met, Wan
was disgusted with the Iraq war. "Saddam Hussein wasn't the greatest guy in the
world, but at least there was stability. Look what has happened now?"

However, unlike many Malaysians we met, Wan had only good things to say
about Singapore. Perhaps because a certain Singapore Airlines stewardess had kept
his bed warm on many-a-cold Kedah night. "There are all these political disagreements, but the people, we still get along well, right?" he smiled sheepishly. Later,
away from the prying mind of our female—and feminist—travel companion, Wan
also revelled in the delights of making love to Chinese women. He clearly didn't let
business get in the way of more carnal pursuits.

He continued to smoke on his *kretek*, and looked even more mysterious as the
smoke rose up past his bluish contacts. Was he wearing those to "match" his political affiliation? It was quite telling that political socialisation occurs early in life in
Malaysia. You grow up, say, becoming a PAS man or an UMNO woman, because
your father and mother are. It is passed on, like a religion.

In Singapore there is no political socialisation per se; most people feel that there
is only one real choice, unlike in Malaysia, where increasingly, and especially during
the 2008 election, each individual had an important choice to make.

Wan was quite sure that BN is the only way forward for Malaysia. "We want to
reduce poverty in this country to zero. That is our aim. BN is the only party that can
do this. The opposition cannot. I think everybody can see that PAS has not brought
any development to Kelantan over the past 18 years that it's been ruling there."

"But isn't that because the Malaysian government has been against PAS, has not given them fair support?"

"No, that's not true. It is actually because PAS knows nothing about business. Those people know nothing about development. They are simply not interested in making money. I have friends in PAS, that's why I know. The old people teach the young from a very early age. They never have a chance to change or to take the lead. They just blindly follow what the elders tell them. That's the nature of their religious beliefs and their politics. That's why nothing ever changes."

Presumably Wan's PAS friends might think that he, too, was blindly following the ways of his UMNO forefathers.

"That is why the Malaysian people have to keep faith with BN. See, it has just come up with the Northern Corridor Economic Region project. The government has a long-term programme to develop Malaysia, to bring poverty to zero. That is why we must let them carry on."

Wan confirmed a lot of things that we had heard on the street: the pervasiveness—and casual acceptance—of patronage politics in Malaysian society; the maturity of UMNO's internal party machinery; the limited career options available to youth; and the Malay boy's fondness for girls of a different colour.

However I wasn't yet certain about the argument that "PAS doesn't know anything about business". No doubt, that was the popular perception of PAS—as right-leaning religious folk who preferred the simple *kampung* life and abhorred the trappings of modern consumer society; apparently they would rather be sitting at home praying than out trying to make a bit of money. But I had to go to Kelantan, the Imam's lair, so to speak, to find out more.

***

Kota Bahru, Kelantan. 7 March 2008.

Just one night before the general elections, Mr Liew, a Kelantanese businessman, was pouring his heart out.

"We cannot eat pork. We cannot drink alcohol. We do not have Chinese temples. We cannot speak Mandarin. We cannot celebrate Chinese festivals. We are forced to wear the *songkok*." Mr Liew, a short, hyperactive man, was working himself into a bit of a frenzy.

"This is what my friends in other states think about us. These are the lies that the government has been spreading for a long time. Whatever you read in the newspapers about PAS, it's mostly lies."

Mun Ching, Sumana and I had met Mr Liew just hours before while looking for a restaurant in Kota Bahru. He was short, spunky, and had no time for nonsense, a sort of Chinese Joe Pesci. Along with directions, we got an invitation for a bit more of a chat later that evening. Mr Liew, his eyes darting around our car as he stood by the passenger's side, had a lot to get off his chest. "PAS is good!" he cried, flashing a thumbs-up at us. "Meet me in Chinatown in the evening, after I close my shop. I'll tell you more."

Kota Bahru's Chinatown is spread along both sides of a single main road in the centre of town, spanning about three blocks. On our two prior visits in 2004 and 2005, we found the same thing there: Chinese businesses, coffee shops and restaurants that looked no different from any others around Malaysia. There was also a large food centre in the middle, with about twenty stalls crammed in, U-shape, with lots of pig all around: roast pork, stewed pork, pork ribs, pork chops. And, to our delight, an abundance of cold beer.

This time, in 2008, there was one difference: election fever. The street, just like every other major one in Malaysia, was festooned with thousands of political flags, banners and ads. Blue and green was draped over everything, everywhere you looked, battling for your mindshare.

Mr Liew, for some reason, had asked to meet in "a quiet part of Chinatown" at 7 pm. When we got there, we realised that no such place existed. The street had erupted at night, with the sights and sounds and smells of a bustling Chinatown. When Mr Liew finally met us in front of a busy coffee shop, he dragged us to the next block, where rows of green plastic chairs had been set up, in anticipation of the evening's *ceramah*.

There were young and old Chinese milling around, all proudly wearing t-shirts with their party insignia. A teenager came up and handed each of us a party pen. We had certainly not expected this event, unfolding in green and white splendour before our eyes—a PAS Chinese political rally.

"Most of what you hear are lies. BN never tells the truth. It controls the media. Look at this, look all around you. All these Chinese people support PAS. Because PAS has been good to us."

Mr Liew, a 47-year-old third-generation Hakka Chinese, owned a clothing shop in Kota Bahru. Business had never been spectacular, but it hummed along, paying the bills and allowing him the occasional weekend jaunt to Sungei Golok, the Thai border town.

"There are no more KTV lounges and girls in Kota Bahru. But why worry? If you really want that, just drive over to Golok!" he said, chuckling, for just a moment, before his sombre side took over. "Anyway, it's better we don't have such things here. Our salaries are not enough to afford that kind of lifestyle."

"Ya, but if Kelantan was more developed, then perhaps you would have higher salaries? If BN wins, it might be able to bring development and prosperity."

"Ha, no," Mr Liew laughed, dismissing the thought. "Those guys are a bunch of crooks. They are dishonest and corrupt. If they win, you know what will happen? All the contracts and money will go to their friends. How will that benefit me? How will that benefit Kelantanese people? That is why so many people here support PAS. The PAS politicians are clean and honest."

"Ya, but PAS does not have as much business experience."

"They will learn, we will develop at our own pace. Anyway, what makes you think that development is so good. If Giant and Tesco come in to Kota Bahru, that will spell the end of small businessmen like me."

As we spoke, different people approached Mr Liew to say their hellos, unperturbed that he was yakking away to us three outsiders. We carried on chatting, about life, love and religion, until the *ceramah* started, hundreds of Chinese in attendance, shouting their allegiance to PAS, in between generous servings of *bihun* noodles, fried chicken wings and orange squash. He certainly seemed to represent the views of many Chinese in Kelantan: content with life, puzzled by why the rest of Malaysia thinks they're living under some sort of Islamic apartheid.

Strictly speaking, Kelantan was certainly not as developed as Malaysia's other states. But this seemingly had less to do with any business naivety, and more to do with the state's history and geography, and also the fact that PAS was simply being excluded from the UMNO patronage loop. Federal contracts and money had been funnelled elsewhere.

The interesting thing is that most Kelantanese we met didn't seem to mind too much—they were happy to thumb their noses at the chichi city boys and girls from KL and their corrupt politicians; happy to occupy the moral high ground, a bit like a proud Cuban *revolutionnaire* sneering at the US.

Listening to Mr Liew, we realised that BN's long history of patronage politics and corruption has had another unfortunate social consequence—it has made sceptics out of a whole swath of Malaysians. People like Mr Liew have simply lost their faith in modern business and development. They view capitalists with great suspicion, and seemingly would rather tolerate slow growth than sell out to perceived crooks.

I asked Nasir Mustafa, a PAS candidate, how he thought the *bumiputera* policy affected the economy in Kelantan.

"There is no development that occurs in other states that doesn't occur in Kelantan. Those are just rumours that are spread by BN. But now, a lot of outsiders

service and knowledge workers. Instead, many companies involved with business-process outsourcing voice work are choosing India and the Philippines.

There is the perception overseas that it is only the lesser-educated rural Malaysians who are keen on Malay. This is clearly not true. Many urban, well-educated Malaysians also do not believe in the primacy of English. Nurul Izzah, for instance, has advocated the teaching of maths and science in Malay, partly so that non-English speaking Malays can cope.

According to Farouk Khan, Malaysia may be the only country where this debate even takes place. The problem, he contends, is not that Malay is Malaysia's first language, but that English is not well taught. "The Chinese learn Mandarin, the French learn French. Why shouldn't every Malaysian speak Malay?"

For those who argue that there aren't enough Malay speakers in this world to justify its importance, he has a simple answer: Indonesia. Farouk argues that Malaysia's great advantage vis-à-vis Singapore is that it is well poised to capitalise on Indonesia's growth. (Unsurprising, perhaps, that Malaysian banks have established such a strong foothold there.)

In a broader sense, it might seem strange to speak of a shortage of talent in Malaysia when the country has produced such exceptional talents including Michelle Yeoh, an actress, Jimmy Choo, a fashion designer, Zeti Akhtar Aziz, Malaysia's central bank governor, and Tony Fernandes, an entrepreneur.

However, it sometimes feels as if half its best people live outside the country. There are some 300,000 Malaysians working overseas. I have met brilliant Malaysians occupying senior executive positions everywhere from America to Zhuhai, China. This brain drain occurs for many different reasons, including frustration at ethnic and social injustices in Malaysia, and the search for better opportunities.

More than 200,000 Malaysians live and work in Singapore. According to Lim Guan Eng, Penang's chief minister, if Malaysia really wanted to sabotage Singapore, it does not have to "turn off the tap" to limit our water supply (a long-standing half joke, half threat). Instead, it should simply recall all its citizens—or turn off the human capital supply, as it were.

A partner at a law firm in KL complained to us that the lure of Singapore is sometimes too great. "Not only do I have trouble finding good lawyers, but my best ones keep getting poached by firms in Singapore. There isn't much I can do—salaries there are so much higher. When they want to go, I just give them my blessings."

Malaysia therefore suffers from all the symptoms of a poorly scripted talent strategy—weak education; insufficient training; mismatch between demand (jobs available) and supply (graduate skills); low wages for skilled workers; retention difficulties; and brain drain.

The government is well aware of this, but the structural hurdles it must overcome are daunting. Meanwhile, Singapore is laughing all the way to the talent bank. Yet it is not just people issues which keep Malaysia stuck in the so-called "middle-income trap".

Low wages in the economy is, in part, a reflection of a broader issue—the failure of many Malaysian companies to boost productivity and move up the value chain. Malaysia has almost been caught in two minds: on the one hand, competing with the likes of China and India for low-skilled manufacturing work; on the other, trying to outdo India and Singapore for higher-skilled service work.

In fact, this overall lack of clear policy direction creates a highly uncertain investment environment. When I visited Ho Chi Minh City, the boss of a large petrochemicals company told us how, "At least here in Vietnam, you are quite clear about the overall direction. There is corruption, and there are wobbles, but the general path is known. In Malaysia, you never know. The worry is that one minister will say something today, and then tomorrow he will be overruled."

This ambiguity leads to inefficiency. Consider Malaysia's high-tech sector. In the mid-1990s, Mahathir decided, with a big song and dance, that Malaysia must promote technology industries, and so he conceived the Multimedia Super Corridor (MSC). However, because of entrenched interests, Malaysia failed to liberalise its Internet broadband market. As a result, broadband charges in Malaysia are much higher than in most IT-savvy markets. Broadband infrastructure build-out has been slow. Malaysia thus has low broadband Internet penetration. Thus, the MSC provides the facilities and tax incentives which dynamic Internet companies love—but the local population is still not really connected. What was mooted as a high-tech adrenaline shot for the country ended up as just another pipe dream.

It is easy to get overly pessimistic about Malaysia. There are several bright spots in the country, which should ensure that, even if nothing else dramatic happens, it continues growing slowly and sustainably. First there is agriculture, including sexy, high-tech agriculture, like genetic dabbling in bovines and oil palm trees.

There is manufacturing, which includes solar panel production, of which Malaysia is now the world's third largest. Malaysia is also consistently ranked third in A.T. Kearney's Global Services Location Index (GSLI), which assesses the attractiveness of countries around the world for locating outsourcing activities and shared service centres.

But will Malaysia ever escape from the middle-income trap? Much will depend on how its identity takes shape. There is this frequent conflict between what the people want, what the government wants, and what the numerous entrenched interest groups want. This leads to inefficiencies in many sectors, including telecommunications, automotive and power.

In other words, instead of becoming more competitive over the years, many parts of Malaysia's economy have been saddled with layers of bureaucracy—and ever more opportunities for a wily crony to make a quick buck. Needless to say, the Malaysian people lose out.

7
Some are more equal than others

Poetry is a luxury we cannot afford.
  —Lee Kuan Yew, in an address at the University of Singapore, 1968[1]

There are a fair number of things that Malaysians don't like about Singapore. Some feel that our society is unfair—"It's a Chinaman's land, right?" or "Singapore's a home only for the rich." Some think that we're snooty. More still that we have no soul, lifeless, boring, devoid of fun, culture and spirit.

But there is one aspect of Singapore that every Malaysian I've spoken to admires, is even envious of—our economic development.

"You know when I walk through your Changi Airport, it feels so great, so fresh, I can go into one of the toilets, they are so clean, even after I've done my business, I just feel like relaxing in there," says Din Merican, the Malaysian blogger. "But back home, in KL, at the airport, the toilets stink, they are so dirty! When I walk in there, I don't even feel like using them!"

Din's grasp of the finer points of lavatories speaks to two ideas I frequently encountered. First, the feeling that Singapore has developed much faster, widening its developmental lead over Malaysia. Second, the sense that, having grown faster and cleaner and more lavish, Singapore now has a much better "maintenance culture".

"In Malaysia, patronage politics has contributed to a short-term culture and mentality. Once the contract is won, and the project is completed, that's it. End of story. There is no follow-up. There is no interest in maintaining the asset," says Din.

The Singapore government, by contrast, is seemingly always one step ahead of the game. At every stage of development, it is already planning for the next. Lee Kuan Yew and his cadres, a generation of brilliant, hardworking technocrats, created a robust economic planning machine that seems to always foretell which way the global economy is going, and then manages to navigate tiny Singapore through it effortlessly; always bearing in mind short, medium and long-term implications. Singapore is *the* economic success story of the past 50 years, bar none.

Nothing is impossible here. If we need more land, we reclaim it from the sea—over the past 50 years, Singapore has added 20 per cent to its total land area through land reclamation—an extra 16,000 football fields worth of space. Since we don't have enough of our own water, we either buy it from our neighbours, desalinise it, or recycle sewage.

When we needed to kick-start our biotech industry, we imported the world's leading experts, paying them enough to feed their next three generations. Once we concluded that having a casino would be good for our long-term competitiveness, we sent our most debonair negotiators to Las Vegas to court their dons, while at home we conducted snappy public consultations to quell age-old apprehensions about gambling.

In the process, Singapore has become not only one of the richest, but also one of the most convenient places in the world to live in. Need to eat some chicken rice at 3 am? No problem. Buy the latest Bang and Olufsen system? Sure. If for some inconceivable reason your home telephone line goes down, just call a 24-hour Singtel hotline, and it will be fixed in hours. There is probably no other place on earth where the latest goods and services from *all over the world* are delivered to your doorstep with such methodical and clinical efficiency. It's infectious and contagious.

As a result, we have been intolerably spoilt by the system. Whenever we're outside Singapore, and something isn't done at the lightning speed we're accustomed to, it irks us. We may have been prepared for it but still, it irks us.

In this ultra-conducive business environment, companies of all shapes and sizes have blossomed. IT behemoths such as Texas Instruments, Hewlett Packard and Microsoft cut their Asian teeth in Singapore. Shipping tycoons made their pretty penny here. In 2007, Citigroup, Standard Chartered Bank and UBS transferred their heads of private banking to Singapore, an indication of the city's growing importance as a centre of private wealth management. Or, in other words, a sign of just how much money is sloshing around here.

In return, Singapore gave the world Sim Wong Hoo, the man behind Creative Technologies, an IT startup that was the first to add good sound to a bland PC experience, courtesy of its Sound Blaster cards. Sam Goi, the plucky, tireless entrepreneur who came to Singapore when he was six—on a small Chinese junk—built his fortune on making and selling the pastry skins around spring rolls and egg rolls. If you've eaten a spring roll in the past ten years, chances are it was made by Sam's firm.

More recent successes include Olivia Lum, the confident, innovative chemist, who found a way to recycle sewage into regular drinking water—in Singapore, what goes around really does come around. Her company, Hyflux, treats water in places as far as Kuwait and Gansu, China.

And of course, the big multinationals keep coming. And coming. They enjoy the stability. They praise the rule of law. They crave the tax breaks. They love the talented workforce.

I learned a bit from Dirk Thomas, president of Greater China for Hitachi Global Storage Technologies, in 2007. The company's "clean rooms"—where technicians motor around in white space-suits, operating US$4 million machines in the production of hard disk drives—resemble the nerve centre of some galactic enterprise.

"This isn't textiles," Dirk said, eyebrows raised, somewhat smugly, as he walked me around the company's high-tech plants in Shenzhen.

Nevertheless, Dirk—a cheery Californian with thinning hair and a creased forehead—was only too aware that the snazzier-than-textiles hard disks occasionally failed. He had to endure a mini crisis at home, when his young daughter's iPod crashed, prompting her to pour scorn on the whole industry. Thankfully he had backed it up.

China, the world's workshop, has come a long way, says Dirk. The latest technology is there, smart companies are popping up, and there are tons of talented people around. Yet he insists that a lot of credit for Hitachi's success must go to the Shenzhen government. It has improved the business climate a lot in the recent past.

"I suppose the most important thing is that they are willing to listen. Whenever I go see them with a problem, they are willing to listen, and willing to make changes. And so, in the process, they have become more like Singapore," Dirk smiled wryly. "You know what I'm talking about."

Dirk had spent many years in Singapore, once the world's hard disk capital. Over the years, much production has been moved out to cheaper locales.

"Singapore is the easiest place in the world to do business," Dirk says. "Your government does all it can to attract businesses and keep them there. Tax incentives. Permits—starting a business is so easy because you can get all the licenses and permits you need within days. There is no bureaucracy, no red tape. The EDB is always talking to businesses, finding out how to make Singapore more attractive, more competitive. Infrastructure is first class—roads, airport, sea port, power, everything."

"And there are talented people. And if you can't find the person you want in Singapore, it's so easy to bring him or her in from outside. It's almost as though the whole country is geared up for business. And Singapore has also become a great place to live. Restaurants, nightlife. Good schools. Very safe. One of the easiest places for expatriates to move to."

Dirk could have gone on for hours.

"You know what's interesting? Even though wages in Singapore have been rising for a while now, there's quite a bit of inertia when it comes to an industry leaving the country and relocating to a cheaper destination. That's because there are so many other advantages of being in the country. It doesn't always make sense to pack up and leave just because wages are lower somewhere else." (That last refrain is something I frequently hear today about China's coastal manufacturing zones, where wages are rising.)

Hearing praise about Singapore always fills me with a fuzzy nationalistic pride, wherever in the world I am, whoever in the world says it. At the same time, I feel slightly embarrassed, because I did not do much in the building of Singapore. My generation was born into relative comfort. We do not know what Singapore was like in the old days. We never experienced the blood and the sweat and the tears.

***

Singapore's economy, and hence society, is constantly in flux. Today, most people work in the services sector—including financial services, trade and transport and tourism—which contributes about 60 per cent of GDP. The manufacturing sector, meanwhile, has been shrinking while moving up the value chain. Today, it is dominated by cutting-edge pharmaceutical outfits and high-end electronics and machinery firms.

But just 30 years ago, many Singaporeans were producing clothes in textile mills. The pace of change in manufacturing, as it quickly moved from menial to high-value work, has been phenomenal. This is in part due to Singapore's rapid growth, driven by the country's efficiency in attracting new businesses and then paving the way for their exit when competitive pressures change.

Over the past 15 years, a lot of low-tech manufacturing work, including electronics assembly, has fled to cheaper locations such as China. All this chopping and changing has, no doubt, led to much upheaval, as old Singaporeans increasingly find they have nowhere to ply their trade. Just as in much of the developed world, the pains of globalisation have been felt keenly here.

But so have the gains. Globalisation is Singapore's lifeblood—after all, our country's wealth is founded on trade. Singapore's geographical position prompted Sir Thomas Stamford Raffles to choose it as the British Empire's main trading station in 1819. In 1822, Raffles declared, "Singapore will long and always remain a free port and no taxes on trade and industry will be established to check its future rise and prosperity." It was as free-trader and middleman that Singapore developed, and so it remains.

This openness to trade and commerce, a willingness to deal with anybody, regardless of political affiliation, has slowly become one of the pillars of Singaporean pragmatism. In recent years some liberal critics have sneered at Singapore's welcoming of Myanmar's military junta: generals visit the country for medical treatment, while their families come to shop and study.

But this Singaporean pragmatism has been around for decades. In the 1950s, even as he denounced communism, Lee Kong Chian, a Singaporean tycoon, told James Michener that: "Well, I do sell my rubber to communist China. To Russia, too. I have to. Singapore is a free port. That's what's made us rich. So if Russia sends a boat down here for rubber, I fill the boat…. if the Government were to pass a law saying that sale of rubber to Russia was forbidden, then the Russian ships would go away empty. But in Singapore there is no such law. Here we trade with everybody."[2]

Today, Singapore's ports handle more containers than any other in the world. At any moment, there are hundreds of ships hovering around this tiny island, waiting their turn to dock, unload, load and refuel. About half of the world's oil flows through Singapore; that spurred the growth of Singapore's petrochemical and refinery plants on its southern islets, where giant smokestacks and gnarling flames frighten the skies, curiosities in a country with no crude of its own.

In fact, unlike Malaysia, there are few natural resources of any kind here. Our land is rarely farmed. There are relics of ancient chicken farms in the outlying areas, while a couple of organic farms have sprouted up too. Other than that, and some fish, there is little primary produce of note. If the world stopped trading tomorrow, Singaporeans would eventually starve.

It is rare to meet a Singaporean whose work depends on the weather. Most Singaporeans are performing similar tasks and following similar service-sector routines on a daily basis. Many of us are desk-bound, and stare at monitors the whole day. As a result, we may have become slightly ignorant about some things.

One person who took great pleasure in pointing this out was Barnabus Son of Encouragement, a tailor Sumana and I met in Taiping, Perak. Taiping was once the capital of Malaysia's tin industry, but today just seems a quaint stopover with grand old buildings in need of paint jobs.

A reformed drug addict, Barnabus Son of Encouragement—that's exactly how he introduced himself—had found religion and changed his name. His cloth-hanger frame sat, one knee-up on chair, near the entrance of a tailor shop that felt more like a Wild West bar.

A few pairs of burning eyes greeted our entrance. Five Indian men near the back of the store were drinking beer. There was dust over all the suits in the display cabinet. Even the mannequins looked aged, as if afflicted by a skin disease that had turned their plastic hides a putrid, patchy shade of brown. The shop, like the town, seemed trapped in the 1960s. The moth-ridden cloth was horribly old, the beer cold and fresh.

Barnabus sat idly, reading the newspaper. He had so little business that his sewing was more hobby than occupation. Halfway through our conversation, we asked him about the differences between Malaysians and Singaporeans. He smiled.

"Aiyah, you two are probably the only two Singaporeans I have seen here since the 1970s lah. What do I know? Back then, they used to call us *sua teng*, from the hills. Let me tell you a story. True story, ah! True story. One or two years ago, there were some young children visiting Malaysia from Singapore, on a school trip. They visited a school in Malaysia. The teacher there asked them to draw a chicken, just a chicken. After five minutes, they were done, and they showed the teacher their drawings." Barnabus' eyes grew big, like giant marbles, "The teacher almost fainted! She almost fainted!"

"Why?"

"Do you know what the children had drawn?"

"What?"

"They had drawn chicken meat in a Styrofoam packet."

The rest of the men in the shop, their faces cherry red because of the alcohol, looked up from their drinks, and cracked up. We hung our heads in gastronomic shame; we were the *sua teng* here. Not the last time, either: we heard variants of that story three more times around Malaysia.

How has living in a city without a rural hinterland affected Singapore? Well, I've always felt that one big difference between Malaysia and Singapore is that people in Malaysia have time. Time to stop for a little chat, time to ask how you are doing, time to answer any questions … time for you. Perhaps it is not fair to say that it is simply a difference between Malaysia and Singapore per se, but rather the difference between a huge city like Singapore and a small town like Taiping. For surely the busy yuppie in KL or Jakarta has no time for you either?

In any case, the sense of urban estrangement in a country like Singapore is heightened because we are only a city—only urban. People are usually in a rush, bogged down by their numerous endeavours. There are no rural areas, where the pace of life slows, and everybody knows your name. We do not go knocking on our neighbour's door or bake *kuihs* for the new kid on the block. We cannot travel an hour to visit our farmers living and working on their plots, to see where our food comes from. They do not exist.

So, while big city dwellers in most countries will have an opportunity to live amongst their countrymen in less stressful environs, Singaporeans do not. Every other Singaporean we meet is living in the same metropolitan pressure cooker.

By the time I entered this world, Singapore's economic wheels had been set in motion. It often seems like we're part of a well-oiled machine that needs little maintenance. Each person just has to grow up, study hard, work well and live happily ever after. And, just like that, we'd be doing our part to keep the great Singaporean machine rumbling on.

When compared with the struggles and anxieties that most of the world face, life in Singapore for most Singaporeans seems rather straightforward. That, perhaps, is our biggest problem.

***

"The culture of creativity does not exist here," lamented Steve Wilson, director of R&D Asia-Pacific at Welch Allyn International, a medical device manufacturer. When Steve speaks, it's not the next table you have to worry about; it's the next building. He is, quite literally, a loud American, and is instantly likeable, with one of those ear-to-ear smiles that seems possible only in caricatures.

Welch Allyn had set up a development centre in Singapore in 2004 to focus on new product development for emerging markets such as Brazil, Russia, India and China. It chose business-friendly Singapore for many of the reasons that Dirk had mentioned. What's more, for the sorts of workers it needed—the PhD, researcher, techy types—labour costs in Singapore are typically half those in New York.

On the whole, Welch Allyn's venture has been successful. For instance, Steve's Singapore team was tasked with developing a prototype for a hospital bedside display monitor, which shows a patient's vital information. They completed it in five weeks. In the US, according to Steve, it would have taken six months.

"Singaporeans are academically brilliant and they have a tremendous respect for authority. They just get the job done. A similar team in the US would keep questioning and want to have a healthy dialogue every step of the way. This may be good in the early stage of a project's development. But it's a real problem during the execution. Singaporeans rarely revisit and question the purpose of a task. They have a great ability to translate something from requirement to developed product. They just get it done."

But, as Steve pointed out, that very strength also presents one of the biggest challenges to performing R&D in Singapore.

"Our teams are very focused on their tasks and as a result do not think much outside of what they have to do. Ideas are seldom generated, as no incentives for creativity exist in the Singaporean education system. In three years of operation, our facility has not produced a single patent, and there is no record of new ideas."

What Steve said should not surprise anybody, really. For at least ten years now, our country has publicly acknowledged that we are not as creative, not as willing to take risks, not as adept at thinking out of the box, not as willing to speak our mind, and not as willing to question as people from many other cultures.

There are many possible reasons for all this: a conformist, authoritarian society; a reluctance to question authority; tight limits, real and perceived, on freedom of expression; a pervasive fear of failure; and the fact that everything is available and provided for by the government, so much so that Singaporeans are rarely forced out of our comfort zone. Decades of spoon-feeding has numbed our instincts—we have forgotten how to hunt.

For instance, in his national day rally speech in 2008, Singapore's prime minister, Lee Hsien Loong, dedicated a chunk of his message to urging Singaporeans to date, get married, and procreate, in light of our low birth rate.

"So the dating agency told me another story. They arranged for a guy to meet a date and the setting was a romantic dinner in a nice restaurant. The guy turned up in slippers. So he counselled the guy. The guy says, that is me, I work in slippers, I walk in slippers, I come in slippers. So they talked to him, finally persuaded him to buy a pair of shoes, keep the shoes in his car. So before getting down at the date, he puts on his shoes, he meets, he goes for the date. And it worked."

If you ever wonder if we Singaporeans are spoon-fed, and lack initiative, think about this: our prime minister, in his once-a-year speech, felt the need to highlight the importance of shoes in dating.

Steve's experiences reminded me that after so many years of pontificating about the problem, things barely seem to have gotten better. This has us stumped. We solve most challenges by throwing money at it, forming a committee and hiring the best people for the job. But how do we make Singapore more creative? We're still not too sure.

One thing that we must tackle is our national fear of failure. In everything we do—school, work, play, whatever—the fear of failure grips us like a disease, paralysing our ability to take risks. Why the fear? It could be due to our "young nation under threat" ethos that has guided us since independence, such that we're afraid to put even one foot wrong.

Or it could be due to our rigid meritocracy that punishes missteps. Or perhaps there are cultural reasons too, a traditional set of beliefs that deems failure unacceptable. Whatever the case, people in Singapore who fail are still treated as outcasts.

Second chances are rare. In such an environment, few dare to try anything out of the ordinary.

But in the first place, why all the fuss about creativity and entrepreneurship now? Well, as Singapore transforms from a manufacturing and service-sector economy to a knowledge-based economy, our labour force has to evolve. The skills and disciplines that served us well yesterday will no longer be enough. Instead, creativity, innovation and risk-taking will come to the fore.

In order to create tomorrow's Microsofts and Facebooks, we need Singaporeans who are, say, willing to drop out of Ivy League schools and pursue wacky business ideas. Bill Gates did just that almost a quarter of century ago. So did Mark Zuckerberg just a few years ago. If a Singaporean tried that today, he or she would probably be grilled alive—by father, mother, and scholarship board.

Singaporean society wants the winners but is not willing to accept the losers. There is little incentive for a bright young person to do anything daring here. Almost everybody from my high school is working for the government or a big private sector firm.

Meanwhile, China's and India's rise has injected some urgency into this shift. As more and more manufacturing has fled to China, and as more and more service work has moved to India, Singapore has gotten worried. We have realised that we have to continually up our game and move up the value chain if we are to stay relevant. Quite frighteningly, China and India also appear to have plenty of innovative potential of their own.

Attempts by the Singapore government to manufacture creativity have been met with ridicule. Sure, it's a bit oxymoronic to try and "manufacture creativity". But that's how most things happen here. Our government decides, and we, the humble citizens, follow.

Singapore's leadership must shoulder some of the blame for not beginning this process earlier. At least it is now taking steps in the right direction. In addition to telling us to be creative, it has also liberalised our educational system, to place less emphasis on rote learning and examinations, and more on creativity, spontaneity and speaking skills.

Lots of money is being pumped into creative industries such as design and animation. Bankruptcy laws have been amended to lessen the financial burden of going broke. And the government has rolled out a slew of incentives for small and medium enterprises (SMEs), to encourage entrepreneurship.

However, according to somebody who works at SPRING Singapore, the agency that promotes SMEs, because of the paucity of genuine business ideas, much taxpayer money is being wasted to support frivolous or unimaginative business plans.

A lot more can be done. Most worryingly, political and civil freedoms are still limited. So while the government has done all it can to make infrastructure, business processes, and other aspects of our country's "hardware" efficient, its policies still stunt our "software"—the ability of our knowledge workers.

According to many human resource directors I speak with, the average Singaporean remains afraid and unable to speak out, challenge convention and voice opinion—crucial elements for a knowledge economy.

Much of that is due to our cultural, political and social restrictions. For long the government has seemed to believe that Singaporeans can grow into creative workers while having narrow, closed political minds. That seems like wishful thinking.

According to Waltraut Ritter, a knowledge management guru. "Although there is no hard substantive evidence, there are signs that a completely free mind—free of fear, free to think or say anything at all—will be able to better innovate than a partially closed mind." As long as chunks of our consciousness are prevented from thinking freely, will the rest of it be able to?

Societal attitudes, meanwhile, will take much longer to change. Even though our government has moved entrepreneurship to the top of its agenda, it will be a few years yet before Singaporean parents readily accept that their bright little girl decided to take a year off school to grow her start-up.

Ultimately, perhaps, the point is probably far more nuanced than simply "Singaporeans cannot innovate". From my experience living and working here, I suspect that Singaporeans are fairly good at incremental innovation but rather poor at disruptive innovation.

Incremental innovation refers to a slow process of making small, gradual tweaks to products, which over time result in radical change. Japan is widely regarded as an exemplar of incremental innovation. Products such as batteries, cars and semiconductors have benefited over the years from incremental innovation.

Disruptive innovation refers to transformational change that can upend entire industries, markets and societies. It is commonly believed that Western societies are more adept at disruptive innovation. Products such as the transistor, low-cost airlines and Google are examples of disruptive innovation.

There is little consensus about which type of innovation is more important to an economy. In March 2011, The Economist Online hosted a debate on the motion, "This house believes Japanese 'incremental innovation' is superior to the West's 'disruptive innovation.'"[3]

William Saito, founder of InTecur, a technology consultancy, and a serial entrepreneur, defended the motion. "A nation needs an environment that supports steady, progressive and perhaps undramatic innovation," Mr Saito, who was raised in America to Japanese parents, says. "It is only by standing on the shoulders of past achievements that a few firms are able to reach for the stars and take on the massive risks associated with disruptive innovation."

Douglas Merrill, founder of Zestcash, an online loan service for the under-banked, and ex-CIO of Google, was against the motion. "Disruptive innovation creates an ecosystem that helps the innovator, other companies, and users across many domains," says Mr Merrill. "The ecosystem adds value to the innovator's customers, to the customers of the other ecosystem members, and lets the innovator learn from the fast followers."

At the end of the debate, after many more exchanges, 43 per cent of the online audience had voted for the motion. Some 57 per cent voted against. Even though there was much contention about which is better, it was generally agreed that both types of innovation are necessary in order for a society to be dynamic and truly creative.

The Singaporean psyche encourages incremental innovation, but not the disruptive sort. From the time we are young, people here are encouraged to constantly better ourselves along certain fixed channels and within specified parameters. But we are reminded not to push ourselves outside those boundaries—society frowns on anything audacious or revolutionary.

Two examples drive home this point. The first is the iPod. In 1998, Creative Technologies, a Singaporean firm, was more valuable than Apple. Creative's industry-standard computer sound cards, such as the Sound Blaster, had established itself as a global leader in digital sound. Creative was in a perfect position to capitalise on the nascent MP3 industry.

Instead of bringing innovative new products to market, however, Creative dithered. Apple, with relatively scarce prior experience in digital sound, released its iPod, which made Creative's players look like museum pieces. Along with its iTunes music distribution model, Apple's resurgence began. In ten years, a Californian company had destroyed Singapore's pride and joy. Few people even remember that Creative once ruled the digital sound roost.

> When you're very structured almost like a religion ... Uniforms, uniforms, uniforms ... everybody is the same. Look at structured societies like Singapore where bad behavior isn't tolerated. You are extremely punished.
>
> Where are the creative people? Where are the great artists? Where are the great musicians? Where are the great singers? Where are the great writers? Where are the athletes? All the creative elements seem to disappear.
>
> —Steve Wozniak, Apple's co-founder, interview with the BBC, December 2011

Furthermore, if Singaporeans were better equipped at disruptive innovation, we would have created Asia's best low-cost airline. As Ryanair was revolutionising air travel around Europe a decade ago, one might have expected its Asian equivalent to be born in Singapore, with our fabulous infrastructure, modern economy, developed financial markets, and great reputation for travel and transportation.

Sheltered by the success of luxurious Singapore Airlines, however, nobody in Singapore was able to recognise and act on this shifting consumer trend. Dynamism and entrepreneurship came instead from the wily Tony Fernandes up north and, just like that, Malaysia, through Air Asia, had stolen a march. Singapore was able only to continually tweak a standard model—premium air travel—not disrupt the entire industry.

Some might argue that Hyflux, the water purification company, is a disruptive innovator, particularly with its recycled-sewage Newater. Perhaps. But its founder, Olivia Lum, was born not in Singapore, but Malaysia.[4] "So what?" one might say. We are all certainly happy that Ms Lum is now a Singaporean.

But her story illustrates another conundrum in Singapore's drive to foster innovation: by pushing creativity without loosening social and political controls, we may be building the ideal environment for foreign innovators—but not local, homegrown ones, who will always have caution hardwired into them.

Fredrik Härén, a Swedish entrepreneur, publisher and writer, moved to Singapore recently. He speaks regularly on creativity. Mr Härén believes Singapore is one of the most creative places he's lived in. "There are 60 per cent Asian locals and 40 per cent foreigners here. This is what the whole world will look like in the future, but it's already here," he told a conference I attended in October 2011. "Because Singapore is so small, one is forced to look outside. Compare that to China or India, where creativity is often inward-looking."

Nevertheless, Mr Härén admits that he will probably send his son to an international school, not a local Singaporean one. He probably doesn't want him becoming *too* Singaporean.

***

[Some participants at the IMF World Bank meetings] were competing with each other to praise Singapore as the success story of globalisation. Actually, Singapore's success came mainly from being the money laundering centre for corrupt Indonesian businessmen and government officials. Indonesia has no money. So Singapore isn't doing well. To sustain its economy, Singapore is building casinos to attract corrupt money from China.

These words were penned not by some deranged critic, but by Morgan Stanley's chief Asia economist, Andy Xie, in an internal memo in late 2006. Andy, who holds a PhD in Economics from the Massachusetts Institute of Technology (MIT), resigned from his post and left Singapore shortly after his comments emerged. He never gave a reason for his departure.

A lot of people I speak to—on the streets, in the bars, in the boardrooms—feel there is "dirty" money flowing through Singapore and getting "washed" somewhere along the way. Where is it coming from? According to them, certainly Indonesia, Myanmar and Russia, but possibly any other country in Asia, and as far off as Africa. Unsurprisingly, given Andy's mysterious departure, none of them want to be quoted on this.

Although it must be difficult to track—how do you tell exactly how the wealthy businessman from Kalimantan made his money?—there are lots of interesting anecdotes around.

For instance, a friend in the luxury watch business is convinced that some of the people buying these fancy timepieces are doing so using "dirty" money. "Singapore has one of the highest per capita sales of luxury watches in the world. Some of these watches run into the hundreds of thousands of dollars, but there's no way a customs guy at the airport would recognise them," he says. Buy a watch, smuggle it out of the country, and your money is clean.

Another friend who works in the luxury jewellery business said that countless Indonesian barons and their dolled-up lady friends have shown up at his shop carrying suitcases of cash. "Business is business. We prefer not to ask questions," he says.

Two years ago, when in Kuala Lumpur, I met a senior executive at a big Malaysian bank who was absolutely certain that Singapore is used to launder money. "Listen, it happens all the time. Some of my friends, top private bankers in Singapore, have told me that if I give them a suitcase of Malaysian ringgit today in KL, by tomorrow they can create a US dollar account for me in Singapore. That's how blatant and easy it is."

Filipino gambling kingpins have certainly laundered money through Singapore, according to the lawyer of a late *jueteng* operator, the illegal numbers gambling game played in the Philippines.[5] In a March 2011 report, the US State Department listed Singapore as one of the "Major Money Laundering Countries in 2010".[6] The report highlighted that "[t]he structural gaps in Singapore's financial regulations make it vulnerable to money launderers, and its financial crimes enforcement should be strengthened."

Of course, none of these things can prove that Singapore is a money-laundering capital. All the same, we shouldn't ignore the fact that there is a perception out there that some ill-gotten money is being attracted here.

Why does this matter? For one it goes against the very grain of squeaky clean incorruptible Singapore. How can we possibly claim to have built a bastion of fairness and justice if crooked capitalists want to ship their money here?

Also, it simply adds to the mystique of an opaque state-led capitalist structure, where ordinary citizens do not really know what goes on in the higher echelons of politics or business.

This feeling stems in part from the relatively secret workings of our two sovereign wealth funds, Temasek Holdings and GIC. Temasek is the holding company for Singapore's government-linked corporations (GLCs), while GIC manages our country's bountiful foreign reserves. Temasek published its first ever annual report in 2004, while GIC did so in in 2007. Up till that point, Singaporeans had little idea about what actually went on with the money they managed.

Many I speak to are extremely concerned about this perceived lack of transparency. Also, they feel that the two SWFs, as they are currently run, have systemic conflicts of interest: Lee Kuan Yew was GIC's chairman till 2011, when he was replaced by his son, the prime minister; the prime minister's wife, Ho Ching, is the boss of Temasek. Together, they form a powerful trinity that sits atop Singaporean politics and business.

Singapore's SWFs decided to reveal details of their performance in part because of global pressure for all SWFs to do so. However, as the electorate matures, it is also going to demand more accountability and transparency. If Singapore Inc. retains its mystique, and if accusations about money laundering do not die down, then ordinary citizens are going to feel increasingly distant from the nation. And that would be a problem.

***

Perhaps the biggest socio-economic challenge facing Singapore is income inequality. The real wages of the lowest earners—the bottom 30 per cent of Singaporeans—have declined from 2001 to 2008. During that time, the wages of the top 10 per cent have soared.

The Gini coefficient, a measure of income inequality, has risen from 0.35 in 2001 to 0.48 in 2010, higher than in China and the US. In other words, during this decade's golden period of growth, when the global economy grew faster than at any other point in history, a yawning gap has been created between Singapore's haves and have-nots.

Some from the establishment do not believe this is a problem. After all, by almost any measure, the "poor" in Singapore are better off than the "poor" in most other countries. Most here have access to relatively decent public services.

Still, in terms of education, healthcare, housing, social security, and transportation, life in Singapore varies dramatically depending on who you speak with. At the upper end are people who enjoy access comparable to the ultra-rich across the world. At the lower end are people struggling to pay the rent for their 400 square foot apartment. Given our density, these two groups can sometimes be found right next to each other.

Moreover, the income gap affects many people, not just the very lowest earners. A large swathe of lower to middle income Singaporeans probably feels that the Singapore dream is slipping away.

Singapore's median monthly income was S$2,710 in 2010. Amid all the hubris about how great our education system is, it is interesting to note that half of Singapore earns, at most, only as much as a university graduate's very first paycheck.

Meanwhile, not only are the spoils of growth more unevenly distributed, it is becoming harder for people at the bottom to ever rise up. Though on par with the US, Singapore's intergenerational mobility is low compared with other developed countries, noted Irene Ng, a professor at the National University of Singapore, in *The Straits Times*.[7]

"Though there has been a significant jump in the earnings and educational status of later generations relative to earlier ones in Singapore, low intergenerational mobility implies that those whose parents were at the bottom tend to also remain at the bottom, while those whose parents were at the top tend to stay there," she says.

In addition, our risk averse culture undermines social mobility in the country, according to Chung Wai Keung, a professor at the Singapore Management University, because it discourages entrepreneurship, which in other countries is a crucial means by which poorer citizens scale the income ladder.[8]

Over the past few years, Singapore's government has become increasingly conscious of all this, and has been trying to address it in its own way. Government-owned newspapers are filled with tear-jerkers about elderly Singaporeans who've been abandoned by their families. Ministers frequently lend an ear—and a hand— to the poor who need help. New goodie bags, filled with rebates and reliefs, are flung out periodically, with a little show of compassion.

However, it is unclear if all this is mostly window-dressing in the name of political expediency. In order to truly address income inequality and its symptoms, the PAP will have to change its own DNA, in particular its growth fetish, and its severe allergy to welfare. Though there are signs it may give an inch or two, it seems incapable of meaningful change in this direction.

On a related note, the issue of income inequality has poisoned two national discussions. The first relates to ministers and government performance.

This is because ministers have been getting paid an obscene amount of money. For instance, ministers earn more than US$1 million a year. The prime minister earns more than US$2 million, which is not only more than 99 per cent of Singaporeans, but also more than all other politicians in the world, and many corporate CEOs. Singapore's prime minister earns five times what the US president does. Ministers' compensation is tied to the top earners in three fields: accounting, banking and law.

The government has always maintained that high pay is needed to attract the best talent into civil service. Many Singaporeans I speak to are sceptical about this argument. "Does that imply that if we halved ministerial salaries tomorrow, some of our Ministers would actually resign and join the private sector?" one friend asked.

Because of this disgruntlement, many discussions on government policies and performance always seem to come back to ministerial pay.

"Oh, sure, we need to raise the GST, but that's only so that we can pay their lofty salaries."

"How could Mas Selamat escape? Why are we paying them such high salaries if they can't prevent things like this?"

"They had to raise car taxes and ERP charges (road tolls) so they could pay their higher salaries."

This issue enrages some people I speak with. They feel that the ministers are creaming off all the spoils. After all, the government's active role in Singapore's economy, and the relatively opaque workings of GIC and Temasek, coupled with the PAP's dominance and the incredible ministerial salaries, are perfect ingredients for a political maelstrom. To some critics, the entire thing stinks. "Legitimised corruption", as *Singapore Review*, an online forum, calls it.

Even worse, almost all Singaporeans I speak to feel that because of the huge disparity between ministerial salaries and the average income, it is impossible for ministers to ever empathise with the trials and tribulations of "the common man". To be sure, ministers do all they can to appear modest—amongst other things, they shun flashy clothes and cars; and they conduct meet-the-people sessions where any Singaporean can meet them.

However, by virtue of how wealthy they are, "How will they ever know what it's like working and living in Singapore with an average income?" asks one friend. In 2007, Sylvia Lim, an opposition politician, pointed out in parliament that a typical worker earning a median salary in Singapore takes one month to earn what a minister earns in half a day. It is a shocking disparity.

Recognising voters' unhappiness with this, in early 2012 the government agreed to salary cuts of between 36 and 51 per cent for political office holders, including the president and the ministers. The framework for politicians' performance bonuses was also broadened from a narrow focus on overall GDP growth to more specific indicators tracking the socio-economic development of lower-income citizens.

About time. Political scientists may one day look back at the period from 1994 to 2012 as an aberration—when an educated, developed democracy decided to reward its senior-most politicians fabulously, even though a significant segment of the population saw hardly any real income growth.

The issue of income inequality also affects how Singaporeans view foreigners. Indeed, there is a growing feeling that the country is becoming a club for the global rich, not ordinary citizens. There are certainly signs of this. Russian tycoons buying up multi-million dollar penthouses in downtown Singapore; Vegas moguls constructing a glitzy casino hoping to pull high-rollers from around the world; and Formula 1, the quintessential millionaire's playground, successfully launching its first ever night-race in Singapore.

"Watch the Formula 1 race tonight? Are you mad?" a friend living in Ang Mo Kio quipped. "Most of the people in my neighbourhood have never even heard of Formula 1." Just like that, one sporting event had sliced our country in two.

Unfortunately, these negative emotions can colour our opinions of all foreigners. More and more of my local friends complain about highly paid expatriates—mostly white—acting arrogantly, and supposedly raising the cost of living by splurging on cars, cuisine and condos. Then there are the talented Asian immigrants—mostly from countries such as India and the Philippines—who are willing to work for lower wages, undercutting Singaporeans, and "stealing jobs".

At the lower end of the ladder are the foreigners who perform manual labour, jobs that most Singaporeans wouldn't want anyway. Even though we don't feel much job competition from them, the way we treat them leaves a lot to be desired. From 2006 to 2009, Singapore's resident employment increased by 73,000. Non-resident employment, meanwhile, increased by 327,000.

This influx of workers, along with rising income inequality, is leading to greater xenophobia. It's easy to blame the "alien" for your woes.

Throughout our travels, Sumana and I met so many Malaysians who were convinced that there is more fairness and more social justice in their country than ours. We were constantly faced with the accusation, "In your country, the rich get richer and the poor get poorer." Time and time again, we defended Singapore. Was it all in vain?

***

"I'm not sure why Singapore needs all these foreigners, actually," says a former colleague who I will call John. "I mean, I understand the need for people right at the top, you know, people with really specialised skills, or with lots of experience. I suppose they're worth the money. And of course we need the low-cost workers, manual labourers, doing things that Singaporeans would not want to do. But what about all the foreigners in the middle? Does Singapore really need them?"

This boom in mid-level executives and service workers has occurred over the past ten years or so, as Singapore gradually liberalised its foreign worker laws. Most recently, in 2006, a law was passed that allowed S pass holders to remain in Singapore even without a formal job offer.

To be sure, foreigners bring a lot of good to Singapore—diversity, talent, innovation, just to name a few. So it was a bit surprising to hear one of my white American colleagues railing against them.

"I know this must be a bit ironic coming from me, but sometimes I really wonder if the huge inflow of foreigners is restricting opportunities for Singaporeans," said John. "For instance, I have an American friend who works for Caterpillar [a large US manufacturer of heavy machinery]. His total cost to the company must be something around US$400,000 a year, if you include relocation, housing, schooling for his kids. And he's not even C-level, he's just one of their senior marketing guys. Now he's my friend, so I'm glad he's here, but I always wonder—why didn't Caterpillar just hire a Singaporean? I'm sure there are tons of guys out there who can do the same job for a third of the price."

"Well, if they can find a Singaporean, then why don't they? Doesn't make sense for a firm to hire the same person for three times the price, does it? If that were happening, the firms that hire Singaporeans will ultimately perform better."

"I know. Maybe there's just a perception that the American can do a better job. But then again, it's a chicken and egg right? If there are so many foreigners around, and Singaporeans are never given the chance to assume leadership positions like this, how will they become better?"

John's argument certainly resonates with me. While working in Singapore over the past six years, I have noticed many foreigners getting the nod over talented locals. Anecdotal evidence suggests that there are three possible reasons for this.

First, in some instances, the foreigner may be willing to work for lower wages. This seems to happen mostly in lower to mid-level service sector jobs, including restaurant staff and junior accountants. As mentioned earlier, these foreigners tend to be Chinese, Indians or Filipinos.

Second, some bosses may have the perception that a foreigner can do a better job, as my friend John thinks. This seems to occur primarily in mid to upper-level service sector jobs, such as corporate executives. The foreigners in question tend to be white or Indian. Why the misconception? There are many possible reasons, ranging from a colonial hangover to the fact that foreigners generally perform better in interviews than relatively reticent Singaporeans.

Third, and perhaps most damaging, is the possibility that the average Singaporean simply isn't equipped to perform at a high level in a knowledge economy.

Several HR directors have told me that many Singaporean employees remain afraid and unable to speak out, don't think out of the box, and are too afraid to challenge convention or question authority, even when we know something is amiss.

Furthermore, the average Singaporean worker often does not have the ability to collaborate across the organisation, and draw on a range of multi-disciplinary skills. Instead, workers are much more comfortable working on set tasks and processes, often in silos. The caricature is of the Singaporean worker's "shield", which is tucked close to the body, and raised instinctively to deflect new "arrows", or responsibilities, which are outside our regular mandate.

The sad truth is that for a lot of us, aspects of our upbringing—rigid educational system, lack of political freedoms, societal restrictions, extreme deference to authority—may have stunted our ability to perform many jobs in our *own country's* knowledge economy.

We Singaporeans may have a solid foundation, but not the spark and lateral thinking required by many great companies. We have technical expertise, but lack the softer skills. To compensate, many firms hire Australians, Americans, Indians, and other bright sparks who were brought up in more open, dynamic systems. Some companies, when seeking to fill specific knowledge-based jobs, have stopped looking for Singaporeans altogether.

***

What then are we to make of Singapore's economic model? A high level summary would suggest that it is a stellar performer, one of the best in the world. Once we dig deeper, though, we find some structural problems which have emerged in the past ten years. These problems, if not addressed, threaten to hamper economic and social development. As with our political system, a model that has served us so well over the past 40 years seems ill-equipped for the future.

At the crux of the issue is groupthink. Whether a result of the PAP's dominance or not, Singapore's economic policymaking is somewhat starved of outside opinions, alternative ideas, and fresh ways of thinking.

As a result, Singaporeans rarely get to consider really radical ideas. Farouk Khan, a Singaporean who lives in Malaysia, described to me an alternative reality, one where Singapore is much more closely linked to Malaysia and Indonesia. This school of thought suggests that instead of latching itself onto the economies of

China, India and many other countries—attempting to be the Gateway to Asia— Singapore should have focussed purely on becoming the pre-eminent city in the Malay-speaking world, where it has a natural competitive advantage.

This would have allowed Singaporean businessmen to capitalise on the huge opportunities opening up in Indonesia, as the Malay-speaking Malaysian business- men have been able to do. Instead, by trying to be a jack of all trades, Singapore will end up being a master of none. Of course, there are many potential pitfalls with this strategy, not least the difficulty in promoting a Chinese-majority city as the hub of the Malay world. But it is one of the many alternative narratives that do not get enough public air time here.

Policy debate here is almost an afterthought, according to a senior American lawyer who has been working in Singapore for ten years. "In Singapore, the govern- ment decides what it wants to do. Then its media lets everybody else know. And then a 'debate' takes place. But the government's already decided."

In the past ten years, Singapore's productivity has fallen, income inequality has risen, and the flood of immigrants has led to severe economic dislocations. In a more open, democratic system, these concerns would have been raised a long time ago.

In Singapore, there was barely a whimper. But of course, now that the govern- ment itself has spoken about these issues, they have been sanctioned and are now talked about everywhere. Sadly, that is not enough—the government's economic foresight of old is being replaced by myopia and hindsight.

That's not to say that the PAP itself has declined—if anything, it remains one of the most efficient, pragmatic parties in the world. Rather, as Singapore's economy and society has evolved, a one-party system, prone to groupthink, is looking more and more archaic and inadequate.

As is the state's heavy involvement in the economy, through industrial policy and via GLCs. Though crucial in Singapore's formative years, GLCs have long hampered the growth of SMEs. While most GLCs are still successful, the paucity of Singapore's SME sector is really starting to show.

From a macroeconomic standpoint, Singapore's economy appears to suffer from too-high savings, an overreliance on investment and exports, and insufficient con- sumption. This is analogous to the structural imbalances which many economists claim plague China's economy. In 2008, private consumption comprised just 40 per cent of Singapore's GDP—compared with 70 per cent in the US, 60 per cent in the EU, and 55 per cent in Japan.[9]

There are many historical reasons for Singapore's insufficient consumption, including an ingrained savings culture. However, in the past ten years, a confluence of different factors has greatly worsened the imbalance.

First, high immigration of low-cost labour has helped hold wages down. As a result, during this golden period of high growth, a disproportionate share of income flowed to corporations. According to Manu Bhaskaran, an economist, in Singapore "profits take about 46 per cent of GDP, which is extremely high in comparison with most developed economies. The available data also shows that foreign-owned companies receive almost half of this extraordinarily high profit share. That leaves an unusually low share of the GDP cake for the average Singapore citizen, whether he is an employee or a businessman. This could be why, even though Singapore's per capita GDP is roughly 11 per cent higher than Hong Kong's, our per capita consumption is about 21 per cent lower."

From 2000 to 2005, at least 40 per cent of Singaporeans saw their real income decrease. In essence, much of Singapore's recent growth has benefited foreigners and the upper crust. In fact, if you're one of those lucky ones, you've probably had a long, fabulous party. In 2008, Singapore had the highest concentration of millionaires in the world. The gulf between the poor and the rich has gotten dangerously wide.

If you want to characterise this cynically—Singapore's economic model has allowed owners of land and capital (i.e., rich people) to reap supernormal profits at the expense of low-income workers whose wages have been held down.

Like China, if Singapore wanted to diversify its economic growth, one way is to allow the wages of workers to rise. The reason is simple: poorer people have a higher marginal propensity to consume. The poorer you are, the more of your next dollar you will spend. If wages are raised, and corporate profits lowered, Singapore will see more consumption and lower savings.

Why hasn't the government allowed this? One reason could be a hangover from the 1980s, when rising wages threatened Singapore's competitiveness. The other possible reason, of course, is that those in power aren't too bothered by the current state of affairs. The lower wages are, the cheaper services are. For example, speak to any waiter in Singapore, and you'll quickly realise that waiters here earn less than they do in any other developed city of similar wealth. That's one reason a champagne and *foie gras* experience may not cost as much.

There is no easy answer to this conundrum. To be sure, higher wages will harm some businesses. Consumers will face higher prices for certain goods and services. Inefficient and low-skill producers will flee to lower-cost locales. Still, it will spur others to move up the value chain, and encourage productivity increases.

Segments of the Singaporean workforce seem to have gotten stuck in a low productivity–low wage rut. "I went to that hotel's bakery for some cake," says Ashish Lall of the Lee Kuan Yew School of Public Policy. "I told the assistant that I would like to buy one whole chocolate cake. She looked at me—I was all alone—and asked if I wanted it for here or to go."

Perhaps the most salient point in this whole income discussion is the first one—the wages of Singapore's bottom third have stagnated over the past ten years. If it's because the productivity and skills of the workers at the bottom have not improved much, well then, the system has failed them. That simply isn't right.

George Yeo, Singapore's former foreign minister, once addressed a class at Harvard Business School, where he argued that one of the great things about the Singapore model is that "the poor" are better off than they are in most other countries. According to him, while many other countries measure success by how well off the winners in society are, Singapore likes to measure success by how comfortable the less fortunate are.

In the past ten years, we seem to have forgotten this.

***

On balance, Malaysia's and Singapore's economies have progressed so much since the oil crisis of the mid-1970s, when Pak Zamin got his lucky break. For anyone who has lived through the past 40 years, the two countries must be now completely unrecognisable.

There are countless symbols of this progress, from the gleaming Petronas Twin Towers, until recently the tallest building in the world, from where one can peer over "Kuala Lumpur", literally a bowl of mud, that has become one of Asia's most dynamic cities; to Singapore's Marina Bay Sands development—an "integrated resort" which just happens to have scores of poker tables—the most bold, brash statement yet that this tiny city state intends to compete with the big boys.

Nevertheless, despite these monuments to capitalism, both countries are still in the midst of massive economic transitions. Malaysia is trying to improve its human capital and innovative capabilities, so as to draw more investment, move up the value chain and become more competitive on the international stage.

Singapore is trying to become more of a service- and knowledge-based economy while switching its source of growth from trade to more domestic demand, i.e. rather than relying on exports to American and Chinese consumers, we want tourists, locals and companies spending their money right here.

As I've travelled through the two countries, and heard about the economic challenges and business risks that both face, it has slowly become clear that a lot of issues hark back to our original developmental blueprint, and the incentives they created.

For instance, consider Singapore, which from the start pursued a dogged, Darwinian meritocracy, where the strongest are rewarded and the weakest sidelined.

Harsh rules govern society, and within that framework, certain companies and individuals have achieved phenomenal success. Singapore's mantra: we live and breathe *efficiency*.

However, the major failure of this supposedly efficient system is that it does not reward ideas and skills outside the rigid framework. Creativity might have been spurred a long time ago if Singapore's educators had known how to reward the stuttering student who fails paper tests, but aces video games.

Instead, our social structure discourages people from attempting anything radical or revolutionary. Just keep your head down, and do your job. Sure, it is efficient, but it is a sort of robotic, numbing efficiency, not a creative, vibrant one.

Furthermore, that hardnosed Darwinian meritocracy has also given rise to one of the most unequal societies on the planet. It is hard to feel smug about "progress" when those at the back are being left further and further behind.

Finally, a series of embarrassing screw-ups, including allowing Mas Selamat, a suspected terrorist, to escape from a detention centre and debilitating breakdowns on Singapore's train system, have raised serious questions about whether Singapore is really as *efficient* as it once was.

On the other hand, Malaysia has been trying to develop while redistributing income via its *bumiputera* policies. Consequently, a lot of problems today stem from this ineffective redistribution—the policy itself has become the problem.

This is a system based on giving aid to a particular group—while this sort of development may eventually reduce economic disparities, it cannot sustain itself, because in the end it leads to *inefficiency*.

Malaysia's system offers relatively few incentives for studying hard, getting the best degrees, and then working diligently towards earning lots of money. Instead, it is often about patronage—finding a political leader who has access to a government contract. And even in Malaysia, there just aren't that many political leaders.

Singapore's system has incentivised a narrow definition of "work" and "success", while Malaysia's system has incentivised a system of patronage. These are both symptoms of our original design—and we have yet to break free.

The main reason is "implementation", the big bogeyman in Malaysian economic discourse. Speak with any Malaysian analyst or commentator, and they will tell you the same thing. Malaysia's problem is not a lack of good ideas about how to develop the economy. In fact, if anything, there are too many ideas floating around—and not enough brave souls to *implement* them. For years, Malaysia has been talking about making itself more competitive. Yet politicians and business leaders, often captured by short-term interest, fail to implement and follow through.

Although Singapore is good at implementing policies, we are less good at reinventing ourselves. Despite the recent hullabaloo about productivity, entrepreneurship, and creativity, these are all issues that have been around for the past decade. In his 2001 national day rally speech, Goh Chok Tong, our prime minister, spoke about how "[i]n the next phase of our development, Singaporeans have to be more entrepreneurial".

For umpteen years now, politicians have been going on about the need to emulate Creative Technologies—it is embarrassing that we keep hailing a decent company that was founded in the 1980s. For a long time now, Singapore has been well aware of the need to liberalise our society and economy. Yet there have been hardly any new "Creatives". For all the talk, we simply have not had the political will or individual courage to open up.

Thus, in order to overcome our economic challenges, Malaysia and Singapore require fundamental changes in the way our societies operate. Our DNAs, formed 40-odd years ago, are preventing us from advancing. Malaysia has to rid itself of the "Malays are downtrodden and they need help" mentality. And Singapore has to move beyond the "government knows best so citizens keep quiet and follow" way of doing things.

When people speculate about the benefits of Malaysia and Singapore reuniting, it is often the visible assets that are presumed worth sharing. Malaysia has lots of land, labour and natural commodities, so it goes, that tiny, resource-starved Singapore needs. Conversely, Singapore has transportation linkages, including a major seaport, as well as skill sets and methods of governance that Malaysia needs.

Less talked about are the mindsets and philosophies that we can share, that will help improve each other's development. Malaysian society appears much more tolerant and welcoming of people with unconventional skills. Malaysians have also long been aware of the need to help those at the bottom of the income ladder (though that agenda has often been hijacked by corrupt elements). Singapore society, meanwhile, has always placed a premium on meritocracy, and on the importance of building a race- and religion-neutral economy.

There must be something there worth copying.

Malayan Civet, one of the many casualties on Malaysia's roads

s shack in Nenasi, one of our best stays (see p. 243)

Young Malaysian boys are often the most excited to see us

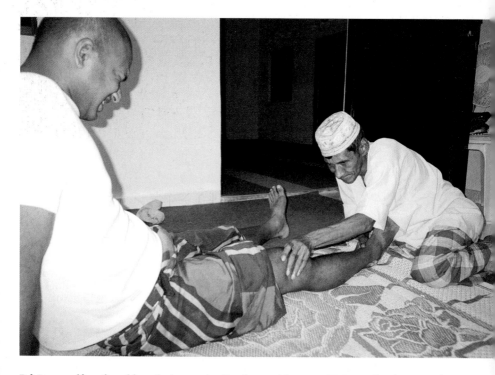

Pak Long, self-professed *bomoh*, shaman, healing Sumana's knee in FELDA Endau (see p. 203)

...nal, our regal host in FELDA Endau (see p. 37)

Chatting with a *nelayan*, fisherman, in Kuala Kedah (see p. 54)

…an lamenting climate change and overfishing, which are depleting fish stocks

…r young Puteri UMNO members in Kota Bahru, Kelantan (see p. 117)

In a Thai border town, a prostitute whose main clients are Malaysians

A doll-maker from Malacca's Chitty Indian community, one of Malaysia's smallest ethnic groups

en Gan, co-founder of *Malaysiakini*, Malaysia's leading alternative news site (see p. 98)

Nurul Izzah, vice president of PKR, one of Malaysia's main opposition parties (see p. 63)

eting a former Communist Party of Malaya guerilla in Betong, Thailand

Where Communist cadres once exchanged vows

Proud mother invited us—and 2,000 others—for her son's wedding in Kuala Kedah

...gs plague Malaysian society; here, a glue sniffer

Days before the 2008 Malaysian general elections

Female PAS supporters dress more conservatively; female UMNO supporters often wear makeup

rate checkout lines for males and females at supermarkets in Kelantan

npoo ads in Kelantan cannot show hair

Malaysia has traditionally sided with Palestine, Singapore with Israel

Painted bamboo shophouse blinds, almost extinct in modern Singapore, but still found all over Malaysia

t Malaysians have a high degree of tolerance for each other's religions

Playing *sepak takraw*, literally "kick cane ball", in Tanjong Tokong, Penang

8
Colour matters

The Malays are spiritually inclined, tolerant and easy-going. The non-Malays, and especially the Chinese, are materialistic, aggressive and have an appetite for work. For equality to come about, it is necessary that these strikingly contrasting races adjust to each other.
—Mahathir Mohamad, *The Malay Dilemma*, 1970[1]

"What race are you?"

Whether it be the old, regal *ketua*, village chief, in the humid *kampung* in Kota Tinggi; the sinewy Malay tobacco picker in Pahang, with blood-shot eyes and home-brew in hand; the sharp-tongued Chinese businessman in Kuala Terengganu, who juggled three mobile phones while offering us "girls from anywhere in the world"; or the chatty, chic twenty-something-year-old Malay bank executive in Kuala Lumpur, who had been "wild" while studying in the UK, but now, back in Malaysia, had become more pious, and had decided to wear a *tudung* to "protect her modesty".

All of them, and many other people I met in Malaysia, wanted to know what *race* I am; it was part of their greeting, the way an airline attendant asks to see your passport. After a while, I even got used to the many stunned reactions—"Huh? Really? You don't look Indian." Many thought I am Arab or White. When I explained that my mother is from North India, a common reaction was, "Oh, you're Hindustani." As opposed to "Indian", which in Malaysia is a term reserved mostly for South Indians.

The awareness of race and religion has been ingrained in us, and underlie every interaction in Malaysia and Singapore. Despite their importance—or, rather, because of—they are rarely discussed in public life, and have become taboo topics in both countries.

How did that happen? The 13th of May 1969, the day Malaysia and Singapore changed. To understand any contemporary issue regarding race or religion in our countries, one has to view it through the prism of that day, when post-election racial riots ripped the multi-ethnic fabric of our countries.

And it wasn't just a case of two, newly independent countries experiencing growing pains—the events of 13 May 1969 would come to define the views and a downhill race on Super Mario Kart, or Speed Racer, slaloming around giant tortoises, but worried about potholes and bumps. One error could send us flying, flailing, at more than 50 km per hour. Sheer adrenaline.

The best moments came when there were two trucks, one in each direction, and we cut between them, through a gap which was wide enough to tempt us, yet narrow enough to kill us, should we put one foot wrong.

But what a gap it is. The moment you enter the space between two trucks, it feels like you are hitting a vacuum, sound just dries up and gets sucked out. All you hear is a burst, similar to that when you first jump into a swimming pool. Or like when you pour Coke into a glassful of ice. A loud fizz that gradually diminishes.

No onomatopoeic device can capture this sound. Each time we treated ourselves to a Coke during the rest of the trip, we would close our eyes and listen, transported back to those few precious seconds in the truck vacuum.

Careening down the chicanes of a mountain does have one distinct disadvantage to climbing slowly uphill. We travelled about the same distance, but the enjoyment was ephemeral. The trip up the hill took hours of strenuous thigh-pumping action. Downhill, however, went by in a matter of minutes. Before we knew it, our downhill race was over, and we found ourselves on the wrong side of Lady Gravity yet again.

The approach to Pulau Banding is dramatic. The island sits in a reservoir that is wrapped around by tall mountains, like a little droplet in a huge bowl.

As soon as we crossed the bridge into Banding, there was a jetty on our right. The boats were mostly painted the same worn and cracked light blue colour. It was late afternoon, and the placid rocking of the boats was the only activity in sight. We rested for a while there, before showering at the only petrol station, a few minutes cycle away, in the middle of the island. Led by our stomachs, and not wanting to worry about where to sleep, we ate at a *warung* nearby.

The sun had set, and darkness was rapidly reaching pitch black. These were not ideal tent-pitching conditions. Worse, there was nowhere to sleep at the *warung* where we had just eaten; we were told to leave.

It seems implausible now that one would be looking for a place to sleep around the physical premises of a restaurant, scouting the place while having dinner, but at that moment, in that frame of mind, it was the most natural thing to do. Seeing that there was no respite for the night, we went back to where we were at dusk, a jetty by the edge of the *Tasik*.

We walked towards the first boathouse, when suddenly two figures emerged from the darkness, coming towards us. One of them was a Malay, dressed in tight jeans, with a red cap that kept his long hair tucked behind his neck. The other was an Indian, and we could barely make out his features because of the low light. Two bulbous eyes stared at us.

"Eh, what are you fellows doing here?" asked the Indian youth, rather forcefully.

"Er … erm … we are two Singaporeans cycling around Malaysia …"

"Two Singaporeans?" He came closer and shone his torchlight at our faces. "Are you Indian?"

"Yes!" we both chorused, triumphantly, excitedly, assuming that this would be a good answer.

He flicked his torchlight across our faces once again, like an immigration officer peeking into a car. Nervous, and with a light in our faces, we just kept quiet. Finally we saw the whites of his eyes bobbing up and down, as he nodded with satisfaction. His torso relaxed, and his voice softened.

"OK, good, you guys want a place to stay? Not a problem, you can stay on the boat. Just go and tell my friend. No problem letting some *machas* [brothers] stay with us. Lock your bicycles somewhere also. I will be back in a while. You guys want some food?" he asked briskly, obviously in a rush.

"No, it's OK, we just ate."

"Are you sure? OK, I see you in a while, I have to go and make a telephone call," Das said as he walked away, hopped onto his Malay friend's motorcycle, and sped off into the darkness.

At that moment, a flood of relief washed over us. It felt nice to be accepted. We were also swollen with Indian pride, and immediately felt a bond with Das and every one of his friends who we had never met. We were swept up in a roaring wave of Indian communalism. It felt great.

Moreover, we felt like insiders because he had called us *macha*. Machan, often pronounced "macha", means brother-in-law in Tamil, but is used colloquially to refer to friends. It connotes a bond stronger than just "friend". We used it in secondary school, both among Tamils and some non-Tamils, but rarely since then. Like so many of Singapore's other vernacular treasures, "macha" seems destined for extinction. It is being replaced, quite worryingly, by "dude".

Filled with gratitude, we quickly locked up our bicycles next to the boathouse, unhinged our bags and brought them onboard. A fat, bearded Indian youth dressed in a white t-shirt and black football shorts was seated in front of a wooden island in the middle of the boathouse, just behind the rudder. He appeared uninterested in us, and the three of us barely talked; the TV proved a welcome distraction, as we focused on a Copa America game in which a young Gabriel Heinze was about to partake in the last act of the drama that is a penalty shoot-out.

In the following days, months and years, as we pondered that racial examination we had been thrust into, it has always filled us with a mix of emotions. What if we were Chinese? Would he have kicked us out? Why did we feel such strong Indian pride? Or was it just relief? Do those communal sentiments linger somewhere deep inside all of us, waiting for the right situation and circumstances?

Forty-five minutes later, Das returned carrying a red plastic bag.

"What did you buy?" asked Elangowan.

"Normal lah, *roti canai kosong dua, tambah gravy* [two plain rotis with extra gravy]," said Das.

After they ate, Das made us all a pot of steaming, hot *teh*, into which he ladled dollops of condensed milk. He was skinny and tall, with a curled moustache destined for handlebar greatness.

"Have you guys ever had *teh* with fresh milk or not?"

"Like from a carton of fresh milk?"

"No lah. I mean fresh like fresh from a cow's *tetek* man," he said, squeezing his own nipples with relish. "That kind of fresh."

"Ah, no lah, never man."

"I *kena* with fresh milk before, that was dang good, man!"

Das' tomfoolery relaxed Elangowan, who began to chat more freely. We spoke a bit about our Singapore Indian backgrounds, and what we were doing in the middle of nowhere in Malaysia.

"This is not like most of the Singaporeans we have met," quipped Das. "You guys are doing this for school? I decided long ago that school was not for me. After Form 5 I decided that it was time for me to work. I went to work at KFC and Gowan went to work at Pizza Hut, so that we could share each other's food. Do you know that I was the top national KFC chef? Yes. I cannot remember when, I think it was in 1997, but I entered the national competition for KFC chefs."

Das was getting revved up as he retold this yarn from yesteryear; Elangowan just smiled, and waited expectantly and excitedly for a story he had heard many times. This is one of the tribulations of not being far from your best friend, but in Elangowan's case, it was a welcome repetition.

"There are two fifteen-minute rounds and we are split into teams of three. One works the register, one does the cooking and one serves. I got the cashier's job in the first round—I finished my job with two minutes left on the clock, so you know what I did?"

"What?"

"I started polishing my boots," Das said, scrubbing the air above his feet with his closed fingers, the same ones which had earlier milked his nipples.

"I thought we would surely win. But the second round, we were up against these Korean girls, and I tell you, I have never seen anything like it, *macha*. When they finished their tasks, you know what they did? They started putting on their make-up for the next round. Bloody hell man, they got to go to the KFC HQ in the US; and we had to go to bloody Sunway College (in KL). No bikini girls there I tell you, no bikini girls there."

Das' hopes of representing Malaysia at the KFC international cook-off had been dashed by Korean efficiency. But he had gotten that far through sheer hard work. "I tell you, education does not matter. Dedication matters, you have to be committed to something."

Das did not care for education? He'd be considered a heretic in Singapore. We all bought into education—perhaps because it offered opportunities to all, or maybe because, as one of our secondary school teachers had said, "[i]t gives us a way of putting inequality into a grading scale." Singapore's educational institutions socialise children into our meritocratic system. Malaysia's educational system, by contrast, makes racial divisions more pronounced.

Das' point, which he reiterated several times during our 18 hours together, was that education did not matter without dedication. However, with dedication, one could overcome a lack of education.

"I am a firm believer in the Indian race. I attend many of these Indian development seminars and I am always disappointed when the speaker says that we have to raise the profile of Indians in the community. I think this is the wrong strategy. We should begin by saying that we are proud of who we are and then only think about how we can improve ourselves."

From our conversations with Das and others, it was clear that many Malaysian Indians lacked self-belief and pride. Why is this? The simple explanation, which we've heard many times, is that in Malaysia, the Malays have the political power, the Chinese have the economic power, and the Indians get stuck with the short end of the stick. Years of living as third-class citizens have drained the energy, confidence and verve of the people.

According to Tommy Thomas, a lawyer in KL, the reality is a bit more complex. "The Indians in Malaysia are not just the Tamils from the South. Those compromise 80 per cent of the Indian population, and the other 20 per cent comprise mainly of Jaffna Tamils, Malayalees and Sikhs.

For reasons pertaining mostly to the way the colonialists divided and ruled, the latter 20 tend to be better off today. They were in administrative positions during the colonial era and that gave them a bit of a leg up. Largely, when we talk about the Indian community that has been left behind, we are talking about the 80 per cent of Tamils. They worked in the plantations. They have not progressed much."

The Indian plantation worker—mostly rubber tappers—once lived decently in cosy, self-contained plantation communities. They were forced out by two broader trends: mechanisation and later, the switch from rubber to more profitable oil palm. Jobless, many were forced to fend for themselves on the fringes of Malaysia's urban societies, often without documentation: nameless, stateless remnants of colonialism.

Lacking money, direction and any form of social capital, they and their descendants have not been able to cope. Some social scientists note similarities between their urban struggle and that of poor African-American communities in large US cities, particularly with the emergence of ethnic Indian ghettos in KL.

It was not surprising that someone like Das might have given up on "education". As far as he was concerned, Malaysia's educational system had done nothing to improve the lot of poor Indians. Better to find a job and work hard.

We didn't quite understand this whole Indian pride thing though. "You say you hold up Ananda Krishnan as a hero, and maybe he is, but for every Ananda, for every Tony Fernandes, there are thousands of Indians who are not doing as well? Surely it's important to deal with that, rather than just saying all Indians should be proud?"

"Eh, what do you guys mean? Typical *mamas* man, let you come into the boat for free, also like that. Why, you not happy ah?" He raised his voice a bit; we couldn't tell if he was trying to intimidate us or not.

"Well, of course we're happy that let us into your boat. But you checked if we were Indian. Would you have turned us away if we were *angmoh* or Chinese or Malay?"

"No … wouldn't have turned you down, but I would have definitely asked you pay like that!" he chuckled.

"But why? Can't you just see us as something else, like just as cyclists? Why must it be Indian or not?"

"*Macha*, we got to take care of our own, *macha*. If we don't, who will?"

"So you are proud of everything that Indians do?"

"No man, not all the time, lah. You know what I don't understand? Why do the Indians always think that life is a bloody movie?"

As we drank their thick sweet tea and puffed on their Dunhill cigarettes, Das entertained us with stories of Indians, those which filled him with shame. One was about a girl who was crying while chugging something on the edge of a football field where Das was playing. "After a while I went over to her and I realised that this stupid bitch I tell you, she had swallowed poison *deh*! Bloody *pundeh*!"

He saved her, apparently, by flushing her with orange juice before another friend drove her to the hospital. "The whole way, aiyoh, saying how her boyfriend had dumped her, how her life was over, she might as well be dead. Stupid girl I tell you, watch too many fucking Tamil movies."

He took a drag of his cigarette, looked at us with a slightly lowered head and raised his eyebrows quizzically while making a small upward gesture with his palm. "You know how the story ends? In the end, she got married to my friend who drove her to the hospital. Amma!" he shouted, stretching his fingers out as far away from each other as possible and slapping his forehead, which, oddly, elicited the exact same response in us.

But with that kind of excitement, why did Das leave the city for the jungle? "Of course life here and life in the city is different. I had this boss in the city when I worked another job, this Chinese man, and when he offered me this opportunity, I straightaway called Elangowan and asked him to come here as well.

I don't want to be stuck in the city for the rest of my life with some low paying job. The pay here is good, not a lot or what, but we save a lot of money here, why? Because there is nothing to spend it on. I want to go back with my savings and open up some 7-11s in the city," Das answered confidently.

"We have many hopes and dreams with this place, we don't want it to be just a tourist boathouse. But the Indians in Malaysia are not ready for this kind of eco-tourism thing lah. They are more content to sit at the *roti canai* store and set records for the best twirling of the *roti canai*," he mumbled with some measure of irritation.

"But also I tell you something," now defensive of his frustration, "Indians do not want to go and do the same thing that other people have done already. They might not have learnt to appreciate adventure travel yet, but also, they do not want to simply go and do the same thing as others, like just simply go and climb Mt. Everest, no ... they want to do something *different*."

At the time, Das could not have known how prescient his words would prove. In 2007, three years after we met him, a group of Indians were doing exactly that—something different. Hindraf was the third group to protest within a period of three months. You could say that it was a season of protests.

With the rise of Hindraf, it looks as though the genie has finally been let out. Fall 2007, the season for protests in Malaysia, precisely 50 years after the country gained its independence from the British, may one day be remembered as the time when its delicate racial experiment began to unravel.

***

Tanjung Tokong, Penang. 2 August 2004.

"Things here are the same as everywhere else. Penang is no different," said 73-year-old Ramli, who had graciously ushered us into the mosque for a chat. His long, wispy white hair seemed to be growing right out of his princely purple and gold *songkok*. Along with a deep brown shirt and black sarong, he was looking resplendent after his late afternoon prayers.

"We love living in Penang. It is a beautiful city. We have the beach, good food, the old city. It doesn't matter if there are more Chinese than Malays here. We have the same government. We have the same policies. Life for Malays is much better in Penang than in Singapore." This was a familiar refrain—many Malaysian Malays we met were sure that they are much better off than their Singaporean Malay brethren.

"But what exactly do you think about the *bumiputera* system? In Singapore, we have a meritocracy. If you're good enough, you'll get in and you can do the job. Since I am an Indian, perhaps Singapore is a better place for me then?"

"Yes, but you must understand why we help the *pribumi*. We are the sons of Malaysia! It is not right that so much of our wealth is owned by other races, people who came here after we did. This is our land! The *bumiputera* policies are to help the people at the bottom, every city tries to do the same thing, right? Once the people are brought up, their minds start to run, their wheels start to turn.

We have the *bumiputera* policy because we believe that the different races should be equal! Our people were disadvantaged to begin with. This is a way of raising our levels to that of the others. That's all. There is nothing unfair about it. It is meant to make people equal, the same.

Last time, there were no Malays working at the bank. Now we do have some. Our studies have improved a lot too. Last time, we had no house, no car. Now we do! Look at that little boy over there, riding his bicycle. We never had a bicycle when we were young."

Two other Malay men had joined us at the table, occasionally chipping in. Encounters with old Malay men were in many ways the most comfortable and informative—they were unburdened by the bravado we faced in younger men, or the shyness we found in women. Each in the group would take great pride in presenting Malaysia to us.

Even the reticent ones eventually opened up. They exuded warmth that made us, their guests, feel at home. Time passed effortlessly between words, there was never a forced conversation to fill a void—old Malay men somehow always felt comfortable in a shared silence.

Tanjung Tokong, the little neighbourhood we were in, had about 5,000 inhabitants, most of whom lived in flats. The community once boasted many fishermen, before development cajoled them away from their nets. The little *masjid* next to us was the focal point, and a slow stream of people shuffled in and out, all saying hello to the old Malay uncles and their strange, sweaty cyclist friends. The *masjid* had served the Tanjung Tokongers well—it was a haven during World War II, when many locals sought refuge within its holy walls.

"I don't know if life is better in Singapore," a Malay man to our right argued, "Singapore is not a real democracy, you can't really say what you want, right?" We met several people in Malaysia who, in the middle of a chat about jobs or development, would start comparing "democracy" in our countries. We could never tell if it is because "democracy" matters so much to them, or if they just needed some justification for their decision to live in Malaysia.

"In Malaysia, we don't really look at somebody's race, this is a democracy. In Malaysia, ten of us can sit together and chat, there's no problem. In Singapore once more than four people are together, there is a problem. Right?" His eyes lit up, wanting us to acknowledge our archaic public assembly law. We kept quiet.

"In Malaysia we all realise that we have to respect each other, that we have to take care of all the different *bangsa* [races]. Otherwise we will never live happily. We always remember what happened in May 1969. Malays in Singapore are different. They have to struggle for everything. It is not the same for us."

Ramli interjected before we could respond, "Yes, but as with everything, there are the pros and cons of our *pribumi* policies lah. We *pribumi* might have certain advantages, but the danger is that everything is spoon-fed to us. You know, a father cannot always give his child food. If you keep giving, the child becomes lazy. So, in a way, many Malays here have become lazy. We take things for granted. That's why the Malays in Australia and Singapore are more capable in a way. They have to take care of themselves, achieve things on their own. They are forced to work harder."

"But we are in a difficult situation lah. If you stop giving, the people here are going to complain! They have gotten used to the support. You know, if a Malay here moves elsewhere, they'll struggle to survive!"

***

In half an hour, Ramli had described the contemporary Malay Dilemma. Many Malays I meet do feel that the New Economic Policy (NEP, the affirmative action policy that gives preference to the *bumiputeras*) has been necessary: because it is, first and foremost, *their* country, and because they are economically disadvantaged.[3] Some form of affirmative action was and still is needed to equalise their lot.

Importantly, most do not see this as an unfair leg up in life. In their eyes, fairness is the impetus behind the NEP, not racism. If left to the free market, the Malays will always be behind. Something has to be done to narrow the gap.

However, many Malays are also acutely aware that the community has become lazy and dependent on state handouts. Many do not want to put in the work required to go the extra yard. Individual motivation and drive have been hopelessly eroded by this collective bonanza. Furthermore, Malaysia's social fabric is being torn apart.

The Chinese and Indians feel like second class citizens, and are not as invested in the pro-Malay country as they might have been in a meritocracy.

All this has left Malaysia in a real social quagmire. Supporters of the NEP say it is a fair way of letting the poorer, weaker segments of society rise up. Critics say it's a racist programme that has done little to raise the standard of living of the average Malay. Rather, it has created systems of patronage, and only benefited a small cadre of Malay leaders. Who is right? From what I've seen, it's done a lot more harm than good.

When the NEP was created, two of its goals were to reduce poverty and inequality, and to "reduce and eventually eliminate the identification of race with economic function".[4] Presumably this would ease racial tensions, and help prevent a repeat of 13 May 1969. Given the rise of Hindraf, and groups like Perkasa, a Malay nationalist outfit, I wonder whether racial harmony has improved at all.

The night before, our charming outspoken young host Sam had revealed a quiet pride that Penangites feel about their identity. But it was KL, not Singapore, that was their mirror, their basis for comparison. KL was too hectic, too urbanised, too polluted. Sure, KL was Malaysia's lead city: business hub, government centre, tallest buildings and Formula 1 races. But it was also a commercialised den whose soul was seeping away. Much too crowded yet somehow everybody seemed further apart.

Penang, says Sam, has the best of both worlds. Developed enough, yet still quaint. Bursting at the seams with a hodge-podge of cultures. Clean, green environment. Lots more greenery. Where you're as likely to spend your Saturday afternoon at a glitzy mall as at the idyllic beach. Penang has it all.

Penang is also the place I have encountered the most support for the *bumiputera* policy.[5] Not only from Malays like Ramli, but from many Chinese too. "Without the *bumiputera* policy, the Malays simply won't be able to compete with us," says Eric, a hip Chinese guy in his mid-twenties. In late 2005, I had spent the evening bar-hopping through Penang with Eric. A little tipsy, having danced the night away, but with his spiky, gelled hair still perfectly in place, Eric spoke freely about how Malays were "racially inferior". This, in his mind, justified the *bumiputera* policy.

Of course, we did bump into a few Chinese along the way, including Mun Ching, who are strongly opposed to the *bumiputera* policy. But the average one accepted it all with a certain measure of sang-froid, either because he/she felt that Malays will find it difficult to survive without it; or because they felt that the Chinese in Malaysia already have enough in their pockets.

***

My biggest dilemma in writing this book has been how to deal with the topic of race. For years, both our countries have conveniently swept it under the carpet.

Our governments, our media channels, our corporations, our civic organisations—everybody, really, prefers not to talk about racial issues.

That may seem at odds with the fact that we have meticulously managed race-based policies. After all, Malaysia and Singapore are countries where race is a cornerstone of an individual's identity, and where each person's life decisions and pathways—from school to housing to work—are profoundly influenced by what race he or she is. Surely in such countries race is a major topic of debate?

In a sense, it is. Our countries' race-based policies are the product of years of thought, conversation, policy discussion, conflict and reconciliation. However, for the most part, these discussions have been conducted by a small cabal of senior policymakers. As a result, Malaysia and Singapore have each created unique ethno religious rulebooks which govern our societies, and by which ordinary citizens live their lives.

For instance, in Malaysia, a bright Chinese student may not get into university because its Chinese quota is used up. Similarly, in Singapore, the government might prevent an Indian family from buying a public housing flat in a particular neighbourhood where there are already too many Indians. Outsiders may find some of our policies bizarre—we take them for granted.

However, nobody wants to discuss or hear about the racial problems with the system. For instance, in Malaysia, I've attended conferences where senior businessmen and government officials talk about the challenges facing the country. In the quiet siderooms and tea breaks, there is a lot of chatter about the need to reform the *bumiputera* system. However, once everybody enters the main conference room, where Mister-So-and-So may be listening, nobody dares whisper the word *bumi*. Since the rise of Hindraf and the 2008 general elections, people do discuss sensitive issues such as race more in Malaysia—but the situation is still far from ideal.

Similarly, in Singapore, we assume that a race-neutral meritocracy will lead to the best socio-economic outcomes for the country. However, nobody wants to compare the real opportunities available to lower-income Indians vs. Malays vs. Chinese. Nobody likes to discuss why we prevent Malay Muslims from enlisting in certain "high-security" branches of our military. And nobody really tries to dispel ethnic stereotypes that float around.

Our governments prefer to dampen discussion of these issues partly because they worry that simple chats can play on grievances and escalate quickly into provocative rhetoric. Every democracy has to find this balance between freedom of speech and the desire not to offend—Malaysia and Singapore have long chosen to lean well in favour of the latter. In this way, we are guided by the passion, the chaos and the paranoia of the 1960s.

This ultra-conservatism may have helped douse the flames of ethnic tensions in the 1960s and 1970s. But it has also prevented a richer, deeper inter-ethnic dialogue from developing.

For example, consider this passage from *Death of a Democracy*, a book about the 13 May 1969 riots:[6]

> In 1950, during the Korean war, the demand for natural rubber caused a boom on the world markets; rubber prices soared. They rose to more than two dollars a pound; the highest figure that year was M$2.38. The attitudes of the three racial groups to this considerable increase were very different and highlight the differences in racial temperament.
>
> The Chinese rubber tappers went out every day in family strength and they tapped every tree as often as they could; they collected every drop of latex they found and many of them quickly made a small fortune. They banked their money or they bought gold which they hid in their houses.
>
> The Indians behaved in the same way, tapping as much and as frequently as possible but few of them made any attempt to save their earnings. With unexpected wealth they bought new clothes, saris for their wives, expensive brands of cigarettes; they bought refrigerators for houses where there was no electricity and then used them as cupboards; some of them bought second-hand cars to drive to the rubber fields.
>
> In contrast to all this activity and business, the Malay villager calculated that if, when the price of rubber was one dollar a pound, he had to work twenty days in the month to make a living, then, when the price rose to two dollars it was necessary for him to work only ten days for the same money. So, while the Chinese and the Indians tapped more and worked harder, the Malays worked less and passed their time in a more leisurely manner. The Malay has an infinite capacity for enjoying the simple pleasures of his kampong life. The rubber boom was 19 years ago. Now he is being forced to become more conscious of his country's economy but there is still no indication that he is becoming more industrious.
>
> The Chinese are far more numerous than the Indians and their control of industry and commerce is greater; for this reason the Malays fear the Chinese more. The Chinese have economic power which the Malays resent.

This book, by John Slimming, was banned almost as soon as it was published, shortly after the riots. Presumably such passages were deemed too inflammatory. The interesting thing is that so many Malaysians and Singaporeans I have met share similar perceptions of the three ethnic groups. With little public dialogue, these stereotypes fester away.

Thus, during our bicycle trip in 2004, through our subsequent research trips and conversations, and ultimately in the very writing of this book, this issue plagued me relentlessly. How much can I talk about "race"? Having grown up here, my instinct is perhaps to not think or say much about it.

Nevertheless, every time I pondered this issue, whether in front of an interviewee or typing at my computer, I came to the same conclusion: I must tell the real stories—which is why I need to talk about Anthony, the church warden in Kuantan.

***

Kuantan, Pahang. 18 July 2004.

Kuantan was the first major city we visited in 2004, while cycling up the East coast of Malaysia—it was there that we first realised how difficult it is to find a spot in a big city to sleep.

Before Kuantan, we had stayed in Kota Tinggi, Mersing, Endau, and Nenasi, relative backwaters with plots aplenty. In Kota Tinggi we pitched our tent on gravel, across from the only *warung* in a small village called Kampung Makam, after an audience with the local *ketua*, village chief, who checked our passports over tea and then welcomed us in; he had tried to squeeze RM40 out of us for a proper room, but then offered the gravel when we mentioned our budget.

In Mersing we stumbled upon a football match at the local stadium. After the game was over and the caretakers had left, we snuck back in and slept on the stands, braving the bite of mosquitoes and the glare of distant street lights. In Endau, we fortuitously met Kamal, who let us sleep in the *surau*, the prayer room, in the village. In Nenasi we had our pick of spots from acres of gorgeous sand by an unspoiled beach.

In Kuantan, we were at a loss. We cycled around the dense streets, soaking in the buzz, finding little in way of accommodation, i.e. a quiet corner where nobody will bother us. We sat on a stand at the central *padang*, field, to plan our next move.

These moments were the most stressful. Drained after a day of cycling, it was tough to muster the drive to go hunting for a nightspot. These mini-expeditions involved a constant scanning of streets; an incredible amount of luck; and numerous conversations with random folk, most of whom had no answer for the 'tired cyclists looking for a free bed'.

On occasion, we were blessed with divine intervention. It happened the night before Kuantan, at the *surau* in Endau, and so we decided to try again, this time entering St Thomas Catholic Church in Kuantan.

It was in this desperate mood that we first saw Anthony. He was standing outside the Father's house in the night talking to a moustachioed Indian friend. They were slightly disgruntled, as they bade farewell to two sheepish looking blokes. "Goodbye, and don't ever come back," Anthony's friend muttered. We later found out that these

Sarawakians were supposed to do some work for the church, but then complained that they "can't work in the sun."

When Anthony saw us, he greeted us with a childlike smile, a luminescent glow we'd see many more times that night.

"Er, excuse me uncle, but do you know where we can find a Mar Thoma Church around here?" we asked.

"Mar Thoma Church?"

Instead of asking for a bed directly, we had the brainy idea of name dropping my Keralan church, in hope of some Christian camaraderie. Both the gentlemen chuckled ever so slightly. We later found out that it was a bit like asking a Mancunian for directions to Liverpool.

"I don't think there is a Mar Thoma Church around here boys, but there might be a Mar Thoma house." We were pummelled with directions: head up this road, hang a left, no stay left when the road goes right, take the hill up, it should be one of the houses there. Go to a house where you can see a cross on the outside and ask.

"Well, we will be here for a while, just go and try and check for the house, if you cannot find it, come back here. We will see what we can do." The gleam of Anthony's smile suggested that, despite our Mar Thoma faux pas, we might have a chance of sleeping there.

After cycling around for 15 minutes without much luck, we decided to do the sensible Singaporean thing—eat a bowl of *wan tan* noodles, at a small roadside stall which, in the dark, drizzly Kuantan night, seemed to scream out our name. Stomachs full, we returned to St Thomas Church, hopeful that Anthony would act as the bed of last resort.

"You found what? A noodle shop?" Anthony smiled. Ten minutes later, we were standing in a room with two steel spring beds with thin, uncovered mattresses on top, a small wooden side table, and several cockroaches scurrying around. In our hierarchy of random Malaysian nightspots, this was a few steps from heaven.

We told Anthony that we'd be off in the morning, perhaps after a quick tour of Kuantan. "Ah, I see, I see. It would be nice if you could wait for Father Eugene to return and just say thank you to him before you leave, that would be nice. And there is a little *roti canai* store round the corner if you want to get a late night snack or something as well, OK?"

Perfect. In the space of two hours, we had gone from bed-less distress to major comfort zone; our month on the road was littered with other similar, violent mood swings. We showered, in a proper shower, and got ready for bed. Anthony returned, to check on us, and was soon yakking away.

Anthony had short, salt-and-pepper hair, and a spiky beard, which looked like it was either unkempt or expertly manicured for a rough look. His ebony skin looked old and tired, and a handsome face sat behind a million wrinkles. He looked like Hemingway's Tamil brother, and in his tattered polo t-shirt, nylon slacks and flip-flops, one could easily picture him stranded on a beach somewhere, holding a bottle of whisky, not a care in the world. As it was, the only spirit he seemed to imbibe was a holy one.

Having lived in Kuantan for more than 60 years, Anthony has seen the place develop from relative obscurity into a bustling city. After half a century of lethargy, according to him, the pace of development spiked after 1997.

"Everything now here is 'development'. Everything. Even the fruit orchards are being destroyed. I tell you, houses here, a terrace house for example, used to cost thirteen kay, a semi-d maybe twenty-five. Now, my goodness, guess how much? $200,000, I tell you."

He spoke quickly, with a typically musical, South Indian intonation. He liked to answer his own questions before we could, after which he'd smile gently, giving his words time to sink in. He also used his smile as a defence mechanism, to parry questions he didn't like.

The villains in this property bubble drama were all too familiar. "There are a lot of foreigners buying land here. Singaporeans especially. Or, it might be Malaysians who work in Singapore, they will be rich enough to afford it."

That includes two of Anthony's three children, living and working in Singapore, supposedly because of the higher pay. Yet Anthony believes they will one day move back. "They miss the land most of all. They are not used to things being so crowded. They work a lot and then come home; they have a few friends, but they don't know their neighbours—that is a very strange feeling for them. I think they might come back when they have kids. Good place for kids, Singapore, but also, very expensive."

Anthony and his family had deep emotional bonds to St Thomas Church. They had all studied at the church school. Anthony himself had literally spent his whole life on the church compounds, in different capacities. The following morning he took great pride in pointing out old photographs of the church which were hanging on a wall, like a drill sergeant showing off his troops.

We asked if his wife, too, had studied there but he just smiled. Parry. When we asked about his third child, the son who lived in Kuantan, again he just smiled.

He smiled a lot during the first hour of our conversation. It was past midnight and it was slightly laborious trying to navigate around these smile parries. Yet as we chatted we realised that Anthony was just sizing us up, slowly revealing more and more of his life. He was guarded, but when he did speak about something, he did not mince his words.

"So what do you think of all these Singaporeans buying land here, Uncle?"

"Singaporeans are all idiots," smile canvassed, "because they think they are smarter than us. Sure lah, in 1969, I went to Singapore, took my one Malaysian ringgit and got one Singapore dollar. Now, I need two ringgit to get one dollar. They are condescending, they think they are all smarter than us. But they are also the ones who are always rushing in life. On the trains and the buses, nobody looks at you, nobody smiles at you ... I ... we, I don't think we could live like that."

Once when Anthony visited his daughter in Singapore, one of her neighbours came over and brought some *kampung* chicken as a gift. "So I told her, see! Some Singaporeans are quite nice. My daughter replied, '*Apa*—she's also Malaysian.'"

Food and food habits can tell a lot about a culture. Consider rice with different delightful dishes piled on top, which is one of the best things you can eat in Malaysia and Singapore. The Chinese, Indians and Malays have their own versions, which may be called, respectively, "economy rice", "banana leaf rice" and "*nasi campur*", mixed rice. Many of us eat simple forms of this at home every day—indeed, rice and curry got me through university abroad.

As we cycled across Malaysia, we would occasionally eat this when we needed a break from *roti canai*. Lots of rice, soaked with curry and maybe just one piece of chicken was about all we could afford. It was economical, carbo-heavy and pretty darn tasty.

But there is a telling difference in how Malaysians and Singaporeans serve these foods. In Malaysia, it is common practice at many food stalls, even restaurants in the big cities, to dish out your own servings from a selection of cooked foods. The stall owner hands you a plate of rice and points you towards the lavish buffet of colours that you've already been salivating over. You take exactly how much or little you want. The owner then performs a cursory calculation, always erring on the low side.

Singaporean chefs have applied an exacting science to this process. A server holds a plate of rice and waits in front of the many dishes for your instruction. You are forced to stand away, and to simply point or say what you want. The server, who must have a degree in food accounting, will then proceed to meticulously spoon an exact, pre-determined amount of the dish. No more, no less.

If the server, heaven forbid, scoops out just a little too much of the dish you want, he or she will carefully tilt the serving spoon over your plate of rice, to ensure that you don't get too much, before putting the rest back in the main dish. It is the "pragmatic" Singaporean at our calculating, Six Sigma best.

And with it vanishes the opportunity for a wonderful interaction between strangers. The Malaysian way of doing things may not make the most immediate business sense, but it pleases your customers and provides a genuine moment of warmth in the randomness of life. Sumana and I visited many small stalls in Malaysian, where the chef—often a charming, elderly Malay woman—would personally usher us in and hand us our plates of rice. You are really just eating in somebody's home.

In Singapore, well, as in so many other facets of life, we've reduced all that food camaraderie to just another transaction. Thank you, come again.

Anthony had lots of stories to tell. We spoke some more about the differences between Malaysians and Singaporeans, the characteristics of Malaysia's West Coast and East Coast, and about the Malaysia Cup, an annual inter-state football tournament. Singapore used to take part, and was actually pretty good, until we pulled out in 1994, in a somewhat foolhardy attempt to jumpstart our own local league.

Despite Singapore's tiny size, we have carved the city up into a fine mosaic of different teams, who then compete against one another. Few supporters feel any allegiance to particular teams—the league has been a dismal failure.

Football was once a great vehicle for Singaporeans to express their passion and national pride. Exit from the Malaysia Cup put an end to that; it also further softened our bond with Malaysia. Thankfully, after a 17-year hiatus, Singapore rejoined in 2012.

Chatting for hours, it seemed as if Anthony didn't often get a chance to open up and speak freely, perhaps because of the strictures of his somewhat insular, conservative church community life. With each passing crack about Singaporeans, which we sucked up in good humour, he was emboldened, and prodded even more.

In a sense, Anthony felt that his life had been on a slow downward trajectory. In the 1940s, as a young boy, he flourished briefly under the British, who "treated Indians very well". Then the "horrible" Japanese arrived. Anthony's family was one of the luckier ones, and they managed to get along by selling cakes.

Independence brought more uncertainty and, as a strapping young teenager, it wasn't at all clear to Anthony what the future held. Thankfully, as in every other difficult period in his life, he relied on God for guidance.

Finally, with the implementation of the *bumiputera* policies in the early 1970s, Anthony was sure that the pendulum had swung—or, as he put it, the bicycle spokes had turned.

"*Those* people," he said, his voice muddied with disdain, "those people, they used to squat by the drains and drink *kopi*. They have no dignity!"

Two hours earlier, when we asked about the different races in Malaysia, Anthony had just smiled.

"Those people were nothing. And then the *bumiputera* policies came, and they suddenly got a lot of money. They were not used to having money. They didn't know how to deal with it. And so they just spend lah. You know if we get some money, we are careful, we save. But they just spend. I tell you, that's why they have all these drug problems. Majority of addicts are the Malays lah."

According to Anthony, the *bumiputera* policies were an almighty injustice, because they amounted to a wealth transfer from the deserving to the undeserving. "I tell you, you see all these problems with teenage pregnancy. It's the same thing. They get money, they don't have to work. All those people, I tell you. *Those* people."

His voice was filled with bitterness, and the smiles had disappeared. He looked different from before, when he had been poking fun at Singaporeans. His face looked pained, angry, serious.

"So are the Indians jealous at all?"

"Jealous? No lah. Why should we be jealous? I call it the bicycle theory. It is like the spokes on a bicycle, with every turn someone else is the leader, with every turn there is a different group that enjoys a good time. Now it is the Malays turn to enjoy, I don't think the Indians are jealous of them."

"Really? We were reading in the newspapers that some Indians are unhappy."

"Of course, but it is not a majority. You could say that the British favoured the Indians also. But when you look at what the *bumiputera* policy has done for the Malays, I think there is no question about it. They have come out of poverty. Now it is their time to enjoy. The Malays used to never be able to afford anything, even to go to a coffee shop. But now, they have money and they are modernising."

"So it's good then?"

"Sure. It's good for *them*. But it's not fair. They don't deserve it. Those people don't deserve it."

Anthony went on for a while more, muttering away about the Malays. Every social and political problem seemed somehow to be related to *those people*. A lifetime of regret and despair bubbled out, and we just nodded our heads in return, prodding him on.

As he had grown older, and lived under the thumb of the British, then Japanese, then Malays, he had felt less and less faith in society; in turn, he had moved closer and closer to God and spent more time in church.

His view of the world, characterised by his bicycle theory of development, was depressing, to say the least. According to this idea, economic opportunity and wealth is a zero-sum game, played out amongst different ethnic groups, based on luck and timing.

The Malay bicycle spoke is up now, so the Indian one must necessarily be down. It is hence impossible for all to develop together. The Indians must simply sit tight and wait for their chance again, which will presumably come long after Anthony is gone.

Perhaps by extension, Anthony also did not think highly of Muslims. He is the only Malaysian I've met who approved of the invasion of Iraq. "We shouldn't judge America. All those Muslim countries have chemical weapons, they hide them, they use them whenever they want, and they sell them to whoever they want. Iraq is not easy to capture—a lot of Americans have died in the war!"

"Actually, if you think about it, America conducts itself honestly and with dignity. I tell you, if they wanted to win the war, all they have to do is drop a nuclear bomb, that's it. And what about those prison photos? People criticise them, but think about it. America had the honesty to show the rest of the world those photos. Can you imagine if it was an Islamic state where it happened? Nobody would have cared! They would have just slaughtered all the prisoners."

That is the only time I've heard the Abu Ghraib incident used to portray America in a positive light. As Anthony said goodnight, at around half past one, he looked calm.

The next morning Anthony showed us around the church. He sat us down underneath Father Eugene's room, where several generations of priests had lived. "In the old days", there was nothing but dirt and foliage underneath the house.

Previous priests had to climb up a rope ladder to get into the room—where they would be safe from all the wildlife that surrounded the church, including "the tigers, the snakes and the elephants". Anthony reminisced about playing alone underneath the bungalow, in the same spot where we were sitting now, catching spiders that hid in the crevices.

It was only days later, after we had interacted with many more Malaysians, that we realised how valuable our late-night palaver with Anthony was. Although we heard stories of disagreement between the races, about unhappiness with this or that policy, we never again got to peer into the soul of resentment.

It's tempting to single him out as the sole bigot in an otherwise calm society. But the truth is that he was simply the most open with us. We have met many others with similarly dim views of other races and religions. Few articulate their feelings as openly or clearly as Anthony. But we hear it, expressed differently, and sometimes get the feeling that there's more buried inside.

Many Malaysians we met believe in the idea behind Anthony's bicycle theory of development. That is one unfortunate consequence of the *bumiputera* policies. By mandating this wealth transfer to the *bumiputeras*, Malaysia has unwittingly cultivated the idea that in order for one race to progress, another one must be put down.

***

Some like to claim that Singapore has achieved some sort of post-racial harmony; a paradise where people of varying backgrounds co-exist peacefully, as our national pledge espouses, "regardless of race, language or religion."

There is some truth to this. Of his many achievements, Lee Kuan Yew's success in building a race-neutral meritocracy stands out—especially considering the race-conscious road which elder brother Malaysia was taking.

In Malaysia, we are much more conscious of our race than we are in Singapore. That's partly because so many people ask us, "What race are you?", a question that we rarely get in Singapore. Upon reflecting on our first racial test—the meeting with Das in the middle of the Belum forest—it struck us that we felt a deep, burning Indian pride when he finally took us in. I've never felt that in Singapore partly because I've never been placed in those sorts of communal situations.

Still, the sort of harmony you see in Singapore is markedly different from what you get in a place such as Cuba. I visited Havana and surrounds in 2002. I was pre-pared for some of the communist oddities that I encountered, like the long ration lines, the parallel monetary systems (official Cuban peso; unofficial peso; US dollars), and the Big Brother paranoia.

However, I didn't expect to see such deep racial integration. Sure, I knew I'd meet blacks and whites and probably some mulattoes. But I had no idea they blended so seamlessly with one another, like a streaked chocolate milkshake. Intermarriage had a lot to do with it.

"We've been sleeping with each other for centuries," smiled one dashing young man, on the edge of a salsa session, right before offering us a bevy of Cuban beauties in exchange for our two Singaporean Chinese female companions. He seemed eager to further diversify Cuba's gene pool.

It was refreshing to walk around in a society where people seemed so com-pletely oblivious to the concept of colour. Things in Singapore are different. Racial self-awareness has been conditioned into us. Ethnic harmony and multiculturalism seem distinctly functional. We get along well with other races because that is the foundation of a successful society. We are taught that integration will ultimately bring collective stability and riches. And so we do it. The carrot, of course, comes with a stick: if we discriminate, we know our government will come down hard.

In other words, the desire to be tolerant, to love thy neighbour, and to learn about each other, does not seem to arise from some innate feeling of oneness. Instead, it is more a pragmatic Singaporean's response to the laws of the land.

This, coupled with the fact that race and religion are barely discussed, leads to a surreal sense of suspended harmony. Multiculturalism here is like a joyous bubble, pumped up by the government, which may one day crystallise into something more genuine. Or it may not.

So is there racism in Singapore? Of course there is—just as there is in many other multi-ethnic countries. In school, I saw how easily racial cliques form. Some teachers cracked jokes about other races. I heard stereotypes repeated over and over. Malays are lazy. Chinese are *kiasu* "scared to lose" (and so will do all they can to get ahead). And we Indians are dirty because, amongst other things, we apparently do not wash our hands after passing motion.

When I grew older, and ventured into the dating arena, new conflicts emerged. I have many friends whose parents did not want them getting together with people of other races. Chinese parents disliking Indian and Malay suitors. Indian parents wanting only Indian partners for their kids. And so on. There may be an increasing number of mixed marriages in Singapore, but some people still harbour ancient prejudices.

In the army, I encountered racism on several occasions. Now, in the workplace, it still persists. It is not overbearing; it does not disgust. But *it is* there. And nobody likes to talk about it.

Some older Singaporeans I speak with long for the pre-war days, when the different ethnicities supposedly mixed around much more. "Life in the old days was different," says a septuagenarian friend. "We played with each other, we visited each other's house, we ate each other's food, and we even spoke each other's languages!"

For years, this has been one of my great "Singapore conundrums": is it true that the Singapore of yesteryear actually had a deeper, more ingrained sense of ethnic harmony? Living in Singapore, and speaking with people of all ages and colours, it's hard to get a perfect picture. For the most part, though, from my conversations, people do believe this story—the Singapore of today, for them, seems less *genuinely* tolerant than the halcyon pre-war glory days.

So, if that be the case, then why have things changed? Some suggest it is because of the independence movement, when race became a marker, a symbol, a pronounced tool which could be used against the colonialists. Others say it's because of the post-independence ethnic policies, which have sharpened the natural divide between the races, in a bid to protect each of them. The recent influx of foreigners might also have contributed to it, when xenophobia and racism are conflated.

Equally worrying is the notion that race consciousness has diffused over the border from Malaysia. According to this idea, no matter how hard Singapore tries to promote its race-neutral meritocracy, our policies are doomed because of how our neighbours treat each other. In other words because Malaysian Malays have an advantage over Malaysian Chinese, Singaporean Chinese are jolted into some sort of Chinese communalism, which they then express locally. It is a tragic race to the bottom of the bigot pile.

Lee Kuan Yew himself, of course, has had an indelible impact on how Singaporeans think about race. Singapore's political stability and economic success, he says, can be attributed in part to the fact that it has a large majority ethnic group (Chinese) coupled with much smaller minorities (Indian and Malay). If it had two or three significant minorities like in, say, Malaysia, then there would be room for much more ethnic tension.

As such, Mr Lee has spoken about the need to maintain a strong ethnic majority. Unfortunately, his powers cannot extend into the bedroom—for a number of years now, Singapore's Chinese have had a lower birth-rate than the Indians and Malays. As a result, the percentage of Chinese in the population has dropped from 77.8 per cent in 1990 to 74.1 per cent in 2011.[7]

To make up for this natural shortfall, many people we speak with believe the government actively imports more Chinese nationals.[8] In 1989, Mr Lee said that the lower Chinese birth rate justified the government's programme of encouraging Chinese immigration from Hong Kong. According to him, the Chinese majority must be maintained, "or there will be a shift in the economy, both the economic performance and the political backdrop which makes that economic performance possible."

Thus, Mr Lee has long believed in the importance of a strong majority. Moreover, he also believes that Singapore is so successful because that strong majority *is* *Chinese*. In a speech to parliament in 1985, he said, "We have a practical people whose culture tells them that contention for the sake of contention leads to disaster. I have said this on many a previous occasion; that had the mix in Singapore been different, had it been 75 per cent Indians, 15 per cent Malays and the rest Chinese, it would not have worked. Because they believe in the politics of contention, of opposition. But because the culture was such that the populace sought a practical way out of their difficulties, therefore it has worked."

Mr Lee's belief in ethnic determinism is even more obvious if one looks a bit further back. In a meeting at the University of Singapore on 27 December 1967, Chandra Muzaffar, a Malaysian political scientist, recalls Lee Kuan Yew sharing this anecdote:

Three women were brought to the Singapore General Hospital, each in the same condition and each needing a blood transfusion. The first, a Southeast Asian was given the transfusion but died a few hours later. The second, a South Asian was also given a transfusion but died a few days later. The third, an East Asian, was given a transfusion and survived. That is the X factor in development.[9]

According to Michael D. Barr of the University of Queensland, based on the available evidence, it is quite clear that Mr Lee has "always had an agenda based on the racial and cultural superiority of Singapore's Chinese population."

I do not really want to debate the merits of these ethnic and cultural explanations for success. Enough has been said, here and elsewhere, about Asian Values and argumentative Indians. Suffice to say that as an Indian who has grown up in a multicultural country, I'd like to think that I'm inherently similar to my counterparts—Chinese, Malay and all the other charming people living in Singapore.

However, what effect has all this ethnic and cultural determinism had on politicians, civil servants, and ordinary Singaporeans? As mentioned, despite our attempts to build a race-neutral meritocracy, it still amazes me how many Singaporeans believe in racial stereotypes.

For instance, I have many highly-educated Chinese friends who believe that Malays are racially inferior. "It's got nothing to do with Islam. The Indian Muslims are bright. Pakistani Muslims are smart. But the Malay Muslims—I don't think they've got what it takes," says a friend of ours, one of the top students in my year at Raffles Junior College.

Have Malays underachieved in Singapore? The statistics suggest so. The average household monthly income in 2000 for the Malays was S$3,148 per year, compared with S$5,219 for the Chinese, and S$4,556 for the Indians.[10] By 2010, it was S$4,575 for the Malays, S$7,326 for the Chinese and S$7,664 for the Indians. Our meritocracy may provide equal opportunity, but that's hardly any guarantee of more equitable outcomes.

Based on my anecdotal evidence, Malays are certainly under-represented in executive jobs in Singapore. In the past six years at the PWC Building in Singapore, where I work, the majority of Malays I have met are lavatory cleaners, delivery boys, and receptionists. Most of the professional workers are Chinese, Indian, or foreign (mostly white). Sure, there are some Malays in senior positions in Singapore—but they are certainly in the minority.

Many people I know would seek a cultural or racial explanation for this. But it's probably simply because of opportunity. The average Malay in Singapore has not had the same benefits of upbringing—including richer, more educated, English-speaking parents—as a lot of Chinese and some Indians.

Of course, that is not the only stereotype out there; it's just one that I hear often. It's possible that many Singaporean Chinese do not think Indians are up to it either, though they may never say it in front of me. In short, this belief in inherent racial and cultural differences is very much prevalent in Malaysia and Singapore, and can be traced back to the time of independence.

Some believe discrimination has recently gotten much worse. In March 2012, Lai Shimun, a 19-year-old Singaporean student, posted comments online expressing her disgust with the smell of Indians. She likened Indians to dogs, and suggested that we need our own form of public transport, or separate train cabins, to insulate other Singaporeans from our stench. Most netizens criticised her comments, but some supported them. The very same month, a group of football fans directed racial slurs at a visiting Liberian player, when Singapore hosted Terengganu.

Early in 2010, I hopped into a cab driven by a Chinese man who looked to be in his 40s. He was unusually articulate and well read. I found out that he was a fairly new cabbie, having worked in banks most of his life. We spoke about the recession, the recovery, the new casinos, the travails of driving taxis in Singapore, and his plans for retirement. Almost from the get-go, he referred to me as "my brother".

"I don't have a family and I hardly spend any money. I rent a small room in Geylang, doesn't cost much. Therefore I can save about S$7,000 a year just driving taxis. I'll do this for ten years, then I'll be old enough to get my CPF money, it's more than S$300,000. Then I'm going to take it all and retire in Thailand."

"Thailand?"

"Yes, Thailand. I like it there."

"Ya, plus it's cheaper than living here."

"My brother, it's not just about cheaper. People there don't discriminate."

"Discriminate? Who discriminates here in Singapore?"

"Ha, of course they do. When they meet me it's fine, but you should see people's reaction when they hear my name."

"Your name?"

"Yes. My name is Ishak … ha, you didn't know I was a Malay, did you?"

Ishak, son of a Malay man and Chinese lady, went on to narrate many stories about how fellow Singaporeans would be shocked, confused, and ultimately disenchanted by his irregular identity, the fact that he didn't fit snugly into one of our ethnic what-you-see-is-what-you-get buckets.

"I tell you, my brother, when some employers find out I am Malay, they lose interest. They think we are lazy and unreliable. At first they smile at me; once they hear my name, they frown."

Instead of getting better, Ishak believed this racism had intensified over the past ten years. "9/11 changed everything. Now that all these stories about Jemaah Islamiyah and Mas Selamat have come out, many people in Singapore don't trust us anymore."

"You know what made me really sad, my brother?" Ishak asked, when I had reached my destination. "Not too long ago, there was a young, sweet PRC girl (i.e. from China) who jumped into my cab. She is studying here. I asked her how she's getting on, whether she's mixing with the local Singaporeans or not. You know what she told me? She said, 'I mix with the locals. Except for the Malays. I have heard they are lazy.'

Can you believe that? Even the new migrants are learning these stupid stereotypes. My brother, hearing all this, I have decided that I must leave."

Ishak harboured no regrets or anger, just a stoic belief that Singapore had become a place where he did not fit in. As he drove off, thanking "my brother", with that big smile still plastered on his face, the irony of his struggle dawned on me: Ishak feels like he is being forced out of Singapore because of racism—when 50-odd years ago, his Malay father had found love in a Chinese lady.

9
The influx of God and migrants

Singapore. 7 July 2004.

One week before we set off on our cycling trip through Malaysia, we met two Buddhist monks at Sumana's house. The monks were from the Sri Lankaramaya Temple, a Sinhalese Buddhist temple in Singapore where Margaret Rajarethnam, Sumana's mum, does a lot of charity work. "Aunty Marge" was very supportive of our trip, and she thought it prudent to have the monks bless us and our bicycles.

The ritual itself didn't last too long. There were chants and blessings where the monks patted our foreheads with holy water and tied thin blue-red-white holy strings around our wrists and on our bicycles' handlebars. Of our many pre-trip preparations, this was the only religious one.

A month later, we and our bicycles were back in Singapore, safe and sound. Except for one flat tyre, one faulty pedal, and one night when I had a fever, our trip had been trouble-free. The multi-coloured strings looked weathered, but still hung loosely around our handlebars and wrists, protecting us.

All over Malaysia, God worked his/her way into many of our conversations. Most of the time, the discussions were about personal fulfilment. Many wanted to save us, perhaps because we look spiritually vacuous.

Few spoke about the intersection between religion and politics. This could be because Malaysians tend to think about political issues more through a racial lens; or perhaps because racial and religious identities have become conflated in our countries.

Chinese are Buddhist/Taoist or Christian; Malays are Muslim; and Indians are Hindu. Those are our simple ethno-religious buckets.[1] So, when somebody like Das, the guy we stayed with in Pulau Banding, speaks about the need for Indians to improve themselves, he is probably speaking about both Indians *and* Hindus, as one.

A few days after we were blessed in Singapore, we found ourselves in the FELDA Endau estate, chatting with Kamal, a Malay man in his forties.

"What religion are you?"

"We do not have any religion."

Kamal frowned disapprovingly. That being our first religious inquiry, we were a bit worried to say "Buddhist" or "Christian", the religions we were born into, and did not want to say "Muslim", lest we get tested.

("No religion", as we later found out, is the worst possible answer, reflective of a godless, soulless being. If you prefer not to reveal your hand—or soul, as it were—better to say "I'm still looking", which suggests some degree of religious exploration. The rest of the trip, we stuck to the truth.)

"Never mind, but do you know who made Heaven?" Kamal asked, two fingers pointing at the sky.

"God made Heaven and Satan Hell?"

"No, God made both. So why do you think he made Hell then?" fingers downwards.

Silence.

"Because he wanted to give us a choice between being good and bad!" he added.

"But I thought you said that we are all born good, and are subject to the influences around us?"

"Yes, yes, but in the end, it is you who chooses what you want!"

"Have you read any Islamic books?"

"No."

"You must read the Qu'ran, and understand it," said Kamal. "If you don't like its message, that's fine! But don't just read it once. You must read it a few times. Better still, study it."

We said we would, and then pressed him to find out about the restrictions that Islam placed on its followers. "Is it true that in the 'more Muslim' states, such as Terengganu and Kelantan, that life there is very different, that they follow stricter laws and codes of conduct?"

Kamal was stunned.

"No, of course not. Who said the laws are different? Everything is the same. Some of the *adat*, local customs, might be different, but that variation exists throughout the whole country. Everything is the same!"

"We've read newspaper articles that talk about how the Northeastern States of Malaysia have a much greater PAS influence, and they have to follow stricter social laws and codes of conduct."

A slightly condescending smile crept up on his face.

"OK, OK, let me tell you a story. I was once on a bus in Terengganu, when a female Western tourist boarded. She talks to the bus driver, and then suddenly starts shouting at him. She points at her little travel book while shouting, and says 'Why isn't the bus fare the same as what is written in this book?' So, moral of the story is, how can you trust what is written? How can you trust a book? Or a newspaper?"

Kamal placed infinite value on direct experience, versus second-hand information. "Anyway, you'll be going there during your trip, right? So just see for yourself. You'll see it's no different." His encouragement gave us a boost, as it was Day 3 of our bicycle journey, and we had yet to overcome our self-doubt about the whole trip.

"But you know, not every Muslim is the same. Not every Muslim follows a *garis panduan* (strict guidelines) when it comes to religion. It's the same with Christians too. Some go to church, others don't. That might explain some difference between Kelantan and Terengganu and other states. Maybe the Muslims there choose to follow a stricter line."

"You've heard the story of Tarzan, right? How he was brought up by monkeys, and learned to behave like a monkey? That's the way it is. Young people follow whatever the old say and do, in the same way, your kids will follow whatever you say and do."

We spoke more about Islamic norms and practices, and inter-religious harmony in Malaysia. As far as Kamal was concerned, Malaysia's different religious groups got along very well. "We respect each other and each other's places of worship. Mosques, temples, and churches exist together in the same town. No problem."

As with many Malaysian Muslims we met, however, his grievances stemmed from events occurring far away. "But I tell you something. Do not believe what the Americans have to say. They only say things to serve their own purpose. They're always saying that Israel is the best, when everybody knows they are evil. Why? Because they [the Jews] control Manhattan! They have no choice but to support them. Do not believe what the Americans say."

The Israel-Palestine conflict greatly influences many ordinary Malaysians' view of the US, and the way it conducts itself internationally. Some we spoke with are convinced that the US is still on a crusade, against Iraq, Palestine, and whichever other Muslim country gets in its way. In 2004, as we cycled around the country, we noticed many bumper stickers and posters calling for the end of the Iraq occupation. In early 2010, Malaysians were absolutely livid over Israel's raid on a Gaza-bound flotilla from Turkey.

This issue has always divided Malaysia and Singapore. Malaysia has tended to side with its fellow Muslim countries. Mahathir has even been accused, somewhat unfairly, of making anti-Semitic remarks. Singapore, on the other hand, is a firm ally of Israel and the US. We cooperate economically and militarily. So, when Kamal spoke about evil America and Israel, we kept quiet.

That first night in the *surau* sparked a series of other religious bedrooms. We got a room at the church in Kuantan where Anthony worked. In Kota Bahru, we tried our luck with a Catholic church as well as a giant mosque, to no avail. Ultimately, we found shelter in the UMNO building, where the *jaga*, watchman, welcomed all and sundry. Each night, on the steps of the building, he hosted a bunch of Malay youth, who were there to strum their guitars and sing songs. It was ironic that in Kota Bahru, one of Malaysia's PAS-dominated religious capitals, we found shelter not in God, but in UMNO.

In Sungai Golok, the Thai border town near Kota Bahru, we slept in a dilapidated mosque run by a glassy-eyed Uzbek who travels the world from mosque to mosque, working in exchange for food and shelter. That was the most unnerving sleep of our lives. The Uzbek was way too friendly, bordering on creepy, insisting on talking late into the night, interrogating us, like an annoying mosquito with devilish eyes. We humoured him only because he had been kind enough to take us in.

There was just enough light for us to notice the many rats scurrying around below our hammock beds—threatening, we feared, to attack at any moment. There was also a humdrum of activity from next door—the innocent hotel transformed at night into a brothel, where Thai girls await sex-starved Malaysian men from across the border.

"In Kelantan they pretend to be pious. Then they come to Golok and have some fun," explained the Uzbek. There we were sitting in the mosque, watching the hotel, listening to the Uzbek criticise the Thai girls, whose country we were in, and the Kelantanese men, who kept the local economy going.

Because of how closely different peoples are integrated in Malaysia and Singapore, such cross-cultural juxtapositions frequently occur. Just like in Sungai Golok, one can find mosques in the heart of Geylang, Singapore's red-light district, where devotees flock, seemingly tolerant of the ungodly behaviour outside.

In Perak we found not just God, but *capati* heaven. First, in Taiping, the tailor Barnabus Son of Encouragement had told us to try the Sikh *gurdwara*. "They never turn anybody away." Sure enough, we were greeted by a charming, old man, whose hair was longer than his loincloth. After signing a travellers' guestbook of sorts, he showed us to a lovely little room. He offered us *capati*, and milk the next morning. "It is part of our culture. *Gurdwaras* are places for travellers to stay. You are always welcome."

Emboldened, we decided to take him at his word, and the next evening, after a day of cycling, we went knocking on the door of the *gurdwara* in Ipoh. Sure enough, there were two well-built men and three plump ladies there who graciously took us in, and plied us with *capati, dhal* and a few winks. We were humbled. Of our many attempts to find free lodging with God in Malaysia, the Sikhs were the only ones to let us in all the time.

Still, we remember that first night in the *surau* fondly—we encountered genuine Malay hospitality, and a bit of black magic. We had stopped at the roadside *warung* owned by Kamal's wife only because Sumana's right knee was hurting.

Word must have gotten around the FELDA estate, because shortly after we settled in, a man by the name of Long showed up at the *surau*. "So, what is wrong with your knee?" pointing at Mana's bandaged right knee. He had a thin, sharp nose and a long jaw that had a life of its own, bouncing erratically whenever he laughed at his own jokes. His ears, little satellite dishes, faced the world with intent, absorbing everything.

"I think I can help you. I can heal people."

"Uncle, are you a *bomoh*, shaman?"

"Erm, yes, *bomoh*, you can say that."

Long knew how to titillate our supernatural curiosities. He had brought two side-kicks; they hardly spoke, happy to look on and guffaw at his jokes, acolytes hanging on his every word.

"OK, why don't you guys make yourselves at home. Put your bikes to the side there and relax! You can bathe over there. There is a toilet too."

"Thanks, thanks so much."

"Yes, and I will go back and change, and will return later to heal you."

"Thanks so much, I hope you can heal me."

"Of course I will heal you."

Was Long a charlatan? Who knows. Just three days into our journey, with the trip's success dependent on Sumana's knee, we were happy to roll whichever die came our way.

Long returned at around 10, having showered and changed into a light green shirt, whose long sleeves were neatly folded till just below his elbows. He had taken off the five gaudy rings he was sporting earlier. He looked ready to perform a miracle.

He ushered us into a side room and sat us down. Long and Mana sat in the middle of the 15-by-10-foot room, on a greenish blue and white striped nylon mat. An ant scurried across the mat, while a couple of flies buzzed around.

Long closed his eyes and began to recite something prayer-like, pausing every now and then to look upwards to Heaven, opening his eyes at the same time, as though seeking confirmation for his ritual. These incantations were indecipherable: he was speaking in tongues to somebody. He continued for about two minutes.

He then whipped out a little bottle of massage oil (Minyak Pengasih—Akar Cenuai) that he had brought along. Was he hiding it in his sarong? Gripping it in his right hand, he showed us the bottle's cap on which was stuck a small label reading

RM12.90. The label looked new. He then placed his index finger over the ".90", leaving us with a view of RM12.

"For you, Pak Long give discount, OK best!" he said, giving us a big thumbs-up. Not so thumbs-up for us. The RM12 was 60 per cent of our daily budget!

"Oh, thank you uncle, thank you."

He asked Mana to raise his sarong a bit, exposing his right knee and thigh more. He then started massaging the area around Mana's knee, using the oil we had just bought. The crickets outside were now in full cry, and they provided a constant high-pitched racket to the healing process, their voices punctuated periodically by a groan, moan or scream from Mana.

The healing session lasted a good twenty minutes. While massaging, he went on about his many exploits. "You know Pak Long used to be an actor in Singapore? Yes! I starred in three films. How else do you think Pak Long gets all the girls? But not just because of the films, no, Pak Long also has a lot of skill in getting girls. Pak Long best!" he said, triumphantly, releasing Mana's leg for a moment so he could flash a thumbs up.

He then opened his mouth wide, exposing an empty, dark cavern. "See! Pak Long does not have teeth but can still get women."

When the massage ended, we had no idea whether it had worked. Sumana did not feel any different. Dissatisfied with a measly RM12 taking, Long then tried to sell us some love potion that would let us get any girl we want. He pulled out a tiny, thin, clear cylindrical bottle with a black screw cap. It was filled with a clear liquid. He insisted that the magic in this bottle is so strong, that the bottle itself can jump up sporadically. "Imagine what it does when you put some on the body," he gushed.

We politely refused. After a moment's hesitation he tried another approach. "Does your knee feel better? I tell you what. Pak Long usually charges RM20 for his therapy. But for you, Pak Long give special price, OK! For you, just give Pak Long RM10 enough. Pak Long give you half price discount, best!"

We were cornered. It is always difficult to negotiate prices after a service is performed, be it a haircut or massage.

We forked over the RM10, and he bid us farewell. RM22 in total for Pak Long's treatment. We said a prayer for Sumana's knee and then fell asleep quickly in the *surau*, about 50 kilometres south of where we had initially thought the day would end. On this ramshackle trip, plans would have to be routinely rubbished.

Prayers awoke us prematurely at 6 in the morning. We rushed to gather ourselves and ready our bikes, not wanting to be any more of a bother, not wanting to irk or scare the dawn devotees, who were kneeling down in the main *surau* room beside us.

Sumana's knee did not act up again the rest of the trip. Black magic? God? We still don't know.

***

Sure enough, when we reached Terengganu and Kelantan, a few days after meeting Kamal, we found few obvious restrictions on peoples' livelihoods. Muslims do seem more conservative, but not in an extremist way. We saw men wearing pants to cover their knees while playing football. All the ladies wore, at the very least, a *tudung*: few had any makeup on. There were separate supermarket checkout lines in Kota Bahru.

And there were visible changes to the landscape. For instance, there is a famous beach near Kota Bahru that used to be called Pantai Cinta Berahi (PCB), the Beach of Passionate Love. "Those days, you could meet so many Malay girls there, all wearing mini-skirts," winked an old Indian man in Kota Bahru, "*those* days."

These days, PCB is known as Pantai Cahaya Bulan, the Beach of Moonlight. It was renamed in 1991 by the PAS state government. That is just one of many changes in Malaysia over the past 50 years, as its Muslim community has become more conservative. This shift mirrors the broader Islamic resurgence that we've witnessed across the world.

It also reflects some local dynamics. Mahathir consciously elevated Islam in the national consciousness. This helped solidify the Malay Muslim identity. It was also tactically shrewd, allowing Mahathir to burnish his Islamic credentials, and co-opt some of PAS' political space.

For some of Malaysia's old guard, this rising Islamisation represents a dramatic change. "Race relations back then were much better," Mustapha Ali, press secretary to Abdul Razak during his tenure as the second prime minister of Malaysia, says. "Tun Razak never played the religious card, in fact he was rather ambivalent on the practice of Islam. Hussein Onn reversed that policy, and then Mahathir."

Like other countries that have experienced rising Islamisation, Malaysia has a religious vanguard that relentlessly seeks to claim the moral high ground. Thus, though there are racial tensions, the only real religious conflict I've noticed exists between the small group of fundamentalist Muslims and everybody else.

The fundamentalists argue with more moderate Muslims as they feel they are not pious enough. Every year, there are stories of religious police crashing into hotel bedrooms to arrest Muslims for *khalwat*—relations between unmarried people. Muslims who drink get prosecuted, particularly in the stricter states. A Muslim woman was sentenced in 2009 to be caned for having a beer (her sentence was later commuted in 2010).

"It's ridiculous," says a Malaysian Indian lawyer working in Singapore, "some of my Malay friends order only gin and tonics, so they can pretend like they're drinking Seven-up. Tunku Abdul Rahman was known to enjoy his whisky. Things are different now. We've allowed the fundamentalists to hijack the agenda."

The fundamentalists, whose influence far outweighs their size, can also ratchet up inter-faith tensions when they want. In 2009, to protest against the relocation of a Hindu temple to their community, some 50 residents in Shah Alam carried a severed cow's head through the streets, and desecrated it in front of the state chief minister's office. In early 2010, a group of extremists fire-bombed several churches in Malaysia, in response to a high-court ruling which allowed non-Muslim faiths to use the word "Allah" to refer to God in their print publications.

These disputes are fomented by the confusion about the role Islam plays in Malaysia. There is a constant tug-of-war between "Malaysia the tolerant multi-religious society" and "Malaysia the Islamic state". The constitution is sufficiently vague, saying that Islam is Malaysia's official religion, but that this does not imply that it is an Islamic state. Politicians routinely play up whichever story is expedient.

Importantly, this affects religious conversion, which is practically impossible for Muslims in Malaysia. Numerous conversion disputes arise each year. Therefore, there is no complete freedom of religion in Malaysia. If Malays could easily convert out of Islam, so it goes, the very essence of Malay Muslim identity would be eroded. What then would happen to *Malay*sia?

Christians are thus very wary of being seen proselytising to Muslims. They tend to focus on other groups. In Kuantan, Father Eugene told us about his church's efforts over a bowl of *Curry Mee*, a thick, spicy noodle dish, which combines the best of Chinese, Indian and Malay cuisines into a bowl of devilish spice. Each sip of the gravy stuns your taste buds, leaving you gasping for air, and hungry for more. As we walloped, alternately dunking our heads in the bowl and then coming up to wipe our foreheads, we listened to him tell us about the church's attempts to help Malaysia's *orang asli*, the native people.

He claimed that the Christian outreach was preferable to the Muslim. "We don't try to convert them; we just want to help them. With the Muslims, they offer help only if the *orang asli* convert to Islam." It seemed strange that the church did not offer lessons about Christ. "Yes, of course we give them free bibles and classes about Christianity. But the point is, they do not *have to* become Christians." Still, most did.

Father Eugene and other missionaries have to tread carefully. Anything that might threaten Islam's dominance in Malaysia can be interpreted as undermining the country itself. A simple discussion about the role of Islam in Malaysia can quickly escalate into an existential debate about the Malaysian state. In that way, race, religion and identity have become so politically charged that it is almost impossible to engage in an honest, reasoned discussion on the issue.

Malaysia's religious agenda, then, is easily captured by some of its fundamentalists. But just how *extreme* are Malaysia's fundamentalists? They are mild compared with the likes of the Taliban and right-wing groups in Indonesia and the Philippines. Yet, from what I saw, they appear much more conservative and deeply religious than Muslims in Singapore. This could, of course, be because Muslims in Singapore feel slightly subdued, as they are in the minority. Hence they are less inclined towards overt displays of religiosity, whether in their dress or in their prayers.

In 2005, I travelled to Pengkalan Pasir, a town on the outskirts of Kota Bahru, to observe a state parliamentary by-election, which was called after the incumbent PAS politician had passed away. UMNO and PAS contingents from far away descended on Pengkalan Pasir, accompanied by television crews, journalists, election observers and nosey parkers like ourselves. It was an absolute carnival: in a matter of days, this tiny, dusty town transformed into a key political battleground, an electoral festival of cameras, lights, posters, flags and *ceramahs*.

The contrast between the two groups was stunning: the rich, urban UMNO guys, wearing dark glasses while barrelling along in their black SUVs, against the white robes and slippers of the PAS devotees, who seemed to walk everywhere, floating along on some spiritual high.

The women, too, had their differences, though one had to look closer. "Look at those UMNO women," said a PAS supporter from KL who was wearing a simple *tudung*, and no makeup, "they flaunt their jewellery and put so much makeup on their faces. Allah does not approve of these things."

I wandered into a little PAS bazaar that had been set up in a half-finished concrete building in the middle of the town. There was a little food and drink stall, as well as a PAS clothing shop, which sold t-shirts, caps and other paraphernalia with the distinctive white-moon-on-a-green-background insignia. The makeshift canteen was filled with about 30 PAS followers, all men, all wearing white, some with turbans too.

What really caught my eye, though, was the CD stall—hundreds of VCDs were sprawled messily across a few tables. While there were regular CDs of Islamic prayers and chants, there were also a whole stack of rather more incendiary ones: VCDs lambasting Mahathir for being anti-Islamic; VCDs of *jihadi* struggles in places such as Afghanistan and Chechnya; and VCDs showing Muslims being ill-treated around the world, some with shocking, violent images on the cover. As I observed these turbaned PAS supporters shuffling through these discs, I started to wonder if this was Malaysia's extremist edge, being schooled right in front of me.

Compared with Muslims I've met in Singapore, some of these PAS followers seemed far more affected by what is happening to the larger Muslim brotherhood overseas. One might assume that they can be more easily influenced by over-zealous Imams eager to (violently) foster a larger Muslim nation. Many people I met in Malaysia's urban centres, such as KL and Penang, worry that there are many radicals amongst the PAS faithful, some of whom can't wait to convert the whole country.[2]

But, despite what I saw at the CD shop, I did not detect any extremism in any PAS members. Instead, they were much more concerned about the injustices in Malaysia's political system.

When we made our first proper field trip to Malaysia, cycling through in 2004, we still held the naïve assumption that there are clean and simple religious fault lines in Malaysia. Urbanites are moderate (or liberal), people from the Northeast are conservative and more prone to intolerance.

I've come to realise that Malaysia's religious mosaic is extremely complex. For instance, there are clear differences between the Muslim fundamentalists, including some PAS conservatives, and the supposedly violent extremists, like the ones who butcher cow's heads and torch churches. The latter group is more opportunistic than religious. "They are just puppets," says a Malaysian analyst, "their masters are using them for political gain."

Most Malaysians actually have a deep respect for each other's religions—so much so that sometimes spirituality is shared in curious ways. For example, in Penang, Malaysians of different religions will drive their new cars to Shree Muniswarar, a Hindu temple, to be blessed by a Car God. Many Malaysians and Singaporeans we know also happily visit each other's homes for religious festivals (the scrumptious food is certainly a draw).

The worrying thing, then, is that far too often, the extremists feel they can run roughshod over the rest of the country. If violent goons are still being hired to stir up religious tensions, how far has Malaysia really come since 1969?

***

In March 2007, Ong Kian Cheong and Dorothy Chan Hien Leng, two Singaporeans in their 40s, handed out *The Little Bride*, an evangelistic comic strip, to Madam Farharti Ahmad, a Muslim Singaporean. Later that year, they gave it to another Muslim, Irwan Ariffin. Following complaints, Mr Ong and Ms Chan were charged in 2009 under the Sedition Act, and sentenced to eight weeks in jail.

Singapore ensures religious harmony the same way it manages everything else—through harsh punishment. *The Little Bride* is published by Jack Chick, an evangelical American known for his vigorous promotion of Christianity and rejection of other religions, particularly Catholicism and Islam. Little wonder, then, that Mr Irwan and Madam Farhati objected to it. Singapore also decided to block access to Mr Chick's website, so that nobody in Singapore, Christian or otherwise, can read his work.

Thus, in the same way we deal with race, we prefer to mute all religiously charged discussions. This approach surely has some benefits. For instance, Singapore is unlikely to experience anything similar to what we've seen in Malaysia: severed cow's heads and burning churches. Religious harmony is maintained through an ever-present deterrent. As long as people fall in line, and do not incite religious tensions, they can practise whatever religion they want (with a few notable exceptions, such as Jehovah's Witnesses, who are banned because their pacifist beliefs prevent their male adherents from joining Singapore's army and carrying arms).

However, as with race, this approach prevents a healthy dialogue from developing. Singaporeans worship in their little silos, without a proper appreciation for each other's religions. This lack of understanding creates an environment in which some religious leaders feel they can disrespect each other—in the past three years, two Christian pastors have been forced to apologise and back down after making derogatory comments against Buddhists and Taoists.

Similarly, Islam is often misunderstood. In 2005, somebody suggested on a pet website that dogs should not be allowed in taxis because Muslims find them unclean. In response, two bloggers criticised Islam. One of them advocated desecrating Mecca. The bloggers were also charged under the Sedition Act.

From my experience growing up in Singapore, Muslims do not mix as much with the other religions. The main reason for this is diet. In school, while the Muslims were able to eat only from one or two stalls, the non-Muslims could choose from about seven or eight. Thus, in our school canteens, where students take a break from their punishing schedules and partake of food together, we often find the Muslims sitting by themselves, away from the rest.

Sometimes I'd sit and eat with them. I knew them better because I was in Malay class, and we used to play football together. On the other hand, many of my Chinese friends hardly interacted with the Muslims.

When I left high school, and went on to the army, my Muslim friends slowly trickled off my radar. Army itself brought separation. Muslims are barred from certain sensitive divisions, such as Armour, where I was based. "Isn't it strange," noted a Malay taxi-driver, "that I sometimes pick up Mainland Chinese PRs who are serving in Armour, when Malays, who have lived here for centuries, are not allowed in?"

Instead, many Muslims tend to get drafted into the Police Force. Thus, while school life led to diet-enforced separation, the two and half years of mandatory national service further cleaves the Muslim community away from the rest. In each cohort, a whole swath of Chinese and Indian soldiers shed blood, sweat and tears—without any Muslims around.

In addition, after high school, many of my social interactions, for better or worse, started to include alcohol. While some of my Muslim friends do drink, many stay away from pubs and bars. Thus, in yet another facet of life, we spend time with our Chinese and Indian friends, without many Muslims around.

Now, in the working world, some of those school-time dietary barriers crop up again. As a result, I find less opportunity to have lunch with my Muslim colleagues. Worse, I have overheard non-Muslims lamenting the lack of options available. For instance, some non-Muslims will complain that "we can't order this cake" or "we can't order food from this caterer" because it is non-*halal*. "It's not fair that the whole office has to accommodate that one person's preference," they moan.

Our Malaysian friends rarely face such situations. Many restaurants there, even some Chinese and Indian ones, serve only *halal* food, which allows people from all religions to eat together. Eating is one of the most basic human rituals, cherished even more so by food-crazy Singaporeans. Sadly, on many an occasion, Muslims have to eat separately.

From our conversations with friends and others, we get the sense that 9/11, its aftermath, and the rise of groups such as Jemaah Islamiyah, an affiliate of Al Qaeda, has led many non-Muslim Singaporeans to question Islam. According to Ishak the taxi driver, over the past ten years, Singaporeans have become more suspicious of Muslims.

Furthermore, some of Lee Kuan Yew's recent comments have undermined relations between Singaporean Muslims and the rest. In the book *Lee Kuan Yew: Hard Truths to Keep Singapore Going*, which was published in January 2011, he says that Singaporean Muslims have not integrated as well as the rest. On what Muslims could do to integrate better, he says: "Be less strict on Islamic observances and say, 'Okay, I'll eat with you.'"[3]

Many Singaporeans were appalled. So were many Malaysians and Indonesians. In December 2011, the Department of Islamic Development Malaysia (Jakim) declared the book "haram". It seems odd for Mr Lee to claim that Muslims haven't integrated when certain national policies—particularly those related to military service—have forcibly kept Muslims apart. Have Muslims not integrated, or has Singapore prevented them from integrating?

PM Lee Hsien Loong, his son, and many other PAP members distanced themselves from the comments. In early March—two months before the general elections—Lee Kuan Yew said that he stands corrected on the statement, which was recorded "probably two or three years ago".

But the damage had been done. Worse followed in September 2011, when WikiLeaks published a conversation between Lee Kuan Yew and then US senator Hillary Clinton in 2005, where he apparently calls Islam a "venomous religion". Mr Lee immediately denied saying that.

Since 9/11, more than 30 people have been detained in Singapore on suspicion of having links to Jemaah Islamiyah. Nevertheless, it seems unlikely that many Muslims in Singapore will ever be seriously influenced by radical elements in their religion. Almost all are moderate and tolerant.

However, a few people I have spoken with, including Donald Low, the former Administrative Officer in the Singapore government, believe that the growing influence and power of evangelical Christians, if left unchecked, could one day pose a threat to religious harmony in Singapore.

Evangelical Christians are increasingly flexing their muscles, as seen by Mr Ong's and Ms Chan's efforts at converting people with *The Little Bride*, as well as the 2009 coup attempt at AWARE (the Association for Women's Action and Research), one of Singapore's most prominent NGOs.

Their influence is one reason Singapore still has an archaic law banning homosexual acts. Private, consensual sex between males is punishable by up to two years in prison. Though the law is rarely enforced, its presence is a stain on the conscience of Singapore, which claims to be an inclusive, modern global city.

Some of these evangelical groups are wealthy. Recent years have seen the rise of Singapore's mega-churches, including City Harvest Church and the New Creation Church, which have more than 20,000 members each.

In the space of 24 hours in August 2010, the New Creation Church raised S$21.1 million for its building fund. The year before, New Creation paid an employee a salary of more than half a million dollars. Rock Productions, its business arm, has invested about $280 million in a tie-up with property giant CapitaLand to develop a $660 million lifestyle hub in Buona Vista.

City Harvest Church is similarly lavish. It invested S$310 million in Suntec City, where it runs its services. Its pastor, Kong Hee, is married to Sun Ho, a singer, who runs a number of boutiques in Singapore, including Ed Hardy and Christian Audigier. Kong Hee is famous for his sermons where he praises wealth and giving to the church, even at the expense of the less fortunate.

"Jesus and his disciples distinguished themselves from poor people," he once told his congregation. "Jesus didn't consider himself poor … Jesus said if you want to help the other poor people like *them*, you can help them anytime. But if you want to worship me, you got to do it now, when the property price is low, and we are getting out of recession, and do it for building in the marketplace, for the marketplace, to penetrate the marketplace."[4]

Such comments can tear Singapore's social fabric, particularly when there is such huge income inequality in the country. To its credit, the government keeps close tabs on the activities of all religious organisations, including evangelical Christians. The worry, according to some people, is what might happen should many evangelical Christians one day enter politics and assume positions of power.

A veneer of religious harmony exists in Singapore, and is likely to persist because of the harsh penalties against anything vaguely offensive. Yet we probably would achieve a healthier balance if we encouraged more public dialogue.

***

Endau, Johor. 16 July 2004.

When Singapore separated from Malaysia in 1965, all of a sudden, the thousands of people working across on the other side suddenly became migrants. It must have been a weird feeling, to have one's job being effectively moved to another country.

Kamal started working in Singapore in 1980, a year after he got married. "I went there as a contract worker, I was a welder in Chai Chee and Loyang. You know lah, Singaporeans don't like us contract workers."

He said this not out of resentment, but what appeared a stoic, seasoned belief that this was his station in life, and if *he* were a Singaporean, he would very much behave like one, the same way they had acted towards him.

He had also worked in Senoko, Sembawang, Sungei Road and Johor Road. "You know? Where Bus 170 ends?"

He seemed to have bittersweet memories of long days, little rest, but good money that supported him and his family. In total, he worked there for seven years. After telling us a bit more about what our country, Singapore, was like in the early 1980s, he got up and walked to a tiny CD stereo set which had been playing slow, smooth Malay ballads—perfect music, as it turned out, for a lazy afternoon under the *warung's* shade.

Kamal wanted to pump it up. Within seconds, "Ra-Ra-Rasputin" was echoing through the afternoon.

He spun around, mouthing the words, and flashed a CD case at us. It was a Boney M Platinum album; "VideoCD" and "CompactDisc" were carelessly printed on the lower right of the sleeve, a reminder of the old days when piracy was still a tad unpolished. The band, pixelated, still looked glamorous.

"I saw them at Kallang, you know."

"What?"

"Kallang. You know, Kallang, Kallang Stadium, your stadium, in Singapore."

"Oh, Kallang ... Oh, really?!? Boney M?!?"

"Ya, I forget exactly when, but I saw them perform at Kallang."

He laughed again, and his eyes crushed under the pressure of his cheek, leaving a narrow slit of a window. He knew all the words to their songs.

"I also enjoyed walking around Orchard Road, but hey! I'm sure there are no Malays who live around Orchard Road."

"Why?"

"Because it's so expensive lah. Only the Whites and Chinese can afford to live there."

There wasn't any short response we could offer.

The *warung* was getting busier, and Kamal made it a point to greet each customer on their way to his wife and an icy escape. His wife oscillated from her seat in front of the counter—where she had been listening intently to our conversation—and her spot behind her little counter, where she prepared the drinks or dessert (Ais Kachang or Cendol).

"So, what do you really think of Singapore?"

"It's good lah, the wages are high, right?"

He repeated it twice later. The only thing Kamal really liked about Singapore was his high salary. Not the people, not the food, not the culture. Not even all those other unique aspects of our city-state about which others rant and rave—cleanliness, efficiency, negligible crime, skyscrapers, public housing, shopping centres and consumerism, the ability to buy almost anything from any place on earth.

No, none of those had left their mark on Kamal. But then again, that was the nature of his job, wasn't it? Kamal was in Singapore on a single-minded mission to earn money. He was thrust into that uncompromising position by his father's death, his mother's return to her home in Terengganu, and the need to provide for his siblings.

For the contract workers who live in Johor and commute daily to work in our industries or construction sites, Singapore is for the most part a film show, moving images and sounds filtered through their bus windows daily. They are shuttled in, work in conditions that Singaporeans never have to put up with, and are then whisked off. They are obviously paid wages better than their next best alternative, but certainly lower than any Singaporean would accept.

Even when they do get a day off, a chance to indulge in concerts at our stadium, prices are prohibitive, locals are indifferent, and the trip is temporary. They build our city cheaply, but then nightfall brings a return to the border, to the other side, pure quotidian immigrants. Singapore is a strange, foreign place to them.

That probably tells the story of any low-cost foreign migrant in the world. What makes it odd for Malaysians and Singaporeans is that just 45 years ago, we were still part of the same country.

Since then, Malaysians' wages have risen as the country has developed. Thus, even as they cross into Singapore, at home they too have come to depend on cheaper imported labour for a lot of menial work. These foreigners—mostly Indonesians—are blamed for stealing jobs, holding down wages and committing crimes.

"Do you know that there are three million migrant workers now in Malaysia? And that's only an official estimate. How about all those unaccounted for?"

"Huh. We didn't know there were that many. Does that lead to friction?"

"Yes, of course it does! But you have to understand them. They are people, like you and me, and they are just trying to live. They come here because they cannot earn enough in their own country—there are no jobs. They come here because they have to find a way to survive. And then, when they get here, they find it's not easy either. They are paid less than us. They are not treated well. So, what do they do? They decide to hide in the jungle and rob people, rob houses. That's a much easier way of life. You can become rich! So, really, they're just like you and me, trying to make a living."

The Asian financial crisis led to serious socioeconomic dislocations in Indonesia. This prompted even more Indonesians to try and sneak into Malaysia. The plight of these workers has become a major point of contention between the countries.

Today, there are many different migrant groups in Malaysia, including the Bangladeshis, Myanmese and Nepalese. Their impact on the country is visible. The restrooms in Malaysia's highway stops, once the stinking scourge of travellers, are now remarkably clean, thanks to the fastidious Bangladeshi cleaners. Eat at some of KL's Chinese coffee shops, and there's a high chance that your noodles will be cooked and served by a Myanmese, speaking perfect Hokkien. The Nepalese, meanwhile, have carved a comfortable niche as KL's security greeters, saluting cars and people as they enter hotels, embassies and other protected places.

Five years ago, these groups were still small and amorphous; today they are noticeable. Still, given Malaysia's size, they have not had a huge impact on the country's complexion or identity. Instead, they form little communities, which dot the landscape, living on the fringes of mainstream Malaysia. When they are discussed, unfortunately, it is usually in relation to the country's rising crime rate.

***

Foreign workers and new migrants have had a much more noticeable impact on Singapore than Malaysia. In recent times, Singapore has witnessed an unprecedented inflow of people. In 1990, citizens made up more than 86 per cent of Singapore's three million people. Today, citizens make up only around 64 per cent of Singapore's five million odd people. In other words, more than one in three people in Singapore today are foreigners (PRs and non-residents, or temporary workers). Meanwhile, more than half of Singaporean citizens are probably foreign-born. This infusion of foreigners is one of the most dramatic social experiments anywhere in the world.

Before, the few immigrants felt a strong need to integrate into Singaporean society. Today, they do not—many immigrant communities have a critical mass and an attendant social support network that newcomers easily plug into. For example, on any given day, one can find a bustling Filipino community in Orchard Road, a Chinese one in Chinatown, an Indian one in Serangoon Road, and a Myanmese one around Peninsular Plaza.

They like to speak their own language, eat at their own restaurants, and buy products and services from their own kind, as with the Filipinos who have their nails cut by the Filipino manicurists plying their trade along the slope next to Rolex House.

They thus feel less need to mix with Singaporeans, and learn the local customs and language. "I am Singaporean and tired of service staff who can only speak Mandarin" is a group on Facebook, the social networking site, with more than 10,000 members. In addition to linguistic confusion, migrants are also blamed for stealing jobs, undercutting wages, and raising the cost of living, especially property prices.

In a way, it's a bit unfair. These new migrants are, as Kamal says, "just like you and me, trying to make a living". They contribute a lot to Singapore, not just economically, but culturally too. Of course, many people now think that mass immigration has happened too fast, too soon, and its repercussions have not been adequately planned for. Even the government has admitted as much. Nevertheless, Singapore is now actually starting to look and feel like a global, cosmopolitan city, a mosaic of different ethnicities.

However, this is where the concept of Singaporean identity comes in. It is unclear what Singapore actually wants to be. Does Singapore want to be a Chinese-dominated Asian city? Or a truly global one? Similarly, does Singapore want to have an integrated population which speaks the same language? Or are we comfortable with a mosaic of different peoples, cultures and languages?

"Yes, I can hire foreign workers from many countries, but it is much easier for me to hire those from China," says a high-end restaurant owner. His restaurant has a "quota of three workers from China"—meaning that three workers from China can have their work permits and paperwork fast-tracked. No other source country enjoys this quota. "If I want an Indian, the person has to have proper qualifications, degrees, and so on. If I want a Chinese, anything goes. No degree, no English, no problem."

As mentioned, Singapore seems to be deliberately targeting Chinese migrants in order to keep the proportion of Chinese in the country high. However, this policy seems at odds with our desire to become a cosmopolitan global city. It seems unfair to treat one foreigner better than another. My friends from places such as Cameroon and Nepal have had a much harder time getting work and residency approval than have my friends from places such as China and the US. As shown by the Facebook group, many people are also uncomfortable with the increased usage of Mandarin in the country—will English standards decline as a result?

Integration has certainly suffered. Even though Singapore is often regarded as a model for ethnic harmony, our traditional channels of integration—including public housing and the delightful food centres—do not really capture migrants. As such, little ethnic enclaves, the government's *bête noire*, have formed.

"The Chinese have taken over an entire block!" says a Malay taxi driver, describing a neighbourhood in Jurong West. (He was referring to Mainland Chinese, not Singaporean Chinese.)

"It happened slowly at first. A contractor rented a four-room flat and put twelve Chinese in it. Twelve people! Can you believe it?" An average four-room flat has about four Singaporeans living in it. By squeezing twelve in, the contractor was unwittingly changing the social dynamics of the area.

"No offense to them, but they are different. Twelve people speaking loudly in their language, cooking their food that doesn't smell very good to us. Soon, the neighbours couldn't take it, so they decided to rent out their own flat, and rent another one somewhere else. This happened one by one—Singaporeans leaving, and Chinese coming in—till the entire flat is now just Chinese!"

Singapore's carefully crafted ethnic housing policies fail to take account of renters, only home owners. By tracking who owns which public housing unit, the authorities can ensure that there is a right mix of Chinese, Indian and Malay in every town. If every homeowner, however, chooses to rent to a Chinese, or Myanmese, there is little the government can do.[5]

Similarly, ethnic enclaves have also formed at the very highest end of the income ladder, none more obvious than the rich Indian communities on the East coast. "The Waterside is just a mini-India," says an Indian acquaintance from Bombay. "Rich, educated Indians move here and realise that they do not need to leave their traditional social circles. Indian schools from Delhi and Mumbai have their own little cliques. Singapore is now known as India's cleanest city, haha."

Ethnic policies do not interfere with the allocation of private condominium units. In that way, we practise a strange double standard—those staying in public housing must integrate, while the richer ones in private do not have to.

There has also been a huge inflow of white professional workers in mid-to-senior management positions. A huge swathe of Singapore's downtown—including retail outlets, clubs and restaurants—cater specifically to this clientele. This has created an elitist, ethnic sort of segregation downtown—in some of the swankiest establishments, there are very few Singaporeans around. The Filipino service staff aside, you could be forgiven for thinking you're in a Western country.

With this huge influx of foreigners has come conflict. According to a Singaporean researcher at one of our think-tanks, "the police have noted a spike in the number of violent incidents between citizens and non-citizens, particularly involving the mainland Chinese and Myanmese."

In 2011, it was reported that Chinese immigrants had lodged a complaint against their Singaporean Indian neighbours because they didn't like the smell of the curry they cooked. Following a "mediation", the Singapore Indian family agreed to cook curry only when the Chinese immigrant family is out of the house.

At first, one might assume that mainland Chinese and India Indians can integrate seamlessly. Those two races have been migrating here for centuries. Surely any problems with integration must afflict other people, such as the Myanmese and Filipinos?

Not anymore. Perhaps perversely, the mainland Chinese and India Indians may find it hardest to integrate because they actually look like Singaporeans, when clearly they are not—they speak differently, dress more traditionally and practise (some) unique customs.

The best way to insult a well-manicured, successful Singaporean lady, is to mistake her for a mainlander. Just as Americans lampoon FOBs, who are Fresh-Off-the-Boat, many Singaporean Chinese I know look down upon mainlanders as slightly backward.

While most new Chinese immigrants tend to be at the lower end of the spectrum, many Indian ones are skilled workers. The common, stereotypical caricature is of the Hindi-speaking, wine-sipping, cricket-watching Indian from India—unable to get along with the Tamil-speaking, beer-guzzling, football-mad Indian Singaporean.

All this has prompted the government to set up the National Integration Council (NIC). Amongst other things, the NIC will help "newcomers and locals move out of their social comfort zones and widen their social circles" says its head, Dr Vivian Balakrishnan, our minister for community development, youth and sports.

Even in Singapore, though, it is hard to force people to mix. "The NIC recognises that integration is a long-term effort, and may take years before success is apparent," says Dr Balakrishnan.

The NIC will have its work cut out. In my opinion, Singapore will not be able to really restrict the inflow of foreigners. Our economy needs them, and our country is all the better for them. What we do need, though, is a much better way of integrating them. What we choose to do, of course, depends on what sort of a Singapore we want.

As I grew up in Singapore, and all the way through university in the US, I would meet many fellow Singaporeans who would look at me, and say, "You don't look Singaporean." After speaking with me, and hearing my instinctive use of "Can lah" and "Cannot lah", they would realise that I am.

Recently, though, we rarely face such identity crises. It is becoming harder to tell a Singaporean based simply on appearance. What does it mean *to be a Singaporean*? My guess is that most people here, myself included, don't really know any more.

This need not be a bad thing. As our country has become more cosmopolitan, Singaporean identity is no longer tied to particular ethnic groups or religions. Singaporeans may sometimes lament the influx of Mainland Chinese, but in truth that is mostly just a reflection of, well, China's growing influence in the region.

Some older Singaporeans reminisce about the pre-Independence days when everybody could speak to each other in Malay. For better or worse, those days will never return. Singapore is fast becoming a melange of Asians, with a sprinkling of Whites and other people.

Lee Kuan Yew's greatest achievement, perhaps, is creating a society where race and religion are de-emphasised and can never be used as tools of business or politics. Different groups are forced to integrate. Each one is given little space to act or organise independently.

Given the recent ethno-religious tensions facing liberal societies everywhere, particularly in Western Europe, Singapore's model of forced integration may look increasingly attractive.

The flipside of the Singapore model is that over time, aspects of an individual's culture, race and religion slowly seep away. An Indian in Singapore can never be as Indian as he or she would in other multicultural cities, where Indians can more easily congregate. Perhaps Singaporean identity will always be in flux, an endless tug-of-war between global currents and specific national policies.

In Ipoh, Pak Zamin had presented us with a simple answer to Malaysia's ethnic, religious and identity conflicts. "Different groups spend time trying to convert people and win them over. Instead, the government should just go all out to encourage inter-racial marriage. That is simply the best way."

According to him, it made no sense to try to figure out what it meant *to be Malaysian*. That would take many hundreds of years of miscegenation. "The true Malaysian has not been born yet."

10
The joy of families and security

In mid-2008, I attended a lunch with Mahathir. The lunch was organised for 20-odd CEOs of companies doing business in Malaysia.

Ahead of the lunch, I tried to find out about his legacy. "India has Gandhi, South Africa has Mandela, and we have Mahathir," gushed an elderly Malay taxi driver. "When he speaks on the international stage, I feel proud to be a Malaysian. He put us on the map," says a young Indian friend.

Others were far less gracious. "He ruined this country," says a Chinese banker at a Malaysian brokerage, lamenting the *bumiputera* policies which Mahathir had vigorously promoted. A senior lawyer concluded that he had "completely destroyed Malaysia's judiciary". Many people spoke about both the good and the bad.

Abroad, Mahathir is generally regarded as one of the toughest, strong-armed autocrats Southeast Asia has ever known. In person, he is like a mouse. He strolled into the meeting room with a huge smile on his face, thanking the hotel staff and welcoming all his fellow lunch guests, as if we were doing him a huge favour. A few days before his 84th birthday, Mahathir seemed to effortlessly afford every single person the utmost respect, regardless of age, rank or skin tone—the perfect politician, perhaps.

Mahathir was great fun. He dodged criticism for the *bumiputera* policies, lamented American financial liberalisation, and, of course, slammed Lee Kuan Yew, who had just concluded an eight-day trip around Malaysia, visiting different states and sharing comments and critiques.

Mahathir saw this as an unwelcome intrusion. According to him, Lee Kuan Yew is a sad, frustrated man. "A man like him needs to govern a country the size of China, yet he is stuck with that small little island." As a result, says Mahathir, LKY takes it upon himself to gallivant around the region, dishing out advice.

"What about yourself?" asked an American CEO, "Do you have any regrets?"

"Do you think I should have any regrets?" Mahathir shot back, in a tone more comic than annoyed. As a stuffy silence fell over the room, the old man obliged. "Well, I suppose there is one thing," he said, clearing his throat. "I am a dictator. And I regret having stepped down."

All the lunch guests looked a bit bewildered, probably having never before heard a dictatorial admission. Mahathir was dead serious. "I left before my job was done." His successor, Abdullah Badawi, had apparently failed to follow through and complete a lot of his brainy ideas. Conversing with him was surreal; he was a history portal, transporting us to different eras and seminal events, in a way my jaunts through old Malaysia never could.

Though he might cultivate the image of the unwilling politician, heaving the burden of his country, he probably really did enjoy being a dictator—as in, *dictating* orders to others—the same way Lee Kuan Yew probably enjoys travelling the region to share his wisdom with other policymakers.

But what about ordinary Malaysians and Singaporeans? Throughout my journeys and conversations, I've spent a lot of time trying to figure out what makes us happy.

Do we dance to the same beat? Do we seek the same rewards, and worry about the same problems? What, essentially, is life for Malaysians and Singaporeans all about?

There are commonalities, of course. For instance, most Malaysians and Singaporeans take certain development basics for granted, such as health, housing, education and national security.[1] Many people living in emerging countries might be "happy" if they had those things alone. Here, they are necessary but not sufficient. Most people are past that, and are looking for further fulfilment in life.

Maybe it is a bit presumptuous to even try and second guess the preferences of people in a country. How could I possibly know? Still, as I made my way across Malaysia, there were several things that kept cropping up—things which Malaysians told me are important. Often, they are different from what one finds in Singapore.

What fulfils your average Malaysian isn't always what fulfils your average Singaporean. Living in a different country these past 45 years seems to have uniquely shaped our view of happiness. These differences affect the way we interact with each other.

***

Endau, Johor. 16 July 2004.

On the third day of our bicycle trip, after showing us the room where we could sleep, Kamal entered the *surau* for one last prayer. Kamal was more reserved than the other men we had met at the FELDA estate, and maybe because of that, he seemed more pious. The *kampung*'s sounds had been swallowed by the pitch black night, leaving only the amplified Muslim prayer that again bellowed out of the *surau*, and the clicks and clacks of insects in the refrain.

The prayers were melodious, but foreign. We were in unfamiliar surroundings, and simply not accustomed to listening to Muslim prayers up close. In Singapore, you could hear them if you were near a mosque. Here, there was always a mosque near you. Five minutes later, Kamal had finished his prayers and headed home.

"Hello!" a voice from behind startled us.

A lanky, dishevelled Malay boy was walking slowly, but confidently, towards us. He had appeared abruptly from behind the *surau*, and we weren't quite sure how he had found his way in. As he approached us, his gait became more hesitant and he put one hand in his pocket, and with the other stroked his puffed-up fringe.

"Ah, hello kid."

"Where are you guys from?"

"Singapore. What's your name?"

"Pip," he answered.

Pip was 17 years old, and was about to sit for a major exam, the SPM, at the end of the year. He already knew what he might do if and when he failed. He had some notion of working in Johor, and if not, he would go to Endau or Rompin.

There was something strange about the way he was looking at our bikes, like he was trying to steal glances instead of just plain stare at it, causing us to be snappier than we needed to be.

Directly outside the *surau*, near this back gate, was a group of male youths chatting and laughing loudly. Loitering in the dark, outside the *surau*, we could only catch glimpses of their silhouettes. We wondered if Pip had been chosen to do some "recce" work in advance of a theft. Without saying anything to each other, we knew what the other was thinking. These guys are after our bikes.

One of his friends joined him, a younger kid, about 13. He shared none of Pip's enthusiasm for conversation, preferring to pull his cap low and just follow the leader.

"So, how much did you pay for this in Singapore?"

"About 400 dollars."

"Singapore money? 400 dollars Singapore money? Wow, that's more than 1,000 here."

"Ya, but we managed to get some money from our universities, wasn't all from our pockets."

"How come university guys are cycling like this? Is it some kind of a ... Hey, are these original Shimano parts?"

"Yes they are."

"Wow, they're nice. We don't get bicycles like this in Malaysia."

When preparing for our bicycle trip, one of the toughest trade-offs we faced was between our bicycles' simplicity and performance. Our intention was to travel as inconspicuously as possible. We had chosen to cycle, after all, partly because we didn't want to be seen as the Rolex-touting Singaporean barrelling through Malaysia in a Mercedes. We certainly didn't want a high-tech, flashy mountain bike.

However, our desire for simplicity had to be balanced with the need for a machine that could get us through thousands of kilometres of Malaysian sand, jungle, road and mountain. In the end, we erred on the side of performance.

As a result, amidst thousands of single-geared bicycles, our 24-speed Giants stuck out like sore thumbs. We also wore ridiculous helmets—shunned even by Malaysian *motorcyclists*—another sure sign that we were slightly out of mind, and definitely out-of-town.

The other major dilemma revolved around our pre-trip dietary plans. I was fairly convinced by the "protein diet" craze that had swept the US, and so decided to cut down on carbohydrates. The aim was to slowly reduce my food intake and therefore shrink my stomach to prepare for our journey where we would be eating much less than normal.

Sumana, being a student of the camel school of consumption, had decided that the only way to prepare for reduced consumption was to eat as much as possible and thus fatten himself up to pre-empt the effects of weight loss. We took to our diets with dogged determination, intent on proving the other wrong. The result of all this waffly nutritional science is that Sumana often felt hungry and I weak.

Our moods were no doubt affected. Hence, that night in the *surau*, with every question from the boy known as Pip, our paranoia deepened, and we had instinctively become a bit standoffish. We kept trying to divert attention and conversation away from our bikes, while monitoring the gang from the corner of our eyes. It drove us mad.

Were we being irrational? Our friends had offered advice before we left. "Malaysia is a crime-ridden country," they had said, "why are you doing something so dangerous? Take this knife, you are going to need it, trust me. You will regret it one day during your trip. You guys are sleeping in a tent? You won't be able to protect your bikes, make sure you sleep on your passports."

We didn't have that knife, but those tendencies were cutting sharp into our minds that evening. If our bikes were stolen, it would confirm another Malaysian stereotype.

This fear did not desert us that night, even as we later shared cigarettes with Pip and his sidekicks. We interpreted all the small talk as him trying to butter us up before the kill. We patronised him, never letting our guard down. Before sleeping, we secured our bikes using reams of rope and multiple locks, like a moth cocooning its baby. We had become the exact stereotype we were trying to dismiss.

It was only days later, after being met with similar reactions from youth else-where, that we realised that Pip's eyes had been filled not with jealous, evil desire, but with adulation and wonder. He was filled with a boyish curiosity, having never seen that kind of cycling technology. He had approached us to find out more, to look at the bike, to meet us, to talk to us.

We feel terrible about not having indulged him. We should have offered a ride on the bike; we should have called in his posse in the background, all probably too shy to approach us. Instead, we acted like the richer neighbour, afraid of getting robbed. It would have been impossible for him to make off with our bikes. Everybody there knew his name, whether he smoked, and how good a football player he is.

As much as we like to think we're well travelled and seasoned, we had fallen into the same trap. Are we conditioned to think of Malaysia as dangerous? We had reacted in a very Singaporean way, having been sheltered under a warm blanket of bliss and security our whole lives. We take it for granted, but that is one of the things that make us happy.

***

We Singaporeans sometimes forget that crime exists. Indeed, the simple rule of law is the result of years of hard work. Lee Kuan Yew's team drew up some of the strict-est laws and harshest penalties known to the post-colonial democratic world. They combated corruption so effectively that the Singapore Police Force and their white-collar crime busters, the Commercial Affairs Department, quickly garnered a repu-tation for moral infallibility and ruthless efficiency.

Bribery is so rare that if and when it does occur, there is a media frenzy. The sort of crime that makes "News!" in Singapore astounds most visitors. Petty bribes, minor drug offences, gang scuffles, unarmed robberies. These newsworthy events in Singapore are but day-to-day hazards of life in many other big cities.

Living without crime is a luxury that Singaporeans only really appreciate when we venture abroad. Then, all of a sudden, we have to be on our guard. Often we forget, and assume the crimelessness of Singapore, and sometimes get caught out. Life is a much more tiresome, bothersome, paranoia-filled exercise when crime lurks.

We long for the sanctity of Singapore's streets, where a lady can walk alone, anywhere, anytime of the night in relative comfort. There is so little crime, in fact, that entire public campaigns are constructed to remind Singaporeans that there is, indeed, such a thing as crime.

The flip side of this strong enforcement is the culture of fear that pervades Singaporeans. This culture of fear has been so deeply ingrained that you rarely see policemen around; there is no need for them. The Singaporean policeman has become a subliminal force that exerts power simply by the threat of its presence.

The classic anecdote is of the obedient Singaporean who, in the dead of the night, standing by a remote road, with not a single car or person in sight, will prefer to wait for the Green Man before crossing, rather than risk breaking the law.

The presence of plainclothes officers and the fear of remote surveillance keep Singaporeans on edge. Big Brother is watching! Many are afraid to publicly discuss even the most banal of government policies, for fear of being recorded. Though certainly not as powerful or brutal as organisations such as the KGB, Singapore's Internal Security Department is sometimes portrayed as a sinister Secret Police.[2] This fear of the unknown, of what can and cannot be said and done, grips and holds Singaporeans in a constant daze of exaggerated self-censorship.

The strict rule of law then has been a double-edged sword. On the one hand, it has created one of the most crime-free and secure bubbles on earth. On the other hand, it limits the free expression of Singaporeans. Afraid to trample on somebody's political toes, we prefer to stay well clear of anything remotely adventurous, spontaneous or uncommon. Our creativity and innovative potential are thus limited.

Outside Singapore, we tend to keep an eye out for the criminal's gun. Inside Singapore, we are wary only of the government's stick. In Malaysia, things are a bit different.

***

The oft-made comparison is between laws and enforcement. Singapore has strong laws and strong enforcement. In Malaysia, there are laws but no enforcement. Once, when two friends of ours were stuck in traffic in Bangsar, a yuppie neighbourhood in KL, a smaller car pulled up alongside. Two men hopped out with baseball bats and started smashing their car.

Stunned, our friends sat motionless. The teenagers kept swinging away, breaking all the glass in and denting the beautifully preserved VW Beetle beyond recognition. The attack lasted less than two minutes. Soon, the teenagers jumped back into their car, and drove off hurriedly, in the process scraping several cars that were parked along the road, all the time laughing loudly, like the psychopaths in *Clockwork Orange*.

Thankfully, our friend jotted down the vehicle's license plate number and managed to get a good look at the driver and his companion. Unfortunately, our friends in Malaysia never heard back from their "so-called investigating officer". The violent louts got away.

Over the years, the police force has lost the trust of many Malaysians I know. Corruption is endemic. Trying to bribe a Malaysian policeman is like closing a deal at a flea market. The only thing in question is the price. And remember, one is never "buying" them off. You are just "settling". Like "service tax" in India, or "coffee money" in Indonesia, the magic word in Malaysia is "settle". The insider phrase to use to get away with most fines in Malaysia is, "Boss, can settle here?"

Singaporean drivers use it frequently on Malaysian highways. So routine is the procedure that many people tuck a 50 ringgit note away in their sun-flap, like change for a toll, an unspoken Autobahn fee. If you haven't had the time to get ringgit, they'll gladly accept 50 Singapore dollars.

These settlements occur when the traffic police erect little bribery drive-throughs on the highway shoulder: green tents, wooden benches, some dubious radar gun machinery and a few of their cronies. A long line of "speeding" offenders, including a few who weren't going fast but made the mistake of driving a nice car, will be hauled to one side.

For all the talk about Singaporean efficiency, nothing in our country is as perfectly streamlined and meticulously managed as the Malaysian bribery drive-through. Drink-driving offenders can also apparently buy their way out of jail, albeit at a much higher price.

When we were driving up to Malaysia to cover the elections in 2008, the customs protocol on the border had been turned on its head. Usually, cars aren't really checked as they leave Singapore. However, just weeks earlier, Mas Selamat, a terrorist suspect, had escaped from Singaporean custody. He broke out of our supposedly watertight detention centre through the lavatory, with the help of toilet rolls, which were used to cushion his fall. The popular view at the time was that he was might be surviving on nuts and small animals in Singapore's jungles, planning a further escape across the border.[3]

What all this meant was that Singaporean immigration and customs officials were extra diligent, sweeping all manner of vehicles on their way out, looking for Mas. On the other side, Malaysian officials could not have been happier. The Singaporeans were doing their work for them. Typically sluggish, now they didn't even have to lift a finger.

We flew through the Malaysian checkpoint in Johor Bahru. Just a few metres past the checkpoint, we drove past an officer, who had gotten off his bike and was attending to someone in a car. As soon as he saw us, he jumped back on his bike, and sped towards us, driving up to the driver's window.

"Hey, hey ... you were talking on the phone. That is not allowed."

"Huh?"

"No, you can't talk on the phone here."

Odd. Clearly Malaysians do not know this law.

"But everyone is doing it. Look there at that car."

The policeman turned around and pretended to look.

"No, I saw you just now talking on the phone. You have to pay a big fine."

"Boss, can settle here?"

"No way. You guys are driving an illegal car as well, you cannot. You have to follow me to the station."

He went on about how we needed a special insurance permit in order to drive our G-plated Singaporean car in Malaysia.[4] We'd seen this kind of play before, trying to drive up the price of the bribe. We were not to be fooled. The cheek of this young officer, to fish for a bribe so openly, so near the checkpoint.

"Boss, no time lah, please lah, let me settle here."

"No time? Eh, how can you say that? You think I care about your time? In Singapore, you think you can tell the police officer no time is it?"

This carried on for a while. We were convinced we could pay our way out of this, as cash strapped as we were, not having changed much cash. And he seemed to have us on some other minor infringement, but we thought it a ploy.

"OK, fine, give me the fine. Write me a ticket. I will pay the fine."

"No, no. Because your car is illegal, you have to come to the station. I cannot issue the thing here."

Reluctantly, we agreed to follow the officer. He called for backup. In our big jeep, we were soon being escorted through JB's main throughway by two small 125cc Honda mopeds, like an oil tanker being ferried by tugboats. It was humiliating. They could have at least given us two proper police bikes with sirens.

If that had been Singapore, we would have been petrified. As it were, we were smiling and joking, concerned only about the slight delay in plans, discussing how much we should offer.

The police station was practically deserted, not a hint of activity anywhere. The cop came up to our jeep.

"OK, you guys wait here, I go and call my boss."

The gate was wide open and we hadn't even switched off the engine. The cop disappeared into the station. We had half a mind to just reverse and drive off. Then, a tinted door at the station entrance swung open, and the cop came out, jogging down the stairs. Just before the door swung close, a boot stopped it, and it flung back open. A thick heavy-set man with short hair walked nonchalantly down the stairs, pulling up his belt, and adjusting his sunglasses. Well, finally they were giving us some respect. This guy at least looked the part. A badge on his left breast said "*Saya Anti-Rasuah*", "I am against bribes".

We weren't too bothered by the badge. We realised it was just another way of jacking up the price. Eager to get back on the election trail, we quickly spewed out the magic words.

"Boss, can settle here?"

"Ha. No way. Handphone is hundreds-of-dollars fine. Other charge is maybe 5,000, I don't know. I have to impound your car. The court is closed on Saturdays. So you have to come back on Monday and you can go to court and pay the fine straight to the judge."

At first, we thought that this was all part of the act. One could not crumble straightaway. The pretence of honesty is as important as the eventual corruption. We smiled, then repeated our refrain.

"Aiyah, like that so hard lah. Are you sure there is nothing you can do? We don't have time lah. Anyway, we have the permit, maybe you can let us go back to Singapore and get it?"

"Are you joking or what? If a Malaysian gets caught in Singapore, you think the police will let him go back and get his stuff? No way. And then you Singaporeans, just go back and ignore all the fines. Think we don't know right? Forget it. Your jeep is staying here. You can come back next week, go to court and talk to the judge."

This went on for about 45 minutes, with long periods of silence in between as either party searched for a way to repeat the exact same thing by changing just a few words—a tautological dance between "Can settle here?" and "You have to go to court." We grew progressively less confident of turning this around, and each new "Can settle here?" was uttered with less conviction.

His "*Saya Anti-Rasuah*" badge grew bigger each time we looked at it, like a demonic symbol sent to pierce our election dreams. Where's a corrupt cop when you need one?

After a sweaty hour under early afternoon Johor sun, and with lunch time slowly approaching, we launched one last desperate appeal.

"Boss, please lah, please," we begged. If he told us to get on our knees, we probably would have. We always listen to cops. "Please boss, we settle here, then we go back to Singapore straightaway, please."

"Hmm. OK, you talk to my assistant. I leave it to him lah."

And with that abrupt final volley, he left, and his assistant came scuttling back. The cop literally sweated us for an hour before walking back into his office. His sudden departure was a bit shocking, but it was a relief at the same time, there was a glimmer of bribe hope. Now all we had to do was negotiate the amount. It was going to be a lot more than the usual, given the extraordinary anti-bribe performance we had just witnessed.

"Boss, no ringgit, American money can or not?" Offering foreign currency puts the cop in the driving seat, as they are always very nationalistic about the strength of the Malaysian dollar.

"US dollars? How much?"

"200 can?"

That was 650 ringgit, enough, we thought, to cover all Singaporean bribers that weekend.

"Ha, ha, ha, ha. The US is in recession, don't you know? The US dollar has dropped already."

What cheek. Not only was he irritating, he also followed the markets. Fed up of the hour long hassle, and sensing that we were well and truly beaten, we didn't have the strength to argue any more. We walked into the station, paid the fine he wanted, and walked out again.

"Make sure you go straight back to Singapore, OK. Your car is not allowed in Malaysia without the permit."

"Yes, OK, thanks."

We drove out of the station and turned left, in the direction of Singapore. As soon as we were out of sight, we made a U-turn, and headed back up north towards KL. We were back in business. Luckily, over the course of the next week, no other cops bothered us.

***

This crookedness leaves the state of Malaysian law enforcement in shambles. Public perception of the state's security is low, and this undermines faith in the government's other institutions. Those with money, like in any society rife with bribery, might believe that they can do what they want and buy their way out. They are, no doubt, also to blame for the current state of affairs.

Therefore, while the Singaporean policeman is revered and feared, the Malaysian policeman is often ridiculed as underpaid, corrupt, parochial and quite simply, a bit of a joke.

When we visited Alor Setar on our bicycles, we ended up at the Police Station—simply because we could not find a free place to stay. We had tried the Hindu temple near the stadium, but the *swami* there told us that he had entertained enough free-loading visitors for this lifetime—apparently the last chap had made off with some temple bounty and, in the process, all of the *swami*'s remaining good karma. The Chinese temple nearby looked fairly imposing—not sure if it was because of the dogs or the line of Mercedes—and so we headed to the sedate looking park that abuts the stadium. Within minutes of sitting down on a bench, we were swarmed. Mosquitoes.

Before we could whip out our insect sprays, we noticed another potential hazard. A bunch of youths were loitering, eyes bloodshot and hands trembling. They might have just been caffeine connoisseurs, but we decided not to take the risk. There was only one place left to go, and we knew it.

And so, with our limbs jellied, and our minds knackered, we trudged over to the police station, tails between our legs. It was a bit of a cop-out.

"What do you all want?"

"We're looking for a place to stay. Can we sleep here?"

After 20 days on the road, we had stopped beating around the bush.

"Here? No, no, you can't stay here. Why don't you go to a hotel?"

"We don't have any money."

Blank stare.

"Where are you from?"

"Singapore."

"So, what exactly are you doing here?"

Within five minutes, he and his fellow officers had collectively decided that they'd rather have us inside the station, than let us loose onto the streets of Alor Setar. So they showed us to a bare room with a fan. It was the reporting room of the police station. We lay down on the floor to sleep, next to a couch. Just as we were about to doze off, a voice whispered.

"Oh, by the way, are these your bicycles?" We had left them right outside the front door, by the side, in full view of the policeman on duty.

"Yes."

"Oh, you better lock them up. You never know who might steal them."

Funny. There were only policemen around.

***

But how dangerous exactly is Malaysia? Singaporeans have long bandied around the idea of a treacherous Malaysia. This notion was given an almighty rubber stamp by Lee Kuan Yew in 1997. In an affidavit as part of a libel case he was bringing against opposition politician Tang Liang Hong, he commented that, "[o]f all places he [Tang] went to Johor. That place is notorious for shootings, muggings and carjackings. It does not make sense for a person who claims to be fearful for his life to go to a place like Johor."

That incensed the Malaysians to no end. Coming from Lee Kuan Yew, the architect of our country, the epitome of our national pride, it was taken to be a statement that represented the whole of our society. UMNO Youths responded with gusto. At a demonstration in Johor, they paraded placards calling Mr Lee "senile", "stupid" and a "pig", outraged that he might have been trying to score political points at home at their expense.[5] Mr Lee's office, fearful of an unnecessary political brouhaha, quickly apologised. What was quite troubling at the time, and is probably still true, is that most Singaporeans share his point of view.

According to the UN, in 2000, Malaysia had, per capita, fewer people brought before the criminal courts, fewer people convicted and fewer people sitting in prison than Singapore.[6] Numbers do not always tell the truth: Malaysia has a lot more unrecorded crime than Singapore, and as the bashed-up Beetle suggests, a low conviction rate.

Malaysia did have a higher per capita rate for homicides, assaults, rape, robbery and automobile thefts. Some occur up to six times more frequently in Malaysia. Singapore, on the other hand, leads in thefts and drug offences, which occur twice as often as they do in Malaysia.

The average Singaporean criminal prefers the behind-your-back elusive theft or a hide-and-seek drug offence. Wander across the causeway and there is a higher prevalence of direct, in-your-face type crime. Based on those facts, you could argue that Singapore is safer than Malaysia.

However, using Singapore as a benchmark for safety is grossly unfair. Perhaps better to look at countries such as Germany, Australia, England, France and Denmark, which had much more total recorded crime, more homicides, more assaults, more rapes, more robberies and more thefts than Malaysia. Thus, statistically speaking, Malaysia is a safe little country to be in.

Yet, Singaporeans happily scoot off to these Western countries even as we bemoan Malaysian danger. Part of it could be that Singaporeans, by virtue of distance, are more attuned to the state of criminal affairs in Malaysia. It seems like every snatched Singaporean purse is reported. There is a tendency to look favourably upon a developed Western country and less favourably upon a less developed Southeast Asian neighbour.

Our own anecdotal evidence suggests that Malaysia is not dangerous at all. In a month, we slept on remote beaches, in quiet parks, by the side of lonely roads. There was ample opportunity for passers-by to assault us or attempt to steal something. Yet not once were we bothered. Perhaps if we flaunted more wealth, we would have been more attractive to would-be-thieves. But that is true of any big city.

As we slowly discovered to our own detriment, the fear of crime bogs the willing traveller down. It makes you paranoid about your fellow human being, and a sub-conscious guard is erected. You interpret slightly ambiguous actions and comments negatively.

Every time somebody wanted to look at our bikes, we got worried. We stopped chatting in our free-wheeling manner and retreated like a snail faced with a hungry Frenchman. Once you fear the people in front of you and the place around you, your mind is simply unable to function. Your soul's despair is all consuming.

Our fear ruined countless social encounters. Worse, we will never know exactly how much we missed out on, how many conversations passed us by. What we learned from all this is that we Singaporeans are somehow conditioned to be too careful. More often than not, our fellow human beings are as well-intentioned as us. The next time we're in an initially troubling social encounter, we're going to take one more step. We'll still be well clear of the touchline.

***

Pontian Kechil, Johor. 13 August 2004 (last day of cycling).

We rolled into Pontian Kechil (Pontian henceforth), just a few hours away from home, relieved to have come through unscathed. Three more hours of cycling and we'd be home and dry. Singapore beckoned! But first we had one more crucial inter-view to get through. In Pontian we went in search of a Malaysian police officer.

Pontian is the sort of cookie-cutter town notable only for forgettable Malaysian town institutions like the busy wet market, polished school and the dominant central police station. It is quiet enough to drive the urban-fed Singaporean mad. At its edge, one can enjoy a decent vista over the Malacca Straits, but that is true of so many towns along the west coast; and the Malacca Straits vista is, really, just decent.

But then again, we didn't have time to dawdle through Pontian. We were on a tight deadline. Singapore was so close, yet in a way so far. The Pontian interview was the easiest because we were nearing the end of the trip, and had accumulated lots of interview experience; but also the hardest, because we were slowing down just hours away from our goal. As it were, we had enough interviews to fill two books.

Sensibility and perseverance won that late morning, and we soon found our-selves sitting in the waiting room of the Pontian Police Station. In a typical show of Malaysian initiative, it took about five minutes for anybody to notice us, then another twenty for somebody to finally help us.

We had traipsed around Malaysia and presented novel headaches to their policemen. In Bandar Permaisuri, Terengganu and Alor Setar, Kedah, we had, like unannounced in-laws, forced them to grudgingly take us in for the night. And now, in Pontian, Johor, we had humbly asked to speak with an officer.

"What? You want to see who?"

"A policeman. Any policeman."

"Why?" she asked, "For what?"

"Just to chat. To find out about his life. And what it's like to be a cop."

The young Malay receptionist sitting behind the glass-walled counter looked up at us with her big eyes and then put up her palm to tell us to be patient. We were kept waiting, as our puzzling request was passed from one incredulous face to another. Finally a tall, middle-aged cop appeared, dressed in a sweater and blue slacks.

"Hello," he said, his voice filled with as much excitement as a Singaporean on election day.

He winced as he talked to us, as if he had drawn the short straw in the back office, and now had to entertain two insects. After ascertaining that we did indeed want to speak about his life, he waved to follow him, leading us on a long walk through narrow corridors full of amused plainclothes policemen and women, up several flights of stairs and into his office.

Isa's office was roomy, and, as with many deskbound cops, it doubled up as his bedroom, wardrobe and study. His blue police uniform hung in the corner, proudly representing Isa's alter-ego, his law-enforcing self, ready to mutate when duty called. He politely sat us down on two chairs across from him, but then an uncomfortable silence filled the room.

"So, yes, ask me, what do you want to know?" He didn't make an effort to introduce himself. He wanted this to be over as soon as possible.

We fired off some banal questions. "It's been 26 years," Isa replied, before pausing and lifting his eyeballs to the ceilings to do the sums again. "Yes, yes, 26 since I joined the police. But you know, by luck lah, I joined."

He'd often reply in English to our Malay comments, and vice versa. It was one of those competitive international social encounters when each party wants to show off their knowledge of the other's language. After a month in Malaysia, we were charged and ready for the battle, and waxed our own delightful brand of the Sultan's Malay.

"Oleh kerana masalah-masalah demikian, Encik Isa memilihi pekerjaan polis, ya?" I asked, accenting the last "a" of each sentence, as we had been taught to do.

"Sorry, what did you say?" Isa asked in English.

"You decided to join the police force, but you said it was by luck. What did you mean?"

"Yes, yes, yes. Like I said, it was a coincidence."

After A Level exams, at the age of 19, Isa enrolled in a *Pengajian Jauh*, Distance Learning Course, which in those days meant a bevy of weekend classes in Kuala Lumpur, 22 km away from his *kampung* home in Kajang. Dreaming of a foreign degree, Isa went for an interview.

However, the acceptance letter arrived only after he had decided to exercise his backup option: join the force, and accept a scholarship to a local university. So instead of an overseas adventure, Isa enrolled in a social sciences course at the Universiti Kebangsaan Malaysia (UKM, Malaysian National University), near his home.

After graduation, Isa started working at the KL Police Headquarters. "Working in KL was very hectic. Some days I only went home to sleep. Wake up, work, go home, sleep. I hardly saw my family. I also did not have much time for my game."

"What game?"

"Badminton. See?" he said, pointing at his rackets, tucked neatly next to the wall, weapons ready for their master's next duel. The rackets clearly took precedence over the pistols.

Isa certainly enjoyed the slower pace of life in Pontian. He also got to jog and play golf regularly. "I get to enjoy my … what do you call it … this 'sports lifestyle'?" he finished, laughing.

He certainly looked the part: he was lean, and his young face was capped by a neatly slicked icing of black hair. ("It's natural. I don't look 48, do I?"). His only "blemishes" were innumerable moles that dotted his face, as if he had just gotten shot in a game of paintball; and a slight paunch that was an inevitable burden of age.

"Thank Tuhan for giving me the chance to stay here," he said, gesticulating to the heavens above the drab ceiling. "I get to spend more time with my family. I get to see my children for breakfast, lunch and dinner," he said, smiling like a little boy.

Isa, awkward and unsure at first, had slowly opened up. Like so many of our other Malaysian interviewees, Isa's character seemed wrapped in a social membrane, comprised of humility, tepidness and a slight insecurity about whether he had anything interesting to say. Once we had reached through, flowery details and absorbing asides came screaming on the tails of personal history. Isa wanted to talk.

Anthony, the church warden in Kuantan, had also told us about the need to find a right work-life balance. His children had moved to Singapore, and though they enjoyed their work, they didn't think Singapore was a great place to bring up children.

They resented the fact that their busy work life left them so little time to spend at home with the kids. This doesn't surprise us. In job satisfaction surveys and happiness indices, Singaporeans frequently complain about the long work day. There are two sides to this. Sure, some people do *need to* work very long hours, either to put food on the table or in their quest for ever more Pradas.[7]

On the other hand, there are also many office workers who want to "show face". They stay late in the office because they believe this will impress their bosses as much as the quality of their work. It's a two-way street: some traditional bosses continue to feed this impression. Thus, instead of working efficiently, these employees drag out their work.

Put together, our deference to authority, the need to "show face" and the existing hierarchical structures make for more time in the office and less at home with the kids.

Anthony's children had also felt that Singapore lacked a sense of communality. Neighbours rarely speak to each other, and many people live in their own little worlds. According to Rajarethnam, Sumana's dad, there was much more camaraderie when he was growing up. He lived in a flat in Macpherson with his parents and 11 siblings. Everybody's flat doors were open, and kids would run from one house to another, sharing food, toys and parenting duties.

How have we lost this? In Singapore, many of us believe that we are caring for our family by spending more time working. We measure love in economic terms, not in badminton games. In that sense, Singapore may just be like any other big East Asian consumerist society.

Singapore is unique in one other way, though—the fact that it is an urban jungle. Hence, the opportunities for outdoor activities are limited. Different people in Malaysia, from Isa the policeman to Steven, an executive with Pfizer in KL, have mentioned how they and their kids love the great outdoors in Malaysia. Jungles, beaches, mountains galore.

Thus many Malaysians we met do not consider Singapore an ideal place to bring up children. This may come as a surprise to the Western expatriates living in Asia who consider Singapore one of the most child-friendly places on Earth—everything is sanitised, schools are top-notch, crime is low and one can easily afford a maid. Of course, Western expats, with generally higher salaries, more flexible work schedules, and the ability to jet their children off at any time, have a very different Singapore experience from many locals.

For most Malaysians we met, life encompassed a lot more than work. The family was of utmost importance, and their life was incomplete if their family played only a bit role. An extracurricular distraction was also crucial, be it badminton, fishing or jungle-tree conservation. It gave one a well-rounded life. You had to have a "sports lifestyle" in addition to your "work lifestyle".

So the average Malaysian policeman might spend less time policing the streets because he's at home teaching his child to ride a bicycle or in the local community centre whacking a shuttlecock at his old chum from primary school. He didn't think of himself as neglecting his work; rather, if he had not been doing these things, he would have been neglecting his life.

In Singapore, work consumes us. Many Malaysians I met, rural and urban, were shocked when I spoke of my busy bee friends who sometimes eat their take-out Saturday dinners alone in their sterile offices. They empathised with the children of busy parents who outsource their parenting to caring but unrelated domestic maids from Indonesia, Myanmar, the Philippines and South Asia, seeing it not as a cheap convenience but as an unfortunate sacrifice.

They looked shocked when I told them that more than anything, top grades, a stellar job and conspicuous consumption—everything from a Vertu to a Mercedes—were the hallmarks of success in Singapore.

"My fourth kid has the same hobbies as me. We even go walking up the Gunung Pulai." The 14-year-old mountain climber is his fourth of five children. His oldest is a 21-year-old computer science student; his second a 16-year-old engineer; his third, the Einstein of the family, a 15-year-old doctor-to-be, currently off at boarding school, in the Sekolah Menengah Sains Muar—he had high hopes for her. The baby of the family was his 12-year-old son.

"I love a big family. When you have a big family, you cherish life more," Isa proclaimed. "You get to see each kid as they are growing up. Each kid has different characteristics, you have to observe, and adapt and respond. Each kid has different needs. You can't treat them all the same, oh no! You have to mould each one ... Do you have any kids?"

"No, we're not married. Maybe in the future."

"Oh, but you have brothers and sisters?"

"We each have two sisters, no brothers."

"Ah, so you know the joy of having sisters."

Joy?

"But your sisters are luckier than you!"

"Why? Because they have such great brothers?"

"Yes, that's it. Your sisters can experience all the relationships of life. They have a sister, and a brother. You only have sisters, you don't have a brother ... or maybe the two of you are brothers, haha."

He didn't know that after a month sleeping together in crappy tents, some time apart was looking strangely attractive.

"So remember, when you have your family, have two boys and two girls, so they can all experience the different relationships of life."

Some 27 years into our life, and that was the first time anybody had spelt out the need for four kids so simply. We had never before heard that line of reasoning. Is that because we grew up in Singapore? Or is it more a general urban, developed condition, as birth-rates decline?

Whatever the case, we were struck by our ignorance. Being able to experience all human relationships seems like such a basic, fundamental tenet of life. In Singapore, parents who have had two children get pats on their back and congratulations for performing "national service". Those who have four may be up for a presidential award.

Singaporean parents will run to the ends of the earth for their children, spoiling and spoon feeding, but few give what Isa considers the greatest gift—a brother and a sister.

Not a *single* friend of ours could speak of their huge families the way Isa did. This is partly due to cost: many Singaporeans cannot afford to have big families. However, many others definitely can—but do not want to, for one reason or another.

We had experienced similar pro-family sentiments along the way, notably in the FELDA Endau estate. After confessing that he was a Boney M fan, flashing a pirated platinum hits album at us, and screaming along to "Ra-Ra-Rasputin", Kamal decided to discuss more personal things.

"So, how old are you guys?"

"Guess lah, uncle."

"Twenty." He had already thought of the answer.

"Twenty?" we both gasped.

"You're 27," said Siti, Kamal's wife, quietly from the corner. Guarded till that point, she spoke with a mystic authority. How did she know?

"Not married right?" asked Kamal.

"No, no."

"What age do you plan on getting married?"

"Don't know actually. Our moms want us to get married now, but we're thinking 32 or 33?"

"Too late," He declared, convinced of our folly. "Too late, you get married too late, you lose out."

We had always thought it was the opposite—get married too *early* and you lose out.

"Lose out? Why?"

"Now you are single, you have only one brain. When you marry, you have two brains, and you can come up with lots of ideas!" bellowed Kamal triumphantly. "You can also have double the income!"

"But won't a wife and family suck up all our income?"

"No, when you get married, you will have a plan. You need a plan. Now, tell me, what plan do you have? You just enjoy here, enjoy there. Are you going to keep enjoying till you're 50?"

"What's wrong with that? Don't we all want to enjoy ourselves?"

"But then you won't have a plan! What about a car? A house? A job? A plan!"

Kamal seemed to be contradicting himself. On the one hand, he was a big champion of our spontaneous romp across Malaysia on bicycles, as unplanned a trip as you can get. Later, he was telling us that we need a plan which included a wife and kids. He clarified things by saying that we should be whoever we want to be, and do whatever we want to do, but without a plan, everything else is pointless. The wife and family have to be the backbone of our life.

Throughout our journey, we met Malaysians, rural and urban, who couldn't believe that we were still single, at the grand old age of 27. As far as they were concerned, we had not planned our life well. We had not given enough priority to starting a family.

Do we Singaporeans value family life less than Malaysians? Quite possibly. After numerous conversations about girlfriends, marriage and children, my sense is that there are cultural and developmental reasons for this.

My anecdotal evidence suggests that Malays treasure big families and family time more than Chinese and Indians. Many Malays I met, including Isa and Kamal, are extremely proud of their big families. Much of their life revolves around their extended families.

I found this to be less so for the Indians, even less for Chinese. This is not to say that Chinese and Indians don't care for their families, just simply that having a big family, and maintaining close ties with the extended family, seems less a priority than it is for Malays.

When we were cycling through Terengganu, we stopped at a tiny *kampung* for a breather, and two very old Malay men immediately chatted us up. They were certain that all the differences between Malaysia and Singapore could be summed up in a neat parable.

Orang Melayu, bini dulu, baru cari harta.
Orang Cina, cari harta, baru bini.

Malays find a wife first, and then wealth.
Chinese find wealth first, and then a wife.

It is interesting to compare total fertility rates—the average number of children a woman is expected to have—among the different ethnic groups in the two countries. In 2010, Malaysia's total fertility rates were: 1.5 for Chinese, 1.7 for Indians and 2.6 for Malays.[8] Singapore's were: 1.02 for Chinese, 1.13 for Indians and 1.65 for Malays.[9]

Thus, in both Malaysia and Singapore, Malays have the highest total fertility rates among the three major ethnic groups. There could be cultural and economic reasons for this. In both countries, the Malays have lower average household incomes than the Chinese and Indians. As incomes rise, people tend to have fewer kids.

This would partly explain why Singapore's fertility rates are today so low. This is a socio-economic phenomenon the world over, particularly with the other East Asian Tigers—Hong Kong, South Korea and Taiwan—who have all recorded torrid economic growth alongside plummeting fertility. (Similarly, the fertility rate in Malaysia's more developed states, such as Penang and Selangor, is lower than other parts of the country.)[10]

What is most surprising, perhaps, is that by 2010 the total fertility rate of Singapore's Malays was almost as low as Malaysia's Chinese. Malay fertility rates in Singapore have dropped drastically from 2.54 in 2000 to 1.65 in 2010.

Perhaps there is something unique about Singapore's pressure-cooker, rat-race, materialist society that has deterred young couples from having children. It is expensive to bring up children in Singapore, particularly with all the extra tuition, expensive pre-school classes, and other personal improvement programmes that parents today deem necessary.

But government policy has also greatly influenced Singaporeans' family values. In Singapore, love and procreation have become somewhat manufactured; transformed from individual decisions and responsibilities into a national obsession. The government has indelibly shaped every Singaporean's conception of love, marriage and children.

In the 1970s, fearful of a population explosion, our government told people to "Stop at 2". As expected, we followed orders. By the early 1980s, it became clear that we were not replacing ourselves sufficiently and so, in a 180-degree turn, the government started to promote bigger families. Tax breaks were offered to parents who had a third child. It didn't make much of a difference.

By 2005, our total fertility rate had slumped to 1.26, well below 2, the "replacement rate" required to maintain a stable population. Our government, desperate, pulled out all the stops: more tax breaks, longer maternity leave, and vociferous public campaigns.

Almost from the day he stepped into office, our prime minister, Lee Hsien Loong, has been urging Singaporeans to make babies. In the space of one generation, the Singaporean family psyche has been switched from big families to "Stop at 2" and back to big families again.

However, our government has tried to manipulate the population in a much more classist fashion—encouraging university graduates to marry other graduates rather than non-graduates. This reflects Lee Kuan Yew's belief in genetic determinism.

In 1967, he said that about 5 per cent of the population "are more than ordinarily endowed physically and mentally and in whom we must extend our limited and slender resources ..." Later, in 1969, he worried that "less economically productive people in the community are reproducing themselves at rates higher than the rest."[11]

Presumably, our government believed it could improve Singapore's gene pool. In 1984 it implemented a programme that tried to increase the fertility of university-educated women while offering subsidies for the voluntary sterilisation of poor and uneducated parents.[12]

Singapore even set up a couple of government agencies to further this agenda. The Social Development Unit (SDU) was formed in 1984 to promote marriages among graduate singles, while Social Development Services (SDS) was set up in 1985 to promote marriages among non-graduate singles.

Sometimes it seems like our eugenics policies were implemented in a bygone era rife with classism. Actually, it was less than 30 years ago. We grew up in a society where eugenics influenced love.

Lee Kuan Yew's views on this haven't changed much. In 2008, he told 700-odd delegates at a Human Capital Summit that Singaporean graduates who marry non-graduates "will worry if their children will make it to the university".[13]

In Singapore, something so natural, so carnal, so innately human as love is transformed into a more structured, formal process. It seems like the only thing the government has yet to do is teach Singaporeans how to give head.

PAP fans love to boast about the party's forward thinking and successful long-term planning. But when its history is eventually written (by somebody neutral), the PAP's misguided population policies of the 1970s–80s will tarnish its legacy. Many of Singapore's current socio-economic problems—including inequality, public transport squeezes and xenophobia—have their roots in our low birth-rate, and the government's attempt to address it with sudden, unsustainably high immigration.

Put another way, when it comes to population policies, the current PAP leadership has created new problems by trying to correct the old problems that are partly the doing of the 1970s–80s PAP leadership.

Malaysia's government, on the other hand, does not try to manipulate its population dynamics so meticulously. However, Malaysia's religious police do frequently try to peer into the private love lives of Muslims in the country, to ensure that unmarried couples are not engaging in illicit physical activity—what is known as *khalwat*, literally "close proximity". These *khalwat* raids can be quite sudden and brutal—Islamic officers are known to barge into people's houses and rooms, looking for immoral activity.

This points to one of the great paradoxes of Malaysian society. The Malay Muslims are afforded special economic rights, but they cannot enjoy certain personal and social freedoms such as the ability to drink and engage in physical relations before marriage. On the other hand, the Chinese and Indian non-Muslims are considered second-class citizens politically, but then are able to lead much freer lives than the Malay Muslims ever can.

It does appear, however, that the Singapore government's constant intrusions into the bedroom may have been counterproductive. At best, they have failed to achieve their goals. At worse, love, marriage and sex, glorious expressions of the human condition, have been reduced to numbers, policies and projections. Procreation becomes a mechanical response, a "national service", akin to paying taxes.

Which begs the question: have we all spent enough time thinking about what makes us happy? For those of us who want huge families, have we really thought hard enough about what else we could be doing with our time if we had a smaller family? Conversely, for those of us who want tiny families, are we missing out on one of life's basic joys?

11
The stress of work and city life

Rural Malaysia has always fascinated us. There is something mystical and charming about it. It conjures visions of a simpler life, of a forgotten age, of padi and wild oxen, of waterfalls and mountains, of bits and pieces of life which we do not know in Singapore, which we'll never have in Singapore.

Malaysia's urban centres, however, do not really inspire us. Many of them, especially KL, are dense, poorly planned heat sinks. They feel like less pretty versions of Singapore: more smog, more heat, more people, more traffic. No thank you.

Still, romanticising the countryside while lamenting urban decay is a luxury of the privileged. It is also an intellectually flimsy exercise—in many countries, rural squalor is often worse, leading to massive urban flight. Therefore, as we traversed Malaysia, we expected to meet many Malaysians who had happily left the *kampung* for the big city's bright lights.

Sure enough, we met scores of Malaysians who had migrated to places such as KL and Penang in search of a better life. However, many we spoke with had mixed feelings about their adopted homes. They longed to return to their birthplaces, whether in Johor or Sarawak.

Some of them have. For instance, Isa, whom we met in 2004, prefers life in sleepy Pontian. If he ever needs something special, he said, he can always get it in Johor Bahru. "No, I don't miss anything in KL. The only thing there is my wife's family," he added dryly.

In Pontian, he held the position of *Ketua Bahagian Pengurusan Daerah*, Head of the District's Public Licensing Department. It was cushy child's play, compared with his time in KL, where he had spent 16 years in the Secret Society Branch of Malaysia's Criminal Investigation Department (CID).

While there, Isa, the accidental policeman, was forced to deal with Malaysia's grimy underworld. The only bonus, he felt, was that his targets seemed to be less race-conscious than the general populace. "In my time, the Indian and the Chinese gangs were together. For example, the Chinese gangs operating in Tapah were headed by an Indian. In fact, the Chinese gangs in Chinatown were headed by a Malay!"

In the late 1980s to the 1990s, there was a lot of construction in Malaysia. According to Isa, many of the gangs lived off "protection money" from these builders. "In KL, there was Wah Kee, they were also dealing in prostitution. And then there was the Ah Ming Hoei, they were involved in everything. Then you had some Indian gangs in Brickfields and Jalan Klang Lama."

"Any others?"

"There were some Indian gangs in Cheras too."

"Any others?"

"No, not really, I don't remember their names, it was long ago. You know, those days, I would work without sleep, sometimes for 48 hours."

Isa had a pensive, distant look in his eyes.

"Were you involved in any fights? Did the gangsters ever shoot at you?"

"No, no, not really. I have friends who were shot, but not me."

Bubbly at first, Isa had grown uncomfortable when remembering his involvement with Malaysia's underworld. A remote, retelling of facts had rapidly become a very personal journey, a return to a place he shunned. He looked at us blankly. Most Malays we have met, when faced with minor social discomfort, rarely say so directly, preferring subtle methods of conveyance. Sensing this, we threw him a lifeline.

"So, what sort of work do the police do here? Is there any crime in a small place like Pontian?"

"The big problem here is illegal immigration and trafficking."

The Pontian police had a tough time catching the illegal Indonesians, some drug traffickers, crossing the Malacca Straits to get from the Riau Archipelago to Malaysia. "We have one police boat to monitor 76 km of coastline. How to check?"

"Other than that, it's like any other Malaysian town."

"Is illegal racing a problem here?"

"Oh yes, that's a problem everywhere. Saturday night is 'race night' for the *kampung* boys," Isa said casually, as if the boys were playing Bingo.

All around Malaysia, we had been broken by woeful stories of a brother or a cousin dying in a horrific motorcycle accident. Drive through Malaysia, and chances are that you'll be taken aback by *Mat Rempit*, reckless speed demons who perform gravity-defying tricks on their miniature two-wheelers.

We had gotten our first taste of the *Mat Rempit* two weeks earlier, far away from Pontian, on Malaysia's other coast. As we cycled into Nenasi, our jaws dropped. Before us lay the most gorgeous beach we had seen, miles and miles of it. A spattering of wooden *kampung* houses sat some distance away from the glittering South China Sea.

Nenasi's residents were served by a row of shophouses, which guarded the town's entrance, most of them Chinese owned. We stepped into one shop, where we were immediately greeted with a welcome curry puff. Food distractions were common on the trip.

"Wah, thanks Aunty, this is *sedap*, delicious!"

"Eh, I no aunty, you just eat," said the Sumo-sized curry puff-maker, who was teaching two attentive young girls the finer points of pastry rolling. After eating, we headed to the beach.

We were approached by an old man with rust-coloured skin and a *parang* in hand, who chatted instantly and soon offered up a dilapidated hut for the night. As we thanked him, a younger man emerged from the hut and stretched lazily as if he had just been awoken. The young man walked towards us. "We're sorry, are we taking your spot?" Our formality caught him off guard; he half-heartedly told us, in the middle of a long yawn, that we were not causing him any trouble.

Mi had wanted to wake before the sunset, and so the timing worked. He was a lean beach bum, and we couldn't tell if it was because of exercise or a lack of food. His moustache thinned and drooped down to the side of his lips, giving it a whisker like appearance. We sat down to chat and he offered us some Gudang Garam cigarettes. He lit his cigarette and stared at the sea with a serene listlessness.

"So what do you think of Singapore?"

"Singapore? I used to work there as a welder. Sometimes I got contracts there legally and sometimes I used to go and work there illegally," he admitted. "Some of my friends have been caught recently and cannot go back to Singapore to work for a while. It is very hard to get a work permit to go there and work now, but still so many people go there lah."

Mi would typically work for three months, before returning home to relax for one to two months. "I like to work in the city, here and in Singapore, but it is so noisy sometimes, it is not peaceful at night," he lamented. "I come back here and I can just *lepak*, laze about, at the beach. Just stare at the water. When I feel like it, I go fishing, but not so much to catch the fish, just to go, you know?"

Not really. *Just to go?* The thought of doing something just for the heck of it seemed reckless. Mi wasn't always so carefree. Ten years before, he had left his small village for Kuala Lumpur, filled with drive and ambition. "I wanted to get a job, live in the city, see what it's like," he said. "KL is the capital city, after all. That's where the biggest and best things in Malaysia are, right?"

Mi quickly felt out of place in KL. Life was a slog. Jobs weren't easy to come by. Things were expensive. People were not straightforward. Friends came and went. And too many women were stuck up. It was all clichéd urban estrangement, except that Mi was real, and we found it easy to empathise with the grief that grows as dreams vanish.

"I realised that the *kampung* life is the best," he said, not really convinced, but at peace with himself.

Some young boys came to the shed and looked around inquisitively. Without a word, they started playing frantically around the shed. One of the boys climbed up the rope to the ceiling and the other two boys were trying to pull him down. There was a lot of laughter. "Look at these kids. I hope you don't mind them. They seldom see foreigners. I think they are just showing off."

The sun was setting. Mi decided we needed to gather wood while there was still some light. "We should build a fire, otherwise the mosquitoes will come and get you."

We helped him, showered in the crimson light of the evening sun, and soon we had gathered a respectable heap of firewood. Mi lit the wood using some leaves. Black smoke rose into the evening. As is common near the equator, dusk was brief, and soon we were enveloped by darkness.

Mi pulled chairs from the shed and we sat in front of the fire. Wan, his friend, joined us in the darkness. As we sat there, the four of us around the fire, able to make out only silhouettes and grainy details on each other's orange-hued faces, Mi and Wan shared chilling stories about Nenasi, fuelled by clove cigarettes and the macabre atmosphere.

Beneath the veneer of a sleepy beach town, old men were raping boys, youth were being drawn into motorcycle gangs, and drugs were paralysing all and sundry. The work cycle was partly to blame, according to Mi and Wan.

"This town is a fishing town, most boys and men work as fishermen, so the work is seasonal. In the off season, there is a lot of crime and drugs. During the season, they work really hard, but off season is a different matter."

Rampant drug abuse had also resulted in a high HIV infection rate, something conservative Malaysia has never been too comfortable dealing with. The first case of HIV infection in Malaysia was reported in 1986. The infection rate peaked in 2002, when almost 7,000 new cases were reported—about 19 each day—of mostly Malay men. By the end of 2010, Malaysia had a total of 91,362 reported HIV infections—or about 1 in every 300 people. By contrast, Singapore had a total of 4,845 HIV infections—or about 1 in every 1,000 people.[1]

"We have a saying here—none of the boys are around, because half of them are in jail and the other half are dead from AIDS. Sometime we are embarrassed to say that we are from Nenasi, this place is notorious."

Rape? Drugs? AIDS? In half an hour, Nenasi had been transformed from a beach paradise to a rural nightmare. We had been cycling only four days at this point, but were further away from Singapore than we thought. Mi looked out into the dark nothingness of the sea, just as he had been doing the whole day. His revelations seemed to bring some inner relief.

"You may hear the sound of motorbikes later at night. That's the crazy young boys racing. It's a big problem here. You know, for some of them, it's their only form of entertainment, that's how they get their kicks."

The same sluggishness and laidback atmosphere that drew Mi back home was proving insufficient to keep testosterone-filled, thrill-seeking youth at home. In other places, they might have channelled their aggression through sports or video games. In Nenasi today, devoid of alternative entertainment, the two-wheeler had stepped in, fuelled by subsidised petrol and insufficient policing. It provided devilish fun and unparalleled machismo, for those who dared.

"No matter how many people die, they never stop. Once there was a horrible accident not far from here: two bikes were racing, and one skidded and lost control. The usual story lah. The guy's girlfriend was watching on the side, cheering him on. After the crash, all she saw was her boyfriend's head, rolling around like a football, eyes wide open."

Mi's eyes grew wider as he said this. Coming from most people, we might have dismissed all this as Malaysian exaggeration. However, Mi—solemn, serious, yogic Mi—did not seem like the type given to drama. He simply narrated life as it is.

Just then we heard some voices in the distance and saw a car driving up to the shed. "Don't worry about that. It is probably the police. If they come and disturb you later at night, just say that you know us and that we let you stay here," said Wan.

Mi and Wan were not pleased with local politics either. Apparently the village chief pocketed any development money earmarked for the area. He did not let anybody else succeed, in their opinion. "Wan and I go to the local meetings, but our voice is never heard," complained Mi.

According to Wan, corruption was ingrained. The former village chief had a spell put on him by a *bomoh*, and then ran away with "a Siam lady" to Kuantan.[2] "Of course, he took all our money and ran. In the end, it is the people who lose out."

"If you could make one change to this place, what would it be?"

"That is easy. You look at us, we have nothing much here. Our only chance is to make it into a resort. That man you talked to earlier, his son used to run the resort here, he did well for a while. We used to go to that shed over there and all get together," said Mi.

"There used to be a karaoke machine there. Those were better times. But his son did not know how to run a business, in the end, he got scared, when he started to lose money, he did not understand things, he just got scared and left. That is why the place looks like it does now. There was hope for a while," said Mi, his voice trailing off.

"Hope?"

"More hope than there is now. This place has become a nightmare. But if I could make one change, it would be a return, I would try to develop this again into a resort, but something that the people did together, not just one person. Otherwise, you come back here in five years and I tell you, the only thing that would have changed is that the beach would be further inshore, we would have to shift our fire."

The four of us talked for a while more and after that we retired for the night. We woke up too late to catch the sunrise but Mi was already there, by the water, flanked by his rods, looking out into the South China Sea, waiting patiently for something to bite.

***

So, where would we most like to live? What makes us happy? This question has been gnawing at us ever since our bicycle trip in 2004. We still don't really know the answer. There are so many places in Malaysia where we would just stop, gasp and think, "What if?" Take the long, unspoilt white-sand beach of Pulau Perhentian Kecil, with its own crystal-clear lagoon, filled with colourful fish. Or the lofty tea estates of Cameron Highlands, where one can eat scones and jam for tea, and then Hainanese pork chop for dinner.

Or, for some "everyday-living", how about a simple, classic Malay *kampung* bungalow in Terengganu, surrounded by acres of lush land, the aroma of fresh *kuih* wafting through the moist morning air. What if we packed up one day and moved to one of those places?

Those are probably the yearnings of two Singaporean boys who've been cooped up in concrete their whole lives. No doubt, if we did move to the countryside, we'd miss our uber-cool, high-tech, run-as-fast-as-you-can city life. And besides, how would we earn a living?

We observed this rural-urban tension across Malaysia. There were rural folk who were fascinated by all things modern, and wanted more of a taste, like the little boy Pip in the FELDA estate, who was blown away by our 24-speed bicycles. Some, like Mi, had seen the city, and then had chosen to return to the *kampung*, only to be forever pained by the incurable squalor.

Then there were urban folk who longed to getaway, like the 50-something-year-old Puru, a retired Motorola executive, who had built a row of chalets near the beach in Cherating, Pahang, where he was going to retire (he returned to city life after four years); or the two Indians on the boat in Banding, delighted to be surrounded by virgin forest every day, but unable to tear themselves away from their cellphones, girlfriends and city life.

Many Malaysians were grappling with the question of where to live—their minds, if not their bodies, seemed to oscillate. Indeed, some of the most contented people we met live in the in-betweens: urban areas that have natural beauty nearby, such as Kota Bahru and Penang—"a city that feels like a *kampung*", Sam, our host there, had told us.

Ultimately, each of us probably sits comfortably at some point on that rural-urban spectrum. As we grow older, the point moves. Lucky ones will get to spend some parts of the year at one point, and others at another.

As we've realised, the problem is that, unlike Malaysians, Singaporeans can't easily experience life in all its different guises. We are perfect urban citizens. No matter how much of a "Garden City" Singapore becomes, it will never be a garden. It will just be a much better city.

In that sense, there is probably a portion of our lives that goes unfulfilled. We are stuck in an urban matrix, and our worldview is limited as such. Singaporeans do not know what life in the country is like. Weekend trips to Margaret River, or even entire summer holidays traipsing across Thailand's beaches, are temporary reprieves.

What is sad is that if international relations between our countries had been better, Malaysians and Singaporeans might have felt a lot closer to each other culturally and socially than we currently do. We'd then probably get more of a fix from Malaysia's gorgeous rural countryside than we currently do. Foolish idealism? Perhaps.

As it is, given the nature of political boundaries and what they mean, endless debates rage in Singapore about whether we should rely on Malaysia as a hinterland. We know of Singaporeans who have sold their HDB apartments and moved to Johor because they can no longer afford to live here. Many other Singaporeans send their parents to nursing homes in Johor because the ones at home are too pricey. Singaporeans are understandably bitter about all this. Nobody likes being priced out of their own country.

But perhaps this shift is inevitable. Every major city, from London to Rio, has a huge hinterland to depend on. City-hinterland relationships can be wonderfully symbiotic.

One of Singapore's drawbacks is that it does not have this hinterland within its borders. The mooted Iskandar Development Project is partly an attempt to create one outside. Yet while businesses seem eager, it remains to be seen if Singaporeans will take to Iskandar with gusto. It is, after all, in a different country.

***

Kelantan. 23 July 2004.

Before our bicycle trip, the Malaysian state we were least familiar with was Kelantan. It had always been a mystery to us. Kelantan was the great beyond, a largely rural state, with many people still living off the land. Physically and socially, it was far, far away from Singapore. What's more, Kelantan has been ruled by PAS, the Islamic Party, since 1990 (in its present term). From what we had heard before going, PAS might equate to "under-development", "conservatism", "gender bias" or "fascism".

And so we were told to watch out. Watch out for fundamentalist Muslims prowling the street, Koran in hand, and mission in heart. Watch out for the men, who wear long, straggly beards and turbans; and the women who wear burqas that expose only their eyes.

And then there are all those peculiarities of a moralistic society. Cinemas leave all their lights on during the show, to deter unmarried couples seeking a secret place for illicit fornication; supermarkets have two separate checkout lines, one for men and one for ladies, lest they mingle while waiting to pay; and there is heavy censorship of the media: for instance, shampoo ads cannot reveal the model's hair beneath her *tudung*; consumers have to assume it is shiny and soft.

Kelantan is where people speak a dialect of Malay that is difficult to decipher. It is wholly and completely different from modern, rich Singapore. Or at least that's what we thought.

The night before reaching Kelantan, we had slept on hard gravel, in the car-park of the sole police station in Bandar Permaisuri, a tiny town in Terengganu. That was the only other time, besides Alor Setar, that the Malaysian police had put us up. In this instance, however, it wasn't thugs and drug pushers we were taking refuge from, but rather giant pythons, indiscriminate elephants, the odd man-eating tiger, and all kinds of other nameless beasts, big and small, that supposedly lurked in the big open field nearby, the only obvious place to pitch our tent.

So we ended up in the car-park, between a motorbike and a small police boat, which was needed only during the monsoon months, when Bandar Permaisuri tended to flood. Sleeping on bumpy Malaysian tar and cement had been so tortuous that neither of us snoozed for more than an hour at a time.

Worse, there was the din from occasional night vehicles whizzing by, and the chatter from policemen coming and going. We were therefore somewhat relieved to pack up our tent and leave, saying a quick goodbye and thanks to the policeman on duty after we brushed our teeth in his bathroom. At least the brisk Malaysian morning air was inviting.

The ride to Kelantan was an absolute treat, cycling through Malaysia's idyllic Northeast, on Highway 3. Because it is less built up—fewer factories, fewer cars—the region feels much cooler. Almost the entire distance from Kuantan to Kota Bahru, we were flanked by rainforest vegetation on one side, palm trees and gorgeous beach on the other. Slicing through tropical paradise, it was easy to forget where exactly we were, what exactly we were doing, how arduous the trip actually was.

Of course, the spattering of human activity reminded us that there *were* others around—we passed little jerry-rigged shacks by the side of the road selling local durians, watermelons and mangosteens, live chickens, and, best of all, hot, sweet *Kuih Akok*, a moist, spongy Malay cake made of egg, coconut and pandan. The vendors and their clients often looked up in surprise when they noticed us. Most offered food eagerly, and simply refused to accept any money.

We also zoomed by numerous *"Banglo untuk dijual"* (Bungalows for sale) signs, an indication of the expected tourist and real-estate boom in the Northeast. A sign on a school screamed out at us, graphically warning all about the dangers of Dengue and the Aedes mosquito—there would be many more such signs ahead of us, many more tales of friends or relatives having been struck down. We had to be careful where we slept.

At Kampung Tok Dor, two youths on single-speed bicycles wanted to race. They shrieked delightedly when they overtook us, having beaten the more seasoned riders on the fancy bikes. Little nincompoops. We were too tired to chase, but eventually did catch up.

We enjoyed the friendly rivalry that these young ones often offered us along the way. Then there were others still who did not want to race, but were content to shepherd us through their tiny *kampungs*, furiously pedalling just to keep abreast, staring at us, smiling at us, admiring our Giant 24-speed hybrids, gossiping amongst themselves.

Every now and then, a rambunctious one would scream out "Hey Brutha! Where you from?" or "What's your name?" in a weird Americanised Malaysian accent. These encounters would never last more than a minute, usually spanning just the length of their *kampungs*. Unofficial chaperones-on-wheels, we loved them.

In Melor, a town just south of Kota Bahru, we got our first proper taste of Kelantanese. Having passed the town centre, we pulled into a tiny *warung* on the left. As we entered the *warung*, a 30-something-year-old Malay lady, bright, cheerful and glowing even in the face of the imminent thunderstorm, greeted us and took our order. Wati had chubby cheeks that were cupped and pressed together by the linen on her *tudung*, like a balloon about to burst. But she did maintain a slim figure that had been inherited by her daughter, who smiled coyly as she served us our *tehs*. Her sharp features magnetized our eyes and dominated our conversation for the next few minutes.

Those *tehs* preceded the most intense, thunderous rainfall we experienced during the trip. The constant din of the falling drops transformed conversations into shouting matches. Visibility was cut to less than ten metres. Lightning crashed in spectacular cartoonish bolts, illuminating giant circles of earth around and below it. The subsequent roar of thunder made you jump out of your seat, petrified at some nebulous evil about to descend. Hard earth softened, becoming mushy mud. Puddles quickly formed in any available crevice or depression.

Dogs and cats scampered for shelter, the uninitiated howling for dear life. Cars slowed to a creep, their hazard-light flashing, while their windscreen wipers moved at blinding speeds, throwing buckets of water with each swipe, yet not nearly enough. All outdoor human activity came to a stop. Inside the house, the television volume was turned up, for no particular reason, as all eyes were now focused on the spectacle outside.

We barely noticed the group of male Malay youth who had walked into the *warung*, breathing sighs of relief as they removed their motorcycle helmets. They all wore dark t-shirts, many emblazoned with the glitzy, decadent logos of 70s and 80s Heavy Metal bands. "KISS", "Iron Maiden" and "Metallica" had all made their way here.

Bob Marley seemed out of place, his worn face smoking a joint on the torso of the group's pretty boy, a handsome Malay who passed time by slicking his long black hair back with a pink plastic comb whose pointed, protruded handle looked like it might double up as an assault weapon. They wore denim jeans of various shades, and had their motorcycle helmets cradled snugly below each of their arms.

Despite the bravado, they were harmless. For the umpteenth time, we were forced to rubbish a silly stereotype that we held. "A group of Malay Motor youth does not a violent gang make."

The next 30 minutes were a blur of laughter, rain and confusion. The Malay youths revolved around a central comedic honcho, who alternated between asking us questions—some genuine, others bait for a joke—and cracking the group up with witty, parochial comments that only they could relate to. Every utterance of ours was seized upon by one of the posse, who proceeded to deconstruct and deride it.

We couldn't compete in this verbal mudfight. We were linguistically lost, unable to decipher their abbreviated Malay, spoken with a Kelantanese slang; and alienated by their very cliquish jargon. Wati and her daughter observed from the sidelines, accompanying the boys' laughter one moment, and the next casting an empathetic glance our way.

It was rollicking good fun, and not for the first time we played the part of the moronic foreigners.

There was also a sexual twist to their tomfoolery. Ever so often, one joker would lift up his right hand, palm up, fingers gripping an imaginary cucumber, while his forearm swung back and forth. We soon found out that this lot actually masturbated together. Before they finally did leave, they told us that they were off to Bachok, a nearby seaside town, for a Friday evening of debauchery. Sex with some young ladies, failing which, another male group therapy session.

In the chaos of the rain, Kelantan had crept up on us. We had been expecting a different environment, a land where radical Islam dominated. Where was the undeveloped, tribal bastion that PAS had supposedly created?

For one, it wasn't clear how suppressed women really are. Kelantan has always been a matriarchal society, and the distinction between ownership and management here was blurred. Wati was running the whole show, while Saupi, her husband, relaxed, playing with his children. He had given her the place when she agreed to be his second wife. We would come to expect this Kelantanese domestic role reversal.

"The women here, they are smart. They can run the business. We men, we can just relax, haha," smiled Saupi.

"So does your first wife have a business too?"

"Yes! She sometimes makes *kuih* from the home and sells it. She is getting older now, so she doesn't work so much."

"Oh."

"But I give her all she needs anyway. Remember, you can't just take a new wife when you want to. You have to make sure you can support all your wives. And you have to make sure that your first wife accepts the second wife, and they can live together."

"And you have to provide for them equally, right?"

"Yes, you must give them the same love, give them the same time, give them the same money. That is what Islam teaches us."

"What if they can't live with each other?"

"Then you must talk to them and teach them how to, let them understand how to."

Whenever Islam meets a matriarchal society, things get a bit confusing. On the one hand, the women have historically owned everything. On the other, Islam allows the man to take up to four wives, on condition that he treats them equally. At the end of the day, we were not quite sure who owned exactly what. But, on the face of it, the dynamic seemed to work. Saupi and Wati seemed very happy. So too, apparently, was his first wife.

Over the next two days, we met many more women running their own food or vegetable stalls, in little *warungs*, and particularly in the giant central market in Kota Bahru, a thronging beehive of activity. We chatted with many of them, and always asked the same thing: "So, how is life different here? We've heard that Kelantan is a very strict place." We were always greeted with the same vociferous response. "Life is not that different! We are free to do what we want. We Kelantanese women are very independent. Do you notice anything different here?"

We were hard pressed for an answer. It's a tricky dilemma. Some liberals might argue that the rights of Kelantanese women have been restricted by customs such as polygamy and conservative dress codes. On the other hand, many women themselves seem perfectly happy with their lives. Why should anybody tell them otherwise?

Moreover, the women aren't living under a shell: there is freedom of information here, with reasonably easy access to the Internet. They are fully aware of how the rest of the world lives. In many parts of Malaysia, we observed these tensions between societal norms, individual rights and happiness.

At the end of the day, we were aching to find the supposed restrictions in Kelantan. No doubt, people do dress more conservatively. We saw the separate supermarket check-out lines, and found the run-down, lights-on cinema, which had by then been put out of business by illegal VCDs and DVDs. But other than a few token things, and the lower level of development, life here didn't seem too different from many other parts of Malaysia. Perhaps one would need an insider's view of a traditional household to feel the restrictions. We certainly did not feel restricted in any way.

***

In our two countries, Malaysia's countryside towns are also the only places where we have found people who seemed content with their jobs.

One of the happiest people we met during our bicycle trip was James Kingham, a planter in Tanjong Malim, Perak. James, a man of imposing stature yet the gentlest of demeanours, is a half-Chinese, half-Ceylonese Malaysian. He was born James Ponapalon in 1935.

Unfortunately, Ponapalon Senior had gotten into some trouble in Sri Lanka before he emigrated and so had to find a way of shielding his family from any cross-Indian Ocean vengeance. Thankfully, the family had made friends with a charming American pastor by the name of Kingham, who graciously let them have a new God and a new name.

In the 1960s, James was considered Malaysia's Orchid King. Today, he is one of the foremost experts on Malaysia's native jungle trees and a conservation advocate. He walked us around his huge nursery in Tanjong Malim, from where many of Malaysia's and Singapore's trees come. As he touched and caressed each seedling—many jungle tree "seedlings" are taller than us—I got the sense that he has a mystical, emotional relationship with every one of them.

Not every rural resident, surely, is on a career high. The Kuala Kedah fishermen's jobs, for instance, are more challenging and frustrating today because of dwindling fish stocks and competition from trawlers. I certainly do not want to trivialise Malaysian rural life. Nevertheless, on balance, I met more people in the countryside who *seemed* happier with their daily work. Job satisfaction there feels higher.

In the rest of Malaysia, and certainly in Singapore, the overwhelming majority of people seem to be grinding through work every day. This could be an urban phenomenon, similar to many other high-pressure cities in the world. However, through our journeys and conversations, we have noticed certain unique characteristics about Malaysia's and Singapore's societies and job markets that seem to confine and constrict individual choice and happiness.

Malaysia's problems seem to stem from the fact that its society is so stratified and fragmented. First, there is an aristocracy here—the Sultans, princes and princesses—that presides over the whole country. They can do pretty much whatever they want. Our friends in KL cringe when retelling stories of sitting in maddening traffic jams, only to find out that traffic has been stopped for royalty—not official business, but rather some princeling racing through in his latest sports car, presumably on his way to some posh party.

Many Sultans use their power and prestige judiciously. However, there are other members of the royal family who appear to treat the country as their fiefdom. Johor's prince Khairil is a particular crowd-pleaser. In 2005, he and a bunch of his friends gate crashed a wedding party in Rawa, an island off Johor's east coast. Unhappy that one of the female wedding guests did not want to boogie with them, the prince ordered the wedding party, many of whom had come from Singapore, to leave the resort. They refused. He and his thugs then attacked the guests with golf clubs and sharp objects. Several of them ended up in hospital.[3]

Meanwhile Mohd Fakhry, a Kelantan prince, was accused in 2009 of abusing and torturing his teenage Indonesian wife, Manohara Odelia Pino. She escaped dramatically from Malaysia, alleging that the prince treated her like a toy. There are numerous other stories of Malaysian monarchs abusing their position and power. They seem to inhabit a parallel world, where the entitlement and privilege of yesteryear's feudal society take great precedence over the decency and respect of modern Malaysia.

A coterie of politicians, businessmen and other distinguished people sit below the monarchs in Malaysia's multi-layered social strata. They are awarded honorifics such as Tun, Tan Sri, Datuk and so on, depending on their position and achievements. There are a bewildering number of titles. A conference organiser from Hong Kong once called us and asked, "In the letter, should I address him as Datuk, Dato, Dato' or Datok?" (The four are different spellings of the same title.)

Many Malaysians pine for these titles, and the opportunities that often accompany them. Some people also crave the respect and adulation. We once observed the boss of a small company, a rotund, cheery Dato', having drinks with his employees, all smart, well-travelled people. They treated him like a demi-god, bowing deferentially whenever he walked by, got up, sat down. His every movement was followed by a suitably obsequious gesture. "Dato' this" and "Dato' that".

Though he clearly loved the attention, the Dato' himself appeared humble enough. True, his employees may have been fawning over him partly because of his genuine achievements. However, his title, Dato', had also created an aura of grandeur and royalty around him. Although some ordinary, title-less, citizens are desensitised to these honorifics, many others are not.

Malaysian society, therefore, has a finely calibrated social ladder, with multiple rungs separating, say, a humble farmer from the Sultan. In addition, society is also fragmented by race and religion.

These divisions lead to a workplace where everybody is acutely aware of his or her social standing. This self-awareness, in turn, influences the way they carry themselves, their work choices, and their job satisfaction.

Importantly, it also reinforces the value of personalities and connections. Young executives want to network with *Datuks* and other members of high society, for they can provide access and opportunities. Chinese and Indian businessmen fuss over their *bumi* connections that help open doors and win contracts.

In such an environment, meritocracy fades. It is not always the most capable who wins, but often the most charismatic, or connected. Of course, personal connections are important for business anywhere—think of the *guanxi* networks in China—but in Malaysia they take on added importance because of the multiple social strata. Politicking becomes as important as doing a good job.

Similarly, it is often difficult in the workplace to distinguish performance from preferential treatment. We have heard Chinese and Indian executives muttering statements such as "Ahmad only got the job because he's a *bumi*" or "Siti only got promoted because she's a *bumi*". A foreign executive once told us, "Johan is a *bumi* hire", implying that there are two classes of Malay executives—one competent; the other, including people such as Johan, merely privileged.

All this affects happiness and job satisfaction—after all, even though you may be doing a pretty good job, you might still get passed over because you do not know the right person or have the preferred skin colour. This inevitably leads to feelings of helplessness and resignation.

Therefore, this fragmentation of Malaysian society—vertically in terms of social standing, and horizontally in terms of ethnicity—has hampered job satisfaction and happiness in the country.

Job satisfaction in Singapore, meanwhile, is one of the lowest in the world, going by a 2009 survey of finance professionals by Robert Half, an HR firm.[4] Just 53 per cent of respondents were satisfied with their jobs, the second lowest globally. Furthermore, only 59 per cent of Singapore respondents claim to be loyal towards their company.

These results support our observations and anecdotal evidence collected while having worked in Singapore over the past five years. We have very few friends or associates who seem to enjoy their jobs. For most of them, work is drudgery, a means to pay the bills. Waking up each weekday morning is tortuous, while Friday brings unbridled relief and joy.

These feelings are somewhat universal. However, Singaporean work stress and dissatisfaction appear more intense. I think there are several reasons for this.

First is money and materialism. Many people here regard wealth accumulation as one of life's primary objectives. "Singapore is a good place to live in if one has money," is a frequent expression heard here. This is true literally—given the high cost of living—and also more philosophically, in the sense that a person is often judged by his or her wealth. Your social standing in Singapore is intimately linked to your income and wealth.

Conspicuous consumption is rampant. "I used to go for the weekly lunches. However, every time we met, it was about this new handbag or that new shoe. It got tiresome," said Soo, a junior college classmate, when speaking about her school friends who had just entered the working world. As I look into my own closet, stuffed with too many shirts and shoes, I realise how easy it is to get sucked into this relentless, contagious material competition.

Singapore sometimes feels like one giant shopping mall. Cynics often say that there is hardly anything else to do here. "Shopping is the opium of the middle class," says one friend, "the government uses it to distract and control the population."

With limited ways to spend our time, and few other means of building social capital, consumerism and materialism reign. They are, of course, fuelled by money, which therefore becomes the primary objective of professional life.

Therefore, perhaps more so than many other developed democracies, Singaporeans work in order to earn money—rarely for love, passion or interest. In the Robert Half survey, the main reason for switching jobs is better pay, with 35 per cent of respondents indicating they would do so.

"The biggest challenge facing medicine in Singapore today is the struggle between two incentives that drive doctors in opposite directions: the humanitarian, ethical, compassionate drive to do the best by all patients versus the cold, calculating attitude that seeks to profit from as many patients as possible," Lee Wei Ling, a neuroscientist and Lee Kuan Yew's daughter, wrote in *The Straits Times* in 2008.[5]

"I have been practising medicine for 30 years now. Over this period, medical science has advanced tremendously, but the values held by the medical community seem to have changed for the worse. Yearning and working for money are more widely and openly practised; and sometimes this is perceived as acceptable behaviour."

Ms Lee may well have a point. In 2011, it emerged that Dr Susan Lim, a general surgeon in private practice, had charged a member of Brunei's royal family an eye-watering S$40 million over four years for treatment.[6] The Singapore Medical Council is still investigating her on charges of overcharging. Dr Lim's rather profitable venture included marking up a S$400 specialist's bill 80 times, and charging the Bruneians S$211,000 for it.[7] Some doctors we spoke to feel she did nothing morally wrong.

When our friends and classmates compare jobs and career options, the single most important determinant is pay. Nothing else even comes close. "Why don't you switch to banking? You could earn a lot more money, you know?" is a refrain that rings in my ear every few months from another concerned soul, reminding me about what's important in life.

Guided excessively by money, few people try to look for a job that might satisfy them in other ways. That is one big reason job satisfaction here is low. On a related note, career choice is much more limited in Singapore than in many other countries.

This is partly because of the structure of our economy, which is heavily dependent on a few industries, such as finance, trade and tourism.

It is also because career choices and definitions of success are more meticulously prescribed here than in many other places. Parents, teachers and other members of society greatly influence—and sometimes dictate—young people's ambitions and dreams.

Therefore, in comparison with many other countries, it far less likely that the average Singaporean will grow up wanting to be, say, a musician, sportsperson, Internet entrepreneur or astronaut. Conversely, we are more likely to harbour dreams of law, medicine or finance. Different characters and personalities, growing up in Singapore, get shoehorned into these popular jobs. In other countries, they may have had greater opportunity to explore alternative careers. It's a good thing Eminem wasn't born here.

Singapore society gives short shrift to the notion of taking time to find yourself, to understand your passions, your abilities and your dreams. University and pre-university students are harangued into thinking and deciding upon a stable career. Few students take time off to, say, spend a year travelling, or work for an NGO. Most have a single-minded drive to maximise earnings as soon as possible. Having decided on something, not many have the gumption to later switch careers if they are unhappy.

Immigration has also dented job satisfaction. First, by suppressing wages at the lower end of the income ladder. Second, the influx of skilled workers has led to structural ethnic preferences in certain vocations. For instance, many friends who work in banks in Singapore have observed how senior Indian bankers will join their firms, and then recruit their entire team from their old-boy networks in India. This has led to a concentration of Indians working in Singapore's financial services industry. The same might be said of Filipinos in certain service industries, such as nursing and restaurants.

Job satisfaction is also low because employees are generally not engaged and invested emotionally in their companies. This is partly due to traditional, hierarchical company structures. Companies rarely empower their workers enough to make decisions and encourage them to question existing processes. Deference to authority is paramount.

Furthermore, employees tend to work in silos without understanding their role in the company from a holistic viewpoint. Few take the initiative to learn more or extend themselves beyond the scope of their job, fearful of piling on added responsibilities. A job, for most of us, is just a job. Nothing more.

Wider opportunities are, however, emerging. We now hear many more stories of lawyers leaving their jobs to cook, young bankers starting their own firms, and students spending extended periods of time outside the classroom, away from their books. The government has been trying its best to encourage entrepreneurs. Still, they are all exceptions to the rule.

The challenge for them is that our society does not tolerate failure. Choose to be different and succeed, and you'll probably be okay. Witness how we praise Lyn Lee, founder of Awfully Chocolate, a cake shop, who left law to bake. Those who fail, however, can be marginalised, and derided for trying to be different. It is a brutal environment in which to experiment.

Some people in other countries face similar challenges and confines. In Singapore they are taken to an extreme. This is largely because these career traditions are a key part of our founding principles—study hard, work hard, get rich, stay out of politics. It is difficult to wean people off a supposedly winning formula.

Perhaps the most tragic consequence of Singapore's materialism and class-consciousness is the discrimination towards particular socio-economic groups, such as construction workers and maids. Many in Singapore tend to regard people in these professions as subhumans, unworthy of eating the same food or sharing the same public spaces.

These biases were unwittingly exposed in March 2012, after Singapore's Ministry of Manpower announced a new rule entitling foreign domestic workers—who come from countries such as Indonesia, the Philippines and Myanmar—to one day off every week.

Although many people cheered the decision, there were many others who expressed concern. "It's not that we are inhumane, but they will be very difficult to control," grumbled banker Jacqueline Ng to a reporter.[8] "What I am saying is with this mandatory day off, as an employer I don't feel secure because we have no control (over) who they mingle with."

The litany of letters and comments protesting the decision cast a dark, shameful shadow over what should have been a proud day for Singapore. This is one instance where we are lucky that no public consultation was ever held. Singaporeans might have been shocked to find out what we're really like.

***

Many Singaporeans we know have never been too bothered about politics. This is probably due to our economic success, as well as the PAP's concerted efforts to monopolise policy thought and discussion. "We decide what is right. Never mind what the people think," asserted then prime minister, Lee Kuan Yew, in 1987.

We have all grown up with the idea that politics is the domain of some higher beings. Every few years, we vote them back into power. They maintain stability, and everybody's happy. It is a mechanical process that has worked smoothly all these years. Ordinary people are rarely engaged in any meaningful political discussion. Our role in society is to work hard and pay our taxes.

Political apathy runs so high that up till the last elections, many Singaporeans might not have been able to name the legislators who represent their district. Some probably do not even know which polling district they live in. We live in an electoral blur born of apathy and never ending gerrymandering.

In 2004, when we first started seriously researching and interviewing people in Malaysia, we found most people there to be more engaged than Singaporeans in politics, both at the local and national level. We had long discussions about town councils, UMNO vs. PAS, Anwar Ibrahim, and many other important issues. Across the country, we saw political flags flying freely, cadres wearing party t-shirts, and stickers—blue (UMNO) or green (PAS), depending where we were—adorning shop fronts, cars and even houses.

Malaysian activism, nevertheless, seemed a bit muted then. Most people we met had strong faith in UMNO and Barisan Nasional. They probably could not contemplate voting for another party. Almost everybody we met was optimistic about Abdullah Badawi, the "Nice Guy" who had just led his coalition to a landslide victory. Even PAS supporters had nice things to say about him. Criticism of the government, if any, was polite and veiled.

Furthermore, not everybody we met was willing to just talk shop with a couple of Singaporeans on bicycles. Some were quite guarded. Many still got their news and information from Malaysia's mainstream media; there weren't too many alternative views floating around.

In the next four years, leading up the 2008 general elections, we witnessed Malaysians slowly getting bolder and becoming more outspoken. This was largely because of dissatisfaction with the leadership—amongst other things, ordinary people got progressively more disgusted with the way Khairy Jamaludin, Abdullah's son-in-law, was perceived to be controlling him and calling the shots.

As we moved around the country in March 2008, some Malaysians would cuss angrily as soon as we mentioned Abdullah or Khairy. These outbursts surprised us. There was a certain feistiness and spontaneity to them, as if dormant feelings had been awakened, and allowed to sprout. Malaysians were cajoled, surely, by the numerous new alternative media channels, including blogs, online newspapers, and even SMS chatter. These outlets encouraged more debate about all sorts of issues.

The election itself was a watershed. BN experienced its worst ever electoral performance—with that, a whole generation of Malaysians suddenly felt the power of the vote. Each individual's decision mattered now. Malaysians had emerged from the political abyss to shock the establishment.

It is hard to overstate the impact of all this. The night of the elections, as the results were announced, and thousands of Malaysians listened and watched in disbelief, our junior college friend, Mun Ching, called us to brag. "So, tell me guys, is this possible in Singapore?" Mun Ching cried emphatically. "This is what it means to be Malaysian!" She went on and on, as if Malaysia had suddenly become a paragon of democracy, while Singapore remained a serf colony.

In the days and months that followed, everybody wanted their voices heard. Taxi drivers, shopkeepers and friends would volunteer information and opinion on issues such as Selangor's outgoing government, Penang's new chief minister, and Najib's supposed involvement in the death of a Mongolian model.

In boardrooms and conferences, meanwhile, local and foreign businessmen and executives started raising their hands and speaking out against particular policies. It was a sea change.

In 2007, the Economist Intelligence Unit (EIU) organised a roundtable with Malaysia's government. While discussing the country's challenges, not a single person mentioned the word *bumiputera*.

By mid-2008, I was attending meetings where people from various companies, local and foreign, would jostle to give their own spin on why *bumiputera* policies were damaging to their business. There are no more sacred cows. Anything and everything is open for debate in Malaysia today.

As a result, we've noticed a newfound joy and exuberance in Malaysians, most of whom feel actively engaged and involved in political processes. Their voices are being heard. Their votes are making a difference. There is less dissonance between the powers that be and the person on the street. Malaysians are, without a shadow of a doubt, much happier for it.

For much of my life, up till 2010, I did not observe any similar political happiness in Singapore. For while most Singaporeans have been generally content with our competent government, most of us have never had much to say about national politics or policies.

When we do speak about issues, it is typically a brief, superficial conversation—for instance, "Too many foreigners" or "Why can't the government control flooding?"—rather than a deep, well-thought out discussion. Furthermore, as most of us get our local news from the same government newspapers, these conversations tend to fall within the same lines. Rarely do we offer new ideas or ways of thinking about national policies. Viewpoints are regurgitated.

Hence Singaporeans have long had somewhat confused feelings towards political fulfilment. On the one hand, we are happy with being governed by one of the
most successful political parties in history. On the other hand, we are somewhat
distanced, and sometimes disillusioned, by its methods of governance. Simply put,
many Singaporeans do not feel that our opinions and voices matter. We have to keep
reminding ourselves that the ends justify the means. (Or do they?)

That said, a lot has changed over the past 20 years. There are certainly more
avenues of discussion available today, thanks to the Internet. Some Singaporeans
are heavily engaged in online discussions, which are usually thought-provoking, and
almost always provide an alternative view of life here.

In that vein, the 2011 general elections will probably be remembered as the
moment when many Singaporeans were politically awakened. For months before
the election itself, Singaporeans started airing their opinions much more freely, both
on new and traditional media channels.

PAP politicians, keen to keep pace with Singaporeans' growing political awareness, have also tried over the past few years to interact more with ordinary people.
This occurs offline, at events like Meet-the-People sessions, and online, through
Facebook and blogs. It is as if the party has had a volte-face from the Lee Kuan Yew
days of not caring about what the people think. The younger generation of politicians appears like it *does care* what we think.

Still, it is unclear if this is all window dressing. Do they really care what we think?
Or are they just pretending to be in touch with the common man? Most people I
meet think the latter. A case in point is the public consultation over the building of
Singapore's casinos. Not a single person I know thinks that it was a genuine consultation. Everybody I speak with believes the government had already made up its mind
to build the casinos. And then it organised a dog and pony show for the people.

More recently, in late 2011, the government seemed to unilaterally decide to
demolish the Bukit Brown Cemetery, one of the last repositories of traditional, intri-
cate gravestones in Singapore. Singaporeans, many of whom had been hoping for a
more consultative approach to governance, were shocked. The Singapore Heritage
Society lamented that it was not consulted in the decision-making process.[9]

For most of Singapore's history, the government went about its business tidily
and efficiently, never bothering about what Singaporeans thought. Now, suddenly,
our politicians say they want to engage us. Should we believe them?

It is unfortunate for the PAP and for Singapore that these doubts exist. A genuine
dialogue would bridge the divide between Singapore's haloed leaders and its citizens. Ordinary people would feel like their voices mattered. They would feel more
invested in the country.

For many of us, voting is also a new phenomenon. For most elections over the past 20 years, about half of Singaporeans did not even have to vote, owing to PAP walkovers. I voted for the very first time at the age of 34.

Moreover, many of those who vote do so out of fear. "Of course I'll vote for the PAP, lah. I'm scared if I vote opposition, the government will blacklist me," a waiter told me before the 2006 elections. I hear similar sentiments every time. Many Singaporeans worry that their vote is not private—a registration number on the ballot ensures that every vote can be traced.

There are of course many Singaporeans who vote for the PAP out of genuine desire. Still, many of them have probably never contemplated anything else. In a sense, they have never really had a proper choice between two competent, respected parties.

Ultimately, Singaporeans do not feel we have much say in how we are governed. The policies, rules and laws which guide and dictate our everyday lives are beyond our control. We simply live, humbly, within the system.

Malaysians, on the other hand, now have a much greater say in their country and in how they live. This provides them with much fulfilment. It would be wrong, however, to conclude that Malaysia's political system contributes more to happiness.

Quite the contrary. Most Malaysians I speak with believe that Singapore has the more stable, clean and reliable political system. Malaysia's political scene is fractious. Prime ministers in waiting are accused of murder. There are the occasional fisticuffs; there is name calling; there are suspensions and all manner of accusations, from corruption to sex scandals to vote-buying. There are resignations and incarcerations, and there are party crossovers and ideological shifts.

To the observer of placid Singaporean politics, Malaysia is an action packed-soap opera. In Singapore, questions are lobbed gently so they can be knocked out of the park. In Malaysia, politicians are prepared for all kinds of curveballs.

The point here is that having witnessed the social and political awakening of Malaysians over the past few years, and the joy and enthusiasm that accompanied it, I wonder even more about how Singapore will evolve. It seems quite clear that part of the reason for Singaporean unhappiness is that we have very little say in our country—who runs it, what they do, how they choose to interact with us, and so on.

This is not a function of how much support the PAP has. Indeed, the PAP will probably be the people's favoured party for the foreseeable future. However, it seems as if Singaporeans would like to be given a proper choice, even if we still end up voting for the PAP. In addition, we want to be involved and engaged in national discussions where we hear alternative viewpoints and arguments—not just government-sanctioned positions.

Sadly, there seems to be little real appetite for that amongst today's leaders. However, until that happens, all the health and wealth that Singaporeans enjoy will not make us completely happy. There is, after all, something intrinsically human about wanting control over your life.

***

In the wake of the 2008–09 financial crisis and recession, many world leaders, from David Cameron to Nicolas Sarkozy, have been falling over themselves to proclaim the importance of happiness to development. Many commentators in Malaysia and Singapore have also recently suggested that the two governments should widen their focus from economic growth to more general well-being.

A few points bear mentioning. First, although there is evidence that indicates that citizens of richer countries tend to be happier than those in poor ones, the jury is still out on how much difference to happiness additional income produces, particularly once a country has achieved a certain standard of living, considered by many to be a GDP per capita of US$15,000 (measured at purchasing power parity).[10]

"The stark fact is that in the world's two leading advanced countries, the United States and Germany, happiness has not risen despite the striking rises in real income," says Richard Layard, professor emeritus of economics at the London School of Economics.[11] Professor Layard chooses these two countries partly because of good data availability: "The data for America go back as far as 1950 and for (West) Germany to 1970."

In 2010, Malaysia's GDP per capita (measured at purchasing power parity) was US$15,540, while Singapore's was US$47,130.[12] Is it time our countries switched gears and placed more emphasis on delivering happiness, rather than just growth? Maybe Malaysia, which has only just crossed that somewhat arbitrary US$15,000 benchmark, has less of a reason to. But surely Singapore, one of the richest countries in the world, should.

Even if our governments did decide to pursue "happiness" in some shape or form, it's worth noting that both our societies have a reflexive allergy to waffly, touchy-feely indicators.

To complicate matters, happiness is extremely subjective, because different things make different people happy. The OECD contends that, among other things, having a job, a short commute, strong social connections, adequate green spaces, and civic engagement make people happy.[13]

A whole range of variables might influence definitions of happiness. For instance, the definition of happiness in an individualistic society, such as the US, probably tends to focus on individual gratification. Meanwhile, the definition of happiness in

In short, a coterie of castaways would emerge every day along the Malaysian railway track, each there for their own reason, but all in search of seclusion. The Malaysians, of course, never minded. I would often stop and chat with the railway officer at the little switching station off Bukit Timah Road, where there were dual tracks, the only point in Singapore where trains could pass. Indeed, the highlight of many a jog was seeing a train passing by as I jogged just a few metres to its side; the driver would often wave.

Narnia's dynamics changed in May 2010, after the Malaysian and Singaporean governments announced that the railway station would be moving to the border. As part of the deal, the Malaysians had agreed to swap the railway land for a few prime downtown lots. The last Malaysian train would travel through the heart of Singapore in July 2011.

In one fell swoop, Narnia was stamped with an expiry date. Many Singaporeans, aware that they only had a year left in which to observe that creaking colonial curiosity called a train, began swarming to the corridor every day, armed with cameras. Wedding couples started turning up, wanting a slice of Malaysian nostalgia in their albums. Several clubs started organising runs along the track.

For the few of us who knew what Narnia once was, all this was terrible. Gone was our little hideaway. The tourists had landed. Worse, land ownership was shifting from the Malaysian to the Singaporean government. That would spell, I thought, the end of the corridor's raw, unplanned beauty. The smiling, affable railway officer would be replaced by security fences and CCTV cameras. Welcome to Singapore.

And yet, a few weeks after the last train had left, some semblance of its former peace had returned. There were far fewer passers-by. There were more construction workers milling around the area, but they seemed to be primarily involved in laying a new green turf where the track once sat. Singaporeans debate over exactly what to do with this land, but whatever happens, it does seem likely that the majority of it will be preserved as a green corridor of sorts. Thank goodness.

Since 1965, Malaysia and Singapore have tried hard to create distinct nation states. For each country, that has often meant defining itself against the other. Each has tried hard to show how it is different.

And yet, as I have discovered, both countries are still struggling to come to terms with their founding principles. Malaysia's constitution guarantees pre-eminence to Islam and Malays. What that means in practice is still a matter of great debate. Malaysians are genuinely torn between running a Malay country and a country for all Malaysians.

Singaporean identity, meanwhile, appears even more vacuous. We all grew up believing in a one-party system that delivers economic growth through a race-neutral meritocracy. All we had to do was keep quiet and work hard and we'd become rich. Cracks are appearing in that philosophy. And without hard work and lots of money, there seems precious little else to being *a Singaporean*. "Malaysian minus hinterland minus history minus soul = Singaporean," Alfian Sa'at, a Singaporean playwright, wrote recently.[1]

Instead of trying to distinguish themselves, perhaps the two countries need to look up and learn more from each other. From Singapore, Malaysia can learn, among other things, the importance of building a race-neutral meritocracy and running an efficient, corruption-free government.

From Malaysia, Singapore can learn, among other things, the fulfilment of non-material pursuits and the need to provide targeted assistance to those who may not be able to compete at the same level as others. Malaysians understood a long time ago that high income inequality is unsustainable (although their efforts to address it have been patchy).

As Malaysia and Singapore embark on their next stage of development, they will have to become a bit more like each other. Malaysians will want more "equality of opportunities" and Singaporeans will want more "equality of outcomes". This will dramatically change the way we think about ourselves and each other.

But these changes will not be smooth. In both countries, authoritarian states born out of post-colonial movements are slowly making way for more democratic societies. Ordinary people are only just finding out that their voices and votes do actually make a difference. The space between public and private actors is being renegotiated. For most people, it is a wonderful, refreshing, liberating and some-what scary journey.

Presumably along the way, through this more collaborative dialogue, Malaysian and Singaporean identity will become stronger and more defined. Or perhaps we might discover that there are very few differences between us. Maybe political boundaries should not affect us so.

Malaysia is no longer just a 15-minute-jog away from my house. In order to visit the country, I now need to spend more time and effort getting across the border. And yet, every time I do, I learn something new.

Notes

Introduction

1. One might reasonably argue that Singapore too joined the Federation of Malaysia only in 1963. True. However, Singapore and West Malaysia have much longer mutual histories, dating back to the Johor Sultanate and the Straits Settlements.
2. In addition to the majority Malay Muslims, Malaysia's definition of "bumiputera" includes a few indigenous minority groups, including the orang asli of West Malaysia and the native peoples of Sabah and Sarawak.
3. Throughout this book, I refer to Malaysian leaders by their names, not by their honorifics, such as Tunku, Tun, Tan Sri, etc. The one exception is Tunku Abdul Rahman, Malaysia's first prime minister, only because he is popularly known as "Tunku". (In a few instances, interviewees refer to people they are talking about with honorifics, which I reproduce verbatim.) The reason for this is simplicity and also for balance with the Singaporean leaders, whom I frequently talk about in the same breath, e.g. Mahathir Mohamad and Lee Kuan Yew. I mean no disrespect to any leader by referring to them simply by their name.

Chapter 1 Forgotten histories

1. "Sedikit", the Malay word for "little", is often pronounced "Sikit" by non-native Malay speakers.
2. Chin Peng, *Alias Chin Peng: My Side of History*, John Wilson Booksales, 2003.
3. Chin Peng, *Alias Chin Peng*, pp. 142–143.
4. Lee Kuan Yew, *The Singapore Story: Memoirs of Lee Kuan Yew*, Times Media, 2000, p. 211.
5. A. Schmid and A. Jongman, *Political Terrorism*, Transaction Publishers, 2005, p. 671.
6. Chin Peng, *Alias Chin Peng*, p. 47.
7. Joseph Knapik and Katy Reynolds, "Load carriage in military operations", Borden Institute, pp. 6 and 11.
8. Though Chin Peng is popularly regarded as the leader of the Communist Party of Malaysia, there were in reality four different camps in Betong, which fell under two broad groupings—a CPM Marxist-Leninist faction, which Betty was under, and a China-backed CPM faction, led by Chin Peng. According to Betty, Chang Chung Ming only occasionally cooperated with Chin Peng. Every time she mentioned his name, she would cite his rank too: "Chang Chung Ming, our leader".

9. "Ex-communist fighters adjust to a life with cash", *Asia Times*, 3 November 1999.
10. "Times have changed at Malaysia's border town", *The Straits Times*, 18 July 1999.
11. We have not been able to verify Betty's claims regarding the difficulty of obtaining a visa. Quite the contrary, it appears as if it has become relatively easy for the ex-communists to visit for short periods. Nevertheless, the fact that Betty and her comrades believed it was difficult, thus preventing her from visiting her father's grave, is interesting.
12. *I Love Malaya*, Asia Witness Production, Objectifs Films, 2006.
13. "Chin Peng apologises for death of innocents", *The Star*, 22 November 2009.
14. "PAS delegates want welfare for Malay Communist soldiers", *Malaysian Insider*, 5 June 2011.
15. "Chia Thye Poh", *Wikipedia*.
16. Both films are available on YouTube. Their popularity has no doubt been helped by the bans.
17. "Ban on Zahari film stays", *Channel News Asia*, 14 October 2009. "Film on ex-leftist leader Lim Hock Siew banned", 13 July 2010.
18. Press release on the prohibition on the film, *Dr Lim Hock Siew*, Ministry of Information, Communications and the Arts, 12 July 2010.
19. Though some of Mr See's other documentaries have been approved for public viewing, MICA's capriciousness in deciding what Singaporeans can or cannot watch contributes to the anxiety amongst filmmakers.
20. "A country's independence cannot be given", *The Straits Times*, 9 February 2003.
21. The Pedra Branca case was resolved in 2008, in Singapore's favour, following mediation at the International Court of Justice. An agreement over the relocation of Malaysia's railway station, and use of the railway land, was reached in 2010.
22. "Malaysia will not go to war with Singapore: Mahathir", *Agence France Presse*, 30 January 2003.
23. "Singapore action criticised (HL)", *New Straits Times*, 28 January 2003.
24. Singapore had declared independence from the British on 31 August 1963. It then joined the Federation of Malaysia. Unable to resolve their differences, this marriage lasted just two years. On 9 August 1965, Singapore separated from the Federation.
25. Lee Kuan Yew, *The Singapore Story: Memoirs of Lee Kuan Yew*, Times Media, 2000, p. 22.
26. One could argue that Singapore effectively separated from Malaysia in the 1940s, well before 1965. In 1941–42 the Japanese invaded the Straits Settlements—Penang, Malacca, Singapore—and began to administer them separately. After the war, the British similarly administered Singapore as a separate entity until partial independence in 1959. Nevertheless, the period from 1941 to 1965 was a turbulent one where Singapore's political future was unclear. Hence, 9 August 1965 should be remembered as the date when closure was brought to this question.
27. V. S. Naipaul, *Among the Believers: An Islamic Journey*, Vintage Books, 1982, pp. 253.
28. Lee Kuan Yew, *The Singapore Story: Memoirs of Lee Kuan Yew*, Times Media, 2000, pp. 22–23.
29. Flags of The World. http://www.crwflags.com/fotw/flags/sg.html and "Tribute to Dr Toh Chin Chye", *Remember Singapore Blog*, 3 February 2012 and "The national flag of Singapore", National Library Board Singapore, 21 December 1999.
30. Lee Kuan Yew, *From Third World to First: The Singapore Story*, Harper, p. 42.

Chapter 2 Two countries separated at birth

1. James Michener, *The Voice of Asia*, Random House, 1951, p. 139.
2. Keith Sutton, "Agribusiness on a grand scale—FELDA's Sahabat Complex in East Malaysia", *Singapore Journal of Tropical Geography*, 22(1), 2001, pp. 90–105; p. 92.
3. "Reinventing FELDA", *The Edge* Singapore, 9 August 2004.
4. FELDA Holdings Corporate Website.
5. "PM: FELDA is a Malaysian success story", *The Sun Daily*, 14 August 2011.
6. "FELDA to market products in African continent", *Pertubuhan Berita Nasional Malaysia*, 11 September 2004.
7. "Call to improve FELDA housing", *New Straits Times Press (Malaysia) Berhad*, 25 September 2004.
8. "Shopping, movie and a FELDA trip", *New Straits Times Press (Malaysia) Berhad*, 23 April 2004.
9. "213 addicts nabbed in FELDA drug crackdown", *New Straits Times Press (Malaysia) Berhad*, 25 April 2005.
10. "Social mechanism against drug menace in FELDA schemes—Abdullah", *Bernama The Malaysian National News Agency*, 8 September 2004.
11. It was shortened to two years in 2004.
12. "Iskandar Malaysia attracts RM77.82 billion cumulative investments", IRDA, 18 October 2011.
13. "Singapore, Malaysia formalise land swap deal", *channelnewsasia*, 28 June 2011.
14. "GTP Briefing", 6 August 2010, and "ETP Update", 26 August 2011, PEMANDU.
15. "DPM: Government to protect Bumiputeras' interest", *Malaysia Today*, 21 August 2011.

Chapter 3 The end of dominance: Part I

1. I explore accusations of judicial bias in Chapter 5.
2. BN later won back one of the opposition states, Perak, following a series of defections and by-elections.
3. Due to their structure, it is easier for bigger parties to win GRCs. This is discussed in greater detail in Chapter 4.
4. No doubt, Malaysian law does not mandate this sort of racial balancing in politics. So, there is nothing stopping, say, a Malay Muslim–dominated party from nudging out BN and gaining power.
5. Most Chinese, Indians and Malays there whom we spoke to said that for the most part, PAS rules fairly, and does not discriminate against minorities. If anything, the one recurring complaint we heard was about its supposed lack of business acumen.
6. Even though public acceptance of PAS has improved since the 2008 general elections, many Malaysians are still wary of their religious motives.
7. According to Malaysia's Department of Statistics, Kelantan's GDP per capita in 2010 was RM8,273 (at Year 2000 constant prices). By contrast, Penang had the highest GDP per capita at RM33,456.

8.   According to the PAS website, the party was started in 1951, and took part in elections for the first time in 1955.
9.   "BN defensive as Penang tops manufacturing investment", *The Malaysian Insider*, 21 February 2012.
10. "Harussani says Malays must defend their land", *The Malaysian Insider*, 21 February 2012.
11. "Waft of scandal choking Anwar", *New Straits Times*, 1 May 2011.
12. Najib appointed Shahrizat to the position in 2009. Because she had lost her parliamentary seat to Nurul the year before, she had to first be sworn in as a senator.
13. Though ethnic parties may well remain, they will no longer be able to succeed by simply appealing to—and working for—one community. The winners will be the ones with a broad-based multi-ethnic appeal.

Chapter 4 The end of dominance: Part II

1.   "Straits Times Review", *The Straits Times*, 25 August 2006.
2.   "Reporting public opinion in Singapore", *The International Journal of Press/Politics*, January 1999, Vol. 4, No. 1, pp. 11–28.
3.   It later emerged that there was no such letter; instead, the IBA's president had praised Singapore's "outstanding judiciary" in a speech at the start of the conference.
4.   Han Fook Kwang, *Lee Kuan Yew: The Man and His Ideas*, Times Editions, 1998.
5.   Channel News Asia, 3 May 2006.
6.   The last election saw a big change, of course, with many more credible, talented individuals representing the opposition, and their support base broadening considerably.
7.   "Obituary: J.B. Jeyaretnam", *The Economist*, 9 October 2008.
8.   Article 39A(1) of the Singapore Constitution.
9.   Why did Singaporeans vote for the late JBJ, as he is fondly known? Maybe they genuinely thought he'd do a better job than the incumbent. Or maybe it was a protest vote, unhappy as they were about the years of single-party rule. Whatever the case, residents of Anson perceived him as the *better* candidate for them, so much so that they returned him to office in 1985.
10. Calculated from "Map of electoral divisions", Elections Department Singapore, http://www.elections.gov.sg/elections_map_electoral.html.
11. "On a high horse called Truth and Right, PAP lost in a changing world", yawningbread. wordpress.com, 21 September 2011.
12. The 2011 presidential election, a four-horse race between very different candidates, further normalised alternative views and opposition politics. Only 35 per cent of Singaporeans voted for Tony Tan, the government's preferred candidate, who won with a plurality in the first-past-the-post contest.
13. Six elected members of parliament (MP) and one non-constituency MP (NCMP), admitted as the "best of the losers".
14. Speech by Lim Boon Heng, 22 July 2011.
15. "Silvester Prakasam, "Evolution of E-payments in public transport—Singapore's experience".

Chapter 5 Not civil enough

1. Half the stories were about BN, compared to 15 per cent about the opposition. Of all stories, BN had about 20 per cent positive pieces and 3 per cent negative pieces. Thirteen per cent of all stories were negative ones about the opposition. Overall, BN had three times as many positive pieces than the opposition.
2. Though Rahman obviously could not back up his claim with any evidence, this quote is included here to reflect an opinion that we hear occasionally in Malaysia.
3. Today it is possible to read each other's newspapers online. But few people bother.
4. Speech at Singapore Press Club, 26 February 1988.
5. I occasionally contribute to *The Online Citizen*.
6. "Judiciary fails to protect minority rights", *Malaysiakini*, 16 September 2010.
7. "Chief jester's circus and charade comes to a close", *The Malaysian Insider*, 15 September 2011.
8. "Hong Kong has best judicial system in Asia: Business survey", *AFP*, 14 September 2008.
9. "Prosperity versus individual rights? Human rights, democracy and the rule of law in Singapore", International Bar Association's Human Rights Institute, July 2008, p. 60.
10. "Lawyers accuse Singapore on human rights", *The Financial Times*, 9 July 2008.
11. "Singapore: Independence of the Judiciary and the Legal Profession in Singapore", Asian Human Rights Commission, 21 October 2007.
12. "Judicial independence in Singapore", Wikipedia, 26 November 2011.
13. "Prosperity versus individual rights? Human rights, democracy and the rule of law in Singapore", International Bar Association's Human Rights Institute, July 2008, p. 59.
14. "Singapore lawyer happily represents thieves and even terror suspects–but no dissidents, please", *Associated Press*, 2 June 2002.
15. "15,000 nays to Lynas project", *The Malay Mail*, 27 February 2012 and "Taking a risk for rare earths", *The New York Times*, 8 March 2011.
16. *Tinur garik* is Kelantanese slang for *tak seronok*, literally "not attractive".

Chapter 6 Alibaba and the thieves

1. Malaysia's New Economic Policy (NEP) was enacted in 1971 and lasted until 1990, when it was effectively replaced by the National Development Policy, which pursued many of the same objectives. In this book, I generally use the terms NEP and bumiputera policies interchangeably to refer to this set of socio-economic policies that continue to give preferences to the so-called bumiputeras.
2. "Malaysia's GDP up 7.2pc, now equal to Singapore", *The Malaysian Insider*, 18 February 2011.
3. Economist Intelligence Unit, 2010 data.
4. Though Indonesia's car market, buoyed by rapid recent economic growth, will likely overtake Malaysia's soon.
5. "The tigers that lost their roar", *The Economist*, 28 February 2008.
6. "Money politics under fire—by Dr M", *The Straits Times*, 29 October 2008.

Chapter 7 Some are more equal than others

1. Kernial Singh Sandhu, *Management of Success: The Moulding of Modern Singapore*, Institute of Southeast Asian Studies, p. 528.
2. James Michener, *The Voice of Asia*, Random House, 1951, p. 128.
3. The Economist Debates, 18 March 2011.
4. As an aside, there is a certain irony that somebody originally from Malaysia should be the one to help solve Singapore's water issues.
5. "Filipino gambling lords launder money in Singapore", *Philippine Daily Inquirer*, 27 September 2010.
6. "International Narcotics Control Strategy Report: Volume II Money laundering and financial crimes", United States Department of State, March 2011.
7. Forum, *The Straits Times*, 16 February 2011.
8. "Risk-averse culture hinders social mobility", *The Straits Times*, 6 April 2011.
9. The Economist Intelligence Unit.

Chapter 8 Colour matters

1. Mahathir bin Mohamad, The Malay Dilemma, Federal Publications, 1981, p. 97.
2. "Malaysian dilemma: The enduring cancer of Affirmative Action", The Center For Independent Studies, 23 February 2011.
3. See Chapter 6, note 1 (p. 273).
4. "The New Development Strategy", Economic Planning Unit (EPU), Malaysia.
5. Not to imply that *most* Penang Chinese are in favour of the *bumiputera* policy. Rather, that from my anecdotal evidence, more Chinese there than anywhere else expressed their support. Since our trip, vocal opposition has grown, particularly since the 2008 general election, when Lim Guan Eng became chief minister. In a conversation with me in mid-2008, he repeatedly expressed his desire to end the "political gravy train" which the *bumiputera* policy has been abused for.
6. *Malaysia: Death of a Democracy*, John Murray Publishers, December 1969.
7. "Population trends 2011", Singapore Department of Statistics.
8. Is the government actually allowing in more Chinese to Singapore to counter the pro-lific Indians and Malays? It is hard to say. While researching an article on immigration in late 2009, and then again in 2011, I had tried to get concrete data on the origin of new citizens. Sadly, I was rebuffed by both the Ministry of Home Affairs and the National Population Secretariat.
9. Michael D. Barr, "Lee Kuan Yew: Race, culture and genes", *Journal of Contemporary Asia*, 29 (2) (1999): 145–166.
10. "Census of population 2010: Households and housing", Singapore Department of Statistics.

Chapter 9 The influx of God and migrants

1. Malaysia's constitution defines all Malays as Muslim. What this also means is that some-body of another ethnicity can become Malay in Malaysia. According to Article 160 of Malaysia's constitution, "... when a non-Malay embraces Islam, he is said to *masuk Melayu* (become a Malay). That person is automatically assumed to be fluent in the Malay language and to be living like a Malay as a result of his close association with the Malays". This constitutional bonding of race and religion affects notions of identity throughout the country.

2. Since the 2008 general elections, when the opposition won more seats than ever before, PAS has slowly become more of a mainstream party, and has made extraordinary efforts to reach out to non-Muslims. This has assuaged some fears about their conservative and orthodox leanings. Nevertheless, the party's more fundamentalist elements regularly rear their head. In 2011, some PAS members were pushing for the implementation of *hudud*, Islamic laws, which allow for, say, the chopping off of thieves' hands.

3. Han Fook Kwang et al., *Lee Kuan Yew: Hard Truths to Keep Singapore Going*, Straits Times Press, 2011.

4. "Jesus do it now by Kong Hee.mp4", YouTube.

5. The government has announced its intention to review this.

Chapter 10 The joy of families and security

1. Many Malaysians and some Singaporeans, however, are dissatisfied with aspects of their educational and healthcare systems, as well as housing, as highlighted in Chapters 6 and 7.

2. See Francis Seow's account of the ISD in *To Catch a Tartar*.

3. This proved to be wrong. When Mas was finally captured, in Johor in 2009, Singapore found out that after escaping, he had fled to Malaysia almost instantly, wading across the narrow Johor Strait. All this showed how lost our authorities were, and was a severe dent to the image of (supposedly) super-secure Singapore.

4. G-plated cars are designated as Commercial Goods Vehicles in Singapore. And yes, one does need separate insurance to drive them in Malaysia.

5. Michael Richardson, "Lee Kuan Yew apologizes for remarks that angered Malaysia", *IHT*, 14 March 1997.

6. The United Nations Surveys on Crime Trends and the Operations of Criminal Justice Systems publishes different crime and justice statistics rates, based on 100,000 people. In 2000, Malaysia had 353.58 total police personnel. Singapore had 324.22. Malaysia had 717.48 total crimes reported. Singapore had 1,202.61. There were 288.76 people brought before the criminal courts. Singapore had 426.51. Malaysia had 192.22 persons convicted. Singapore had 292.71. Malaysia had 339.90 people incarcerated. Singapore had 411.55.

7. There are also a few who simply enjoy their job so much that they keep working, not for want of fame nor fortune. However, in our opinion, Singapore does not have many such souls.

8. Preliminary figures from Malaysia's Department of Statistics.

9.   "Population in brief 2011", Singapore Department of Statistics.

10. Tey Nai Peng, "Social, economic and ethnic fertility differentials in Peninsular Malaysia", June 2002.

11. "Eugenics in Singapore", Singapore Democrats, 9 November 2008.

12. J. John Palen, "Fertility and eugenics: Singapore's population policies". *Population Research and Policy Review* 5(1) (1986): 3–14. The more controversial aspects of the Graduate Mothers Scheme were ended in 1985.

13. "Playing cupid once more", *The Star Online*, 1 November 2008.

Chapter 11 The stress of work and city life

1.   HIV statistics from Malaysia's and Singapore's respective Ministries of Health. 2010 Malaysia population: 28.3 million, Singapore: 5.1 million, according to the Economist Intelligence Unit.

2.   Many Malaysians we met, particularly in the North and East, refer to Thais as "Siam" people.

3.   "Malaysian royal arrested over wedding brawl", *Sydney Morning Herald*, 18 October 2005 and "Victims of Pulau Rawa brawl refuse to come forward", *New Straits Times*, 20 November 2005

4.   "Singapore ranks second-lowest for job satisfaction", *The Business Times*, 18 April 2009.

5.   "Medicine is not just a career, but a calling", *The Straits Times*, 9 December 2008.

6.   "Surgeon billed Brunei patient $40m over 4 years", *The New Paper*, 1 March 2011.

7.   "Surgeon inflated $400 bill to $211,000", *The Straits Times*, 24 February 2011.

8.   "Cheers and jeers for maids' day off in Singapore", *AFP*, 7 March 2011.

9.   "Heritage Society 'not consulted' on Bukit Brown plans", *My Paper*, 21 October 2011.

10. "Money and happiness", *The Economist Online*, 25 November 2010.

11. "Letters", *The Economist*, 9 December 2010.

12. The Economist Intelligence Unit, March 2012.

13. "How's life?", OECD, 12 October 2011.

14. Jas Jaafar, Haslina Muhamad, Shajaratu Hanapiah, Tina Afiatin, Yogi Sugandi, "The index of happiness of the Malaysian and Indonesian peoples", *Academia.edu*.

Epilogue

1.   Facebook Status Update, Alfian Sa'at, 26 February 2012.

Index

United Malays National Organisation
      (UMNO), 57, 59–60, 66–67, 106,
      130–32, 134–37, 170–72, 202, 207,
      259
   Puteri UMNO, 117–20
   UMNO Baru, 60
United Nations (UN), 28, 44, 230
Universiti Kebangsaan Malaysia, 233
USA. *See* America
Utusan Malaysia, 27, 101, 136

Vietnam, 7, 21, 32, 126, 141, 143

Wain, Barry, 132
Wan Azizah, 90
Welch Allyn International, 151–52
WikiLeaks, 68, 97, 211
Woon, Walter, 96
Workers Party (WP), 76, 85
World Trade Center, 37
World War II, 18, 28, 180
Wozniak, Steve, 155

Xie, Andy, 156–57

Yap Mun Ching, 47–50, 55–56, 116–17,
      138, 182
Yayasan Strategik Sosial (YSS), 111
Yeo, George, 129, 166

Zabur Nawawi, 26
Zahari, Said. *See* Said Zahari